W9-AZF-756

tear here

Safe Cooking Tips

Without exception, poultry must be cooked to a temperature of 180 degrees to destroy any harmful bacteria that might be present. To be absolutely safe, you can use a digital instant-read thermometer in the thickest part of the meat (being careful not to touch bone), or use the chart below to gauge minimum cooking times for unstuffed poultry, roasting at 350 degrees, grilling over medium coals, or frying at 350 degrees.

Cut	Weight	Cooking Times
Whole Broiler-Fryer	2–4 lbs.	Roast: 1 1/4–1 1/2 hrs. Grill: 1–1 1/4 hours
Whole Roaster	5–7 lbs.	Roast: 2–2 1/4 hrs. Grill: 1 1/2–2 1/2 hrs.
Breast halves, boneless	4–6 oz.	Roast: 20–25 mins. Grill: 12–15 mins. Fry: 10–15 mins.
Breast halves, with bone	5–8 oz.	Roast: 30–40 mins. Grill: 20–30 mins. Fry: 20–30 mins.
Drumsticks	4 oz.	Roast: 35–45 mins. Grill: 15–25 mins. Fry: 20–25 mins.
Whole Legs, Thighs	4–8 oz.	Roast: 40–50 mins. Grill: 20–30 mins Fry: 20–30 mins.
Wings	2–3 oz.	Roast: 25–40 mins. Grill: 15–25 mins. Fry: 15–25 mins.
Rock Cornish Hens	1–2 lbs.	Roast: 50–60 mins. Grill: 45–55 mins.

Super-Simple Marinade

Makes about 3/4 cup, to marinate a 2–4-pound chicken
1/2 cup extra virgin olive oil
1/3 cup lemon juice
2–3 cloves garlic, finely chopped
1/2 teaspoon salt
1/4 teaspoon freshly ground black pepper (or more to taste)

1. Mix all the ingredients together in a bowl.
2. Place the chicken parts in a gallon-size zipper-lock plastic bag, pour the marinade over the chicken, and seal the bag.
3. Turn the bag several times to coat well, and marinate for 1–2 hours at room temperature, or up to 24 hours in the refrigerator.

alpha
books

Foolproof Roast Chicken

Serves 4

1 3–4-pound broiler-fryer	1 medium onion, quartered
Salt and pepper	2 tablespoons softened butter
1 lemon, halved	

1. Preheat oven to 450°. Remove the giblets and rinse the chicken inside and out. Pat it dry with paper towels and sprinkle with salt and pepper inside and out. Rub all over with softened butter and place the lemon halves and onion quarters in the cavity.
2. Place the chicken breast side down on a rack in a roasting pan. Place in the preheated oven and roast at 450° for 30 minutes. After 20 minutes, baste once.
3. After 30 minutes, lower the heat to 350° and flip the chicken over so it's breast-side up. Cook for another hour, basting every 10–15 minutes, or until the legs move easily, the juices run clear, and there's no hint of pink in the meat.

Recipe for Mom's Fried Chicken

This is the simplest way to fry chicken. There are all sorts of things you can add into the flour, such as celery salt and cayenne, but purists prefer their fried chicken to taste of nothing but chicken.

Serves 4

1 2–3-pound broiler-fryer	1 1/2 teaspoons salt
1 cup all-purpose flour	1/2 teaspoon black pepper
1 tablespoon paprika	Vegetable oil for frying

1. Remove the giblets and save them for stock (p. 137). Joint the chicken into 8 pieces as described on p. 24. If desired, leave the pieces to soak for 2 hours in a saltwater solution. (If you do brine the chicken, rinse in cool water when finished.)
2. When ready to fry, pour oil into a heavy skillet till the oil is 1/2-inch deep, and begin heating over medium heat to about 350°, or until a tiny pinch of flour or a cube of bread will sizzle when dropped into the oil. It should not be hot enough to smoke. If it is smoking, remove pan from heat and cool for a few moments.
3. Combine all dry ingredients in a paper bag such as a brown lunch bag or a plastic zipper-lock bag. Drop in four chicken pieces at a time and shake until well coated with flour. Slip the floured chicken into the hot oil and repeat with the remaining pieces. All eight pieces should fit into the hot oil, even if they're crowded.
4. Increase the heat slightly to keep the oil hot enough to sizzle. After 5 minutes, turn all the chicken pieces and brown on the other side. Lower the heat and cover with the lid slightly askew so that steam can escape, and cook for 25–30 minutes.
5. Remove cover and increase the heat slightly. Turn the chicken pieces again and fry for another 5–10 minutes to crisp up the crust. Both sides should be a rich, golden brown. Remove to a paper-towel-lined platter and place the platter in a warm oven (180°) until ready to serve.

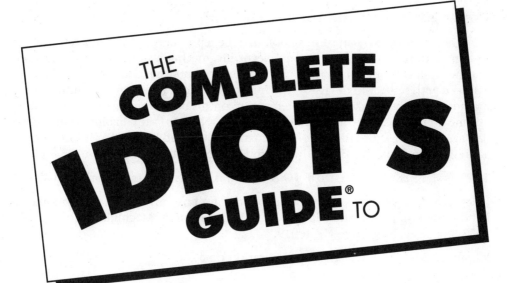

THE COMPLETE IDIOT'S GUIDE® TO

Cooking Chicken

by Sharon Bowers

alpha books

A Division of Macmillan General Reference
A Simon & Schuster Macmillan Company
1633 Broadway, New York, NY 10019-6785

Macmillan Publishing books may be purchased for business or sales promotional use. For information please write: Special Markets Department, Macmillan Publishing USA, 1633 Broadway, New York, NY 10019.

Library of Congress Cataloging-in-Publication Data

Bowers, Sharon
The complete idiot's guide to cooking chicken / Sharon Bowers p. cm.
Includes Index.
ISBN 0-02-862331-2
1. Cookery (Chicken) 2. Chickens. I. Title. TX750.5.C45B86 1998
641.6 65—dc21

01 00 99   8 7 6 5 4 3 2 1

Interpretation of the printing code: the rightmost number of the first series of numbers is the year of the book's printing; the rightmost number of the second series of numbers is the number of the book's printing. For example, a printing code of 99-1 shows that the first printing occurred in 1999.

Printed in the United States of America

Contents at a Glance

Contents

Foreword

Sharon Bowers is absolutely right that you can eat chicken seven nights a week and barely notice it's the same meat from meal to meal. I speak from experience, because my family and I ate chicken nearly every night during the year I wrote my chicken cookbook, *The 15-Minute Chicken Gourmet.*

The versatility of chicken took on a new meaning for me, and I discovered the possibilities to be unlimited. No other meat can be prepared using as many cooking methods, and the mild flavor of chicken is compatible with an almost endless variety of herbs and spices, fruits, and vegetables. No doubt this is why chicken plays a starring role in many of the world's cuisines.

Chicken is the perfect choice all year round, because it can be enjoyed hot, at room temperature, or chilled. It can be the answer to satisfying the entire family on a busy weeknight with a quick-to-prepare recipe such as chicken burgers, creating an impressive entrée to serve discriminating guests, like an elegant chicken in wine sauce, or as the basis for the ultimate comfort food, chicken soup. For the health conscious, chicken can be cooked with little or no fat. To fit into today's busy lifestyles, many chicken dishes are ideal as they incorporate vegetables and a starch to create a complete one-dish meal. And many chicken recipes can be prepared quickly, like those I included in my 15-minute recipes.

The Complete Idiot's Guide to Cooking Chicken also offers an extensive array of speedy dishes and includes some delectable slow-cooked dishes, too. Here you will find recipes for every style of cooking: roasted, oven-braised, baked, stewed, and slow cooked.

This book not only dishes up tasty chicken recipes but also serves as a complete guide to buying chicken and other poultry, handling it safely, and cooking it to perfection.

—Paulette Mitchell

Paulette Mitchell is a cooking instructor, lecturer, restaurant consultant, food columnist, and the author of many books including *The 15-Minute Chicken Gourmet.*

Introduction

Tastes Like Chicken!

Chicken—it's the hamburger of the '90s. Low in price, low in fat, incredibly versatile, and endlessly forgiving, we turn to it again and again when the dinner bell rings. The US poultry industry produces some three billion chickens for consumption annually, and Americans eat approximately twenty chickens a year per person, which means a family of four can count on seeing chicken on the table at least once a week and probably more.

No matter how much you love it, though, all that chicken can start to look and taste the same after awhile. Fortunately, there's hardly a cuisine in the world that doesn't use chicken in some form, from the great Chinese delicacy of chicken feet (we won't be using those) to classic French Coq au Vin (or chicken simmered in red wine) to all-American Buffalo Wings. And it certainly helps to really know your chicken, not only in terms of getting the best value at the store and consistently producing nutritious and healthy dishes at home, but also in keeping the interest level up tastewise.

With the recipes here, you can eat chicken seven nights a week and barely notice it's the same meat from meal to meal. Once you know all the different sorts of chicken available, from stewing hens to capons, broiler-fryers to Cornish Game Hens (which are actually little chickens), and take into account the differences produced by battery-raising compared to organic or free-range, you can shop for chicken like a pro. You'll know how to prepare a top-quality chicken for holidays and festive occasions in ways that will enhance its delicate flavor, and also how to create delicious everyday meals when bags of drumsticks are on sale at the supermarket for 29¢ a pound.

A special section on international recipes offers easy-to-follow instructions for repro-ducing the exact flavors of chicken favorites from around the world, from an authentic Indian Chicken Curry to a fabulous Italian Chicken Cacciatore, to a Moroccan Chicken Tagine and a version of Swedish Meatballs made with ground chicken. As an added bonus, we'll hunt and peck our way safely and successfully through that holiday rite of passage, roasting the Thanksgiving turkey, and also make sure you're never at a loss should someone ask you what to do with a quail, squab, or pheasant.

How to Use This Book

We're going to look into chicken from all the angles (including some places you never thought you'd be looking), and explore preparation from all sides: by chicken type, by the cooking method, by the chicken part, by the course in a meal, and by the country.

Part I: Getting to Know Chicken: In this section we'll discuss commercial production and what it means on the labels, buying, storage and handling, and cutting up chickens both raw and cooked.

Part II: Chicken Wrangling: Major Cooking Methods: Every way to cook chicken, from making the best stock to grilling without charring, from perfect frying to the excellent texture obtained by poaching.

Part III: Chicken by the Part: I Saw a Sale on Drumsticks for 39¢ a Pound! Or, What to Make When There's Nothing to Cook but Chicken Thighs: A joint-by-joint look at what to do with different chicken parts, and what types of cooking best suit individual pieces.

Part IV: Chicken by the Course: You can use chicken in pretty much every course and food type except dessert, from sandwiches and appetizers to stews, salads, soups, and more. You'll find excellent versions of traditional recipes, such as Ladies Lunch Chicken Salad, as well as chicken dishes to make with pasta or pastry, in a casserole dish or a stewpot.

Part V: Chicken Around the World: North, South, East, West, we'll travel the world in search of the best chicken recipes, including fabulously flavored Asian noodle soups and deliciously rich European dishes such as Poulet a l'Estragon.

Part VI: Beyond Chicken: Playing the Game: You need never fear turkey again with this step by step guide, and you'll never wonder what to do if someone should give you a brace of pheasant (or quail, squab, duck, grouse, goose, or Cornish game hens).

Extras

Don't Fowl Up

Don't Fowl Up cautions you with safety details for handling chicken, cooking utensils and appliances, and materials (such as never serving or saving a marinade in which you soaked raw chicken).

Wing Tips

Wing Tips will help you soar over the more difficult parts of preparing chicken, with hints and suggestions for getting the most out of each recipe.

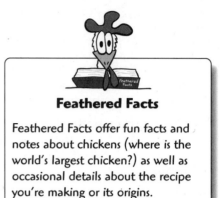

Feathered Facts

Feathered Facts offer fun facts and notes about chickens (where is the world's largest chicken?) as well as occasional details about the recipe you're making or its origins.

Roost Rap

Roost Rap helps you talk turkey and get your beak around the poultry terms and phrases.

Acknowledgments

Special thanks to Elizabeth Morgan for her help, advice, and suggestions for countless ways to roast chicken, and to my mother, Carolyn Parrish, who is always ready to drop everything and answer or research an obscure chicken question.

Many thanks to Lydia Wills, my reassuring and rational agent, and to Jim Willhite at Macmillan, always ready and able to answer questions.

Most of all, I owe a particular debt of gratitude to Jennifer Griffin, whom I'm proud to call my editor but best pleased to call my friend.

Part 1
Getting to Know Chicken

Know your chicken. Before you start to cook it, get to know the parts of the bird, what exactly you're buying, and the best ways to cook and store it. How careful do you have to be when handling raw chicken? Is there a way to make a mass-produced chicken more flavorful? A quick glance through these chapters will tell you everything you need to know to get a chicken from the supermarket to your refrigerator to the stove, including tips on jointing and carving like a pro.

Chapter 1

The Chicken and the Egg

In This Chapter

➤ Chicken production in the US

➤ What's got into your chicken? Antibiotics and growth hormones

➤ Ruling the roost: USDA standards

➤ The difference between organic, free-range, and battery

Americans love chicken, and its popularity has boomed in the last decade or so, as we've become increasingly aware of the need to eat less red meat. Chicken is a readily accessible, economical, and deliciously healthy alternative, but the boom in chicken production in the US has, paradoxically, made our chickens in some ways not quite the same tasty creatures that our grandmothers remember. Fortunately, the US Department of Agriculture (USDA) closely monitors the poultry industry to provide the safest possible product, but it's also good for you as a consumer to know what you're getting from the start when you're buying chicken. This way you can make sure you always eat chicken that's not only safe and healthy, but also moist and yummy.

A Growth Industry

The concentration of grain production in the midwestern United States made it, at the turn of the century, the starting point of the chicken industry as we know it today. For the most part, families who ate chicken grew their own, and it was regarded in many homes as a Sunday dinner, not a nightly repast. But as with grain co-ops and creameries, small-town farmers (or more particularly, farm wives) eventually banded together to process and sell not only their eggs but their chickens through local hatcheries.

Initially, chicken producers were independent growers who essentially sold through local consortiums, but as the industry flourished in the early 1920s, farmers began to rely on feed dealers to bankroll chicken production, and dealers in turn looked to feed manufacturers for funding. To share the risk, manufacturers and dealers integrated production with hatchers and processors, leading to the production of chicken by huge conglomerates as it's done today, with company-owned or -contracted farms producing chicken from hatching through delivery.

Feathered Facts

When the USDA began keeping records on commercial broiler production in 1934, the total number raised in the U.S. annually was 34 million birds. In 1989, the annual total of birds produced was over 5 billion.

With mass production, however, came mass problems. Railroad cars transported hordes of live chickens to distribution centers, New York City being one of the largest, and in 1924 in the New York Central Railroad Yards, there was an outbreak of fowl plague, a highly contagious respiratory disease that can kill entire flocks (though not humans) in weeks.

From this outbreak came modern inspection programs, first organized by the New York Live Poultry Commission in 1924, then taken over by the US Department of Agriculture in 1926. In 1928, the program was expanded to include inspection of dressed poultry and by-products before they left the processor, though all inspection was still voluntary. Not until 1956 was inspection compulsory. The Poultry Products Inspection Act was signed in August 1956 by President Dwight D. Eisenhower, requiring inspection of poultry.

What's Got Into Your Chicken? Antibiotics and Growth Hormones

Feathered Facts

As the modern poultry industry developed, science helped it along by producing hybrid birds that grew bigger faster and were more resistant to disease. Today's bird is generally a cross between the Cornish and White Rock breeds.

Chickens once pecked for food in the farmyard, eating corn and insects and even leftovers from their owners' tables. This laissez-faire approach to chicken-raising is now known as "free-range" and is generally agreed to produce the best-tasting meat. Mass production does not allow for free-ranging chickens, however, and modern growers need to get their birds to market as quickly as possible, so most chickens are kept in confined spaces and given feed that has a carefully calculated nutritional content.

In an effort to decrease the potential for widespread diseases and bacteria in chickens, the USDA has approved a number of additives to chicken diets. Growth hormones are not allowed by the USDA in the production of poultry (or pork, for that matter, though they can be used in beef) so you may be reasonably assured that your chicken contains no added hormones. Antibiotics are a different matter, however, and unless the package specifically states "no antibiotics added," you may reasonably assume that the bird's feed did contain them. The birds must not be slaughtered before they've had a "withdrawal" period from ingesting antibiotics to prevent residue. Though the government tests to insure that antibiotics are not present in the commercially purchased chicken, it's naive to believe that a chicken raised on antibiotics will have absolutely no trace of them in its system.

Although there is much benefit to be derived from killing certain strains of bacteria off at large, the US poultry industry is starting to see a backlash by way of the development of resistant strains of bacteria in chickens, and thus resistance in humans to the antibiotics used to treat these illnesses when they appear in humans (for more on that, see Chapter 3.

Ruling the Roost: USDA Standards

All commercially processed agricultural products are required to meet specific standards set by the USDA. Live chickens in their crates are visually inspected by a federal or state poultry inspector before entering the processing. The birds are then inspected on the processing line for any signs of contamination or diseases.

Inspection is mandatory but grading is voluntary. If you buy a Grade A chicken, expect it to be plump, unbruised, with soft, smooth, unbroken skin that is not discolored, and flexible, unbroken cartilage and unbroken bones. All feathers must have been removed.

Feathered Facts

Where it once took fourteen to sixteen weeks to bring a commercial broiler to its market weight of three to four pounds, requiring about four pounds of feed per pound of chicken, today's hybrid breeds and feeding systems can bring a 3- to 4-pound bird to market in six to eight weeks, requiring less than two pounds of feed per pound of bird.

Roost Rap

Any poultry product labeled "basted" or "self-basted" has been injected with or marinated in a solution that probably contained salt, oil or butter, water or stock, and seasonings or flavor enhancers— a solution intended to keep the bird moist while it cooks. The maximum amount of weight that can be added with this solution is 3%, and that's included on the label weight. The label must also include a list of what the basting solution contains. It's okay to buy these self-basters for roasting, but you'll find they're not really necessary if you baste the chicken yourself.

Feathered Facts

The USDA does not allow the word "organic" to appear on poultry labels at this time. A proposal is in the works so that growers who raise organic livestock and poultry may so label their products, but until it is finalized by the USDA, don't go looking for organic labeling. Occasionally markets will advertise the availability of organic poultry. This generally means that the store has a relationship with a local supplier whom they trust. Ask questions and find out where the chickens came from before you buy at those elevated "organic" prices.

Roost Rap

Domestic chickens don't do a lot of flying, so the breast and wing meat is relatively unused muscle, and hence white because of a different structure requiring less oxygen. The legs, which they use to run around, are dark—moister, more flavorful, and somewhat more chewy when cooked. Most game birds, such as ducks and geese, actually do fly, so their breast and wing meat is dark.

Inspectors also regularly check processing plants and farms, including personnel as needed, to make sure everything meets sanitary requirements.

The Food Safety and Inspection Service (FSIS) is a branch of the USDA that ensures accuracy of labeling in meat and poultry, and insures that a chicken labeled, say, "natural" contains no artificial ingredients, added colorings, and has been minimally processed.

The Difference Between Organic, Free-Range, and Battery

The vast majority of poultry in the US is battery-raised, meaning that the birds are kept in a confined space for the duration of their lives and fed and watered within their cages. This is done to bring the bird to market weight as quickly and efficiently as possible.

Free-range chicken no longer has quite the meaning that it once did, when chickens roamed free around the back door of the house and ate whatever they could find. To label a chicken free-range now, a manufacturer merely has to demonstrate to the USDA that the bird has been allowed access to the outside. These birds may also be labeled "free-roaming," and the distinction may or may not result in a better-tasting chicken. Generally, chickens labeled free-range are more expensive and the taste is not always worth the extra price.

True organic chicken has been raised using pure grains and feeds instead of processed food pellets. The best organic chickens will have been raised in a free-range environment, and they will not have been given antibiotics. This is not to say that the birds have not had any chemicals whatsoever (the FSIS does not allow the label "chemical-free" on any poultry), but the grower who bothers to raise his poultry organically will generally have a far more flavorful, plumper, and more tender product to bring to market. Real organic chicken will cost substantially more per pound, and the best way to be sure you're getting it is to buy directly from the producer, if you're lucky enough to live where that's available, or from a trusted gourmet store, or at a farmer's market or greenmarket.

The Least You Need to Know

➤ The increase in chicken consumption by Americans has led to phenomenal growth in the poultry industry and hence to a more uniform taste and some loss of flavor.

➤ Be aware that most commercially produced chickens have been given chemicals and possibly antibiotics in their feed.

➤ Organic chickens have been fed on natural ingredients, without antibiotics and synthetic chemicals. Organic chickens may also be "free-range," meaning that they were allowed more freedom of movement and possibly access to the outdoors.

➤ The US Department of Agriculture inspects all chickens processed commercially to ensure their safety and freedom from illness.

Chapter 2

What's A Capon? Buying and Handling

In This Chapter

➤ Understanding chicken types

➤ Special cuts

➤ Giblets and what to do with them

➤ Rotisserie chicken

Although the majority of chickens at the grocery store are broiler-fryers, there's a lot more to it than that—there are different types of whole chickens, each intended for different uses. You can buy all sorts of parts and pieces separately, but you have to know what you're looking at.

Rock Cornish Game Hens and Other Mysteries

Nearly all chicken classifications are based on weight. Age used to be more of a defining factor, but with modern production, a chicken can be ready for market practically whenever the producer wants. So check the weight on the label depending on what you're making.

Baby Broiler, Squab, or Rock Cornish Game Hen

The tiny little birds that usually linger, frozen, near the end of the poultry section of the grocery store are nothing more than very young chickens, 3/4 to 1 1/4 pounds. The "Rock Cornish" designation means it's a hybrid White Rock and Cornish, but so are most other birds on the market. The name adds a touch of mystery to the little creatures, but what you'll get is simply young meat. They can be a little bit tasteless, without that chicken-y punch of flavor, but the meat is juicy and tender and they take well to roasting with herbs or fruit sauces, broiling, and grilling. Plan on serving one per person.

Broiler-Fryer

The usual chicken you'll buy at the store, broiler-fryers, range from two to four pounds. This type of chicken is suitable for nearly any cooking method, from frying to steaming, roasting, sauteing, grilling, and broiling. The flesh is not suitable for long stewing, however, and will become stringy and tasteless if overcooked.

Wing Tips

Nearly all chicken parts can be bought with the skin already removed, but removing the skin hardly warrants the extra cost. Buy meat with the skin on and simply pull it off and discard if you don't want skin.

Roaster

The roaster is slightly bigger than the broiler fryer, from four to six pounds, and tends to be a little older, too, maybe ten weeks instead of six to eight. Most roasters are labeled, not surprisingly, "roaster," and the extra breast meat and bigger drumsticks and thighs make them ideal for whole roasting, with more breast meat to slice.

Stewing Hen

Stewing hens are distinguished by their age, which is usually eight to twenty-four months (though likely closer to twelve than twenty-four). Generally, they have been raised to lay eggs and are butchered when they become infertile. The meat tends to be quite tough and stringy, and they are best suited for long, slow cooking in liquid, such as a stew or fricassee. Their age also makes them more flavorful, however, and because of this they're the best choice not only for stews but for stocks. Slightly smaller hens, closer to five pounds than seven, are likely to be more tasty.

Wing Tips

Giblets are generally only fried or boiled for stock. To boil, place everything but the liver (which doesn't taste good in stock) in a small saucepan with 2 to 2 1/2 cups of water, add half an onion, a piece of celery, and half a carrot if desired, and simmer over low heat for about an hour (see p. 137 for a Giblet Gravy recipe).

Capon

Capons are male chickens that have been castrated and fattened. They are much more expensive to produce and their flesh is tender, juicy, and marbled with fat, which makes them especially flavorful and suitable for special meals. They tend to be larger than broiler-fryers, ranging from four to seven pounds. Capons are almost always roasted whole, and still treated as something of a "special-occasion" bird, rather like a duck or goose. Since they tend to be rare in US supermarkets, you'll probably always find them frozen. Since they're not always a fast-moving item in stores, check the packaging and sell-by date before buying, in case your capon has been sitting in the freezer section a little too long.

Don't Fowl Up

Larger and older birds should never be roasted, fried or sauteed, but stewed or fricasseed. Occasionally you may find something labeled "rooster," "stewing hen," or even "old hen." Old birds tend to be tougher and stringier and need the long cooking to tenderize. (After all, they didn't call it a spring chicken.) Take the labeler's tip and cook slowly in liquid or use for stock, for best results.

Special Cuts

In the old days, you bought a whole chicken, cut it up yourself as you saw fit, and found some way to use all the parts. Now you can buy any part of a chicken already cut up and packaged. Often they can be a significant bargain, as with "family packs" of drumsticks or thighs that can run as low as 29¢ a pound. Or they can run to the opposite extreme. Generally the more work that has been done for you, the more money you pay. For instance, chicken breasts that have been skinned and cut into bite-size squares cost substantially more than an ordinary package of breasts, which you have to skin and chop up yourself.

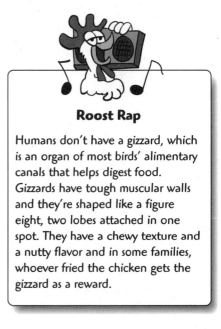

Roost Rap

Humans don't have a gizzard, which is an organ of most birds' alimentary canals that helps digest food. Gizzards have tough muscular walls and they're shaped like a figure eight, two lobes attached in one spot. They have a chewy texture and a nutty flavor and in some families, whoever fried the chicken gets the gizzard as a reward.

The portion of chicken that is commonly known as a breast is actually one half of the whole breast of a chicken. When sold on the bone, these breast portions will usually be labeled "split breasts," meaning that the entire breast, the front of the bird, has been halved down the breastbone. When boned and/or skinned, however, the pieces are labeled "boneless, skinless, chicken breasts," though the package may specify "six pieces," and mean three split breasts. You're more likely to see whole turkey breasts on the bone than whole chicken breasts, but if you do buy one (see illustration), it's good for roasting or poaching for salads and sandwiches.

When you cut a raw breast off the bone, there will be a long narrow strip of flesh on the back that comes away easily from the rest of the breast. This is the fillet, and you can buy a whole, quite expensive, pack of these, usually under the label "breast tenders." It is a very tender piece of meat, but it's not so very different from the rest of the breast that it's really worth all the extra money.

Legs can often be bought cheaply whole, with the thigh and drumstick still attached, to be cooked whole or jointed. A whole package of thighs is perfect for baking, and if you can find boned thighs, it's a much lower cost, though slightly higher calorie, alternative to breast meat.

Chicken wings used to be the discarded leftovers of packaged chicken, sold cheaply for making stocks or soups. Then Buffalo Wings became a rage across the country, and now chicken wings are among the more pricey cuts, sometimes costing up to $2 a pound.

Roost Rap

One of the great chicken mysteries for the average buyer is how the rock-hard frozen chicken in her hands can be plainly labeled "Fresh." According to the Food Safety and Inspection Service, poultry can be labeled fresh if its internal temperature has never been below 26°. Anything colder than that and it must be labeled as "hard chilled."

Whole chicken breasts on the bone.

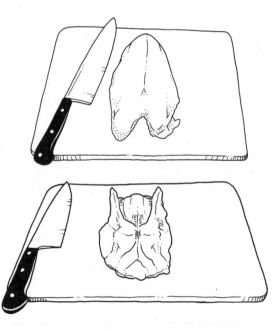

Don't Fowl Up

Don't buy packaged chicken with a pool of liquid in the package. It probably means that the bird was thawed and refrozen. As the liquid in the cells freezes repeatedly, it expands and ruptures the cell walls. When the bird is thawed, the liquid—and a good bit of the flavor—seeps out of the cells. The result is flabby, dull-tasting meat.

Giblets and What to Do with Them

Giblets are the chicken's edible organs and they are included with the purchase price of nearly every whole chicken. This comes as a surprise to many a first-time chicken roaster or carver who had no idea that there was a little paper or plastic pack of stuff in the cavity of the bird.

Giblets consist of the heart, the liver (which comes in two lobes), the gizzard, and the neck, which isn't an organ but is packaged with the giblets. Some people prefer to throw the whole package in the garbage without examining it further, but the giblets are not only edible but quite tasty.

The gizzard is tough and chewy and very good when fried, as are the heart and liver. Some people fry the neck and pick bits of meat off it, too. Perhaps you had to grow up eating these parts to really appreciate them, but the organ meats are full of iron and quite good for you. All the giblet parts can be bought separately, including tubs of chicken livers, which are wonderful for making pates or chopped liver or hors d'ouevres. A tray of hearts and giblets can be more intimidating, but if you don't want to fry and eat them all whole, you might try a down-home Southern dish called Dirty Rice, which incorporates deep-fried and finely chopped hearts, gizzards, and livers into spicy Cajun-seasoned rice (see p. 138).

Wing Tips

Giblets are especially good when fried. Toss the individual pieces in a little flour and fry in the same pan in which you're frying the chicken. The liver will be done in three to four minutes, turned once, but the heart, gizzard, and neck should cook about ten minutes or so, until nicely browned.

Wing Tips

Rotisserie chicken is great sliced and served, but it's also terrific stripped off the bone and used in other dishes. Try rotisserie chicken in your own homemade pot pie with a biscuit crust, curry, chicken salad, or any dish that uses cooked meat. The high-heat rotisserie process adds an extra flavor layer to the finished dish.

Rotisserie Chicken

It's best to avoid tasteless, precooked, ready-cooked chicken that comes in shrink-wrapped packages and lies in the refrigerated case next to raw chicken. The packaging always touts the convenience of having it already cooked, but unwrapped, you end up with pallid, often dry meat. However, precooked is a good thing when it comes off a rotisserie.

The proliferation of rotisserie chickens across America is a blessing for the busy cook. Besides several national chains, many grocery stores and delis now have a case of glistening birds turning before a heat source as their skin crisps and browns. Usually packed in foil-lined, heat-proof envelopes, a rotisserie chicken can stay warm on the counter for twenty minutes or so while you boil a few potatoes (or better yet, bake them in the microwave) and throw together a salad. Carve the chicken and voila! Dinner is served.

The Least You Need to Know

➤ Most of the names for chickens are based on size, from little Rock Cornish Game hens, weighing in under a pound, to huge, 7-pound stewing hens.

➤ Chickens can be bought whole or cut into any shape, from whole packs of wings or thighs to the expensive little fillet on the back of each breast piece, usually sold as a "breast tender."

➤ The single portion that we all refer to as a chicken breast is actually one side of the bird's whole breast. The whole breast is made of two plump sides.

➤ The giblets are the bird's heart, liver, gizzard, and neck, usually found in a paper or plastic package in the cavity of a whole chicken. Don't automatically throw them away, because they can be fried or used for stock to make giblet gravy.

➤ If you're buying chicken ready-cooked, your best bet for moistness and flavor is rotisserie chicken, available at national chain restaurants as well as in more and more grocery stores and delis.

Chapter 3

Playing Chicken: Safe Handling of Raw Poultry

In This Chapter

➤ Bacteria in raw chicken

➤ Transportation, storage, and preparation of raw chicken

➤ Safe cooking tips

➤ Storing cooked chicken

Any raw meat can pose serious health risks if handled improperly, but chicken is a source of special concern. The variety of bacteria that can affect raw chicken can pose a significant threat to children, the ill, and the elderly, so a little extra care is needed to ensure safe handling.

We Are Not Alone: Bacteria in Raw Chicken

For the most part, harmful bacteria present in raw chicken has come to be there due to improper handling or transmission from hands, as opposed to being already present in the chicken. Thus, careful handling and avoidance of contamination on the part of the food preparer as well as cooking to a safe temperature will almost always ensure that all bacteria have been destroyed in the cooked meat.

There have been a number of scares relating to salmonella in the media over recent years, but salmonella can easily be killed by cooking to the proper temperature. Although salmonella is largely associated with poultry, it is also present in beef and can be more of a threat to those with a taste for rare meat than those with a taste for well-roasted chicken. While salmonella gets all the press attention, only recently are we becoming more aware of campylobacter as the most common bacterial cause of diarrhea in humans. Campylobacter can be present in the intestinal tracts of both animals and humans without causing illness, but if humans consume the live bacteria, as they might in undercooked poultry, campylobacteriosis may result. (Other sources are contaminated milk or water.) The symptoms include fever, headache, muscle pain, then nausea, stomach pain, and diarrhea. Antibiotics once used to treat campylo-bacteriosis in humans have become increasingly ineffective as the bacteria have become resistant, possibly due to the fact that the antibiotics are given to poultry in their feed. In rare cases, campylobacter infections can be fatal.

For safety reasons then, chicken should be cooked to an interior temperature of 180°. Many cooks find that the meat is moister at a slightly lower internal temperature, such as 160° to 170°, but if you're cooking for children, sick people, or the elderly, it's always safer to go for the higher temperature and destroy any bacteria by cooking.

Transportation, Storage, and Handling of Raw Chicken

Wrapped packages of chicken at the supermarket can often be wet with raw juices and blood, and many stores will put the packages into a separate plastic bag. Don't allow a clerk at the supermarket to pile raw meat on top of raw vegetables, and don't do it yourself. Be sure that the packs of raw chicken do not come into contact with other food products, especially fresh fruits and vegetables. Never let meat or poultry sit in grocery bags in the car while you run other errands. Bacteria can start to grow if the meat or poultry is left outside of a refrigerated case for any lengthy period, and have a strong foothold before you even get home. Refrigeration and freezing will not kill many bacteria, especially campylobacter. Only cooking to the proper temperature will do that.

Never buy a prestuffed chicken. Although these items are occasionally available, the risk of bacterial infection is high. Stuffing is usually partially cooked before being placed in the raw bird, and when you do it at home, you know that you're about to put the poultry right into a hot oven to cook it through. If a bird was stuffed and then packaged, however, the stuffing becomes a veritable petri dish to cultivate any bacteria that might be in the bird, and it's very difficult to get the stuffing hot enough (180°) to kill the bacteria without way overcooking the bird. You might see a stuffed frozen bird, which is a safer choice. Those usually require cooking directly from the frozen state. You'll find, however, that homemade stuffing is just as easy, and far more delicious, than anything you could buy ready-made.

Once home, store packs of meat or chicken in clean, dry plastic bags and place in the refrigerator where they can't drip onto other foods. If raw meat juices do drip onto other foods in the refrigerator, especially a product previously cooked, discard the contaminated food.

Don't Fowl Up

TV advertising has been assuring consumers for years that a yellow skin on a chicken was a sign of a good, healthy bird. And that's true if the yellowness in the skin is attributed to long, happy days in the sunshine, pecking at yellow corn. But modern manufacturers have found a way to mix natural yellow coloring into chickens' feed without having to report on the label that the color didn't simply develop on its own.

The trick is a heavy infusion of marigold leaves, cheap, full of yellow color, and apparently tasty to chickens. The pigment in the marigolds collects in the chickens' skin and tinges it yellow.

So don't be fooled. If a chicken came by its yellow skin from a healthy life, the fat will also be bright yellow. If it got that way from marigolds, the fat will be pale and whitish.

Refrigerate chicken in the coldest part of the refrigerator, preferably at 40° (a meat storage drawer is good if you have one), and freeze meat that you do not plan to use within two days. You can freeze chicken in its original packaging, but to protect it from freezer burn, you may want to wrap it in heavy aluminum foil or in another layer or two of plastic bags. Large packs of chicken, such as "family packs" of legs or thighs, can be separated into meal-sized portions in a freezer bag and frozen separately, making them easier to thaw and use. If you're freezing whole chickens, do yourself a favor and remove the giblets first. It will speed up defrosting later and save you the frustration of trying to get still-frozen giblets out of a mostly thawed bird.

For optimum safety, the USDA recommends that frozen chicken should be thawed slowly in the refrigerator, not at room temperature. However, at some point every cook has faced a solidly frozen chicken that must be cooked for dinner that night. Microwave defrosting is the fastest but also gives the poorest results in terms of the finished bird. Because the microwave partially cooks the chicken while defrosting, when you finish the dish in whatever manner you originally intended to cook it, you can end up with dry, overcooked meat.

The quickest option after that is submerging the icy bird in hot water, but resist the temptation. The sudden rush of hot water will not only thaw the outside too quickly while the interior is rock hard, but it will damage the cell structure of the frozen bird. You'll likely end up with mushy meat, not to mention risking the danger of bacterial growth.

Feathered Facts

The USDA offers a toll-free hotline to answer any questions about food safety you may have, with a large selection of recordings about food safety that can be accessed with a touch-tone phone, and a staff of dietitians, food technologists, and home economists to answer other questions. The staff is present from 10:00 a.m. to 4:00 p.m. (Eastern time) year-round. The number for the Meat and Poultry hotline is 1-800-535-4555.

For best results if you need to increase the speed of defrosting, submerge the chicken in cold water in the kitchen sink. Temperature equalizes more quickly in water than in the air, so although the water seems cold, it's much warmer than the frozen meat. Cold water speeds up the thawing process gently and safely, and you can have a usable bird in three to four hours.

Wash your hands for at least twenty seconds with soap and water before touching the raw meat, to ensure that any possible bacteria present on your hands is not transferred to the meat, then wash hands again for twenty seconds, with soap and water, after handling the raw meat, so that any bacteria on the chicken is not transferred elsewhere in your kitchen. If you wear kitchen gloves while cutting up or handling raw chicken, wash your hands while still wearing the gloves. Clean all utensils such as knives or poultry shears well after contact with raw chicken or meat, and be sure to wipe the counter space with soap and water around where you were working. Remember, bacteria is not always present in chicken, but if it is, the touch of raw juices onto, say, the lettuce for your salad, can transmit bacteria to an entire family.

Don't Fowl Up

Many experts recommend keeping a separate cutting board solely for meat and poultry, and a different board for vegetables and bread and other uses. After years of discussion over whether plastic cutting boards are safer than wood, it is now generally agreed that either are acceptable as long as they are cleaned regularly. Plastic boards were once believed to harbor fewer bacteria than wood, but research has shown that the deep grooves in the plastic made by knives are just as likely to hold bacteria as the grooves in wood.

Each time you cut meat or poultry on your meat board, wash the surface and all related utensils with water and soap, and once a month, rinse the board with a weak bleach solution (a tablespoon of bleach in a quart of warm water).

Safe Cooking Tips

After sanitary handling and careful cleaning upon touching raw chicken, the key to preventing the spread of bacteria and infection is safe cooking. Without exception, poultry must be cooked to a temperature of 180° to destroy any harmful bacteria that might be present.

Children, the elderly, and the ill or disabled are at the most risk when it comes to bacteria in food. Healthy adults may experience nothing more than a slightly upset stomach, or even feel no symptoms, while a child could become gravely ill from the same bacteria.

To be absolutely safe, you can use a digital instant-read thermometer in the thickest part of the meat (in the thigh for a whole chicken) to make sure that the chicken is cooked to a full 180°, or use the chart below to gauge minimum cooking times for unstuffed poultry, roasting at 350°, grilling over medium coals, or frying at 350°.

Table 3.1

Cut	Weight	Cooking Times
Whole Broiler-Fryer	2–4 lbs.	Roast: 1 1/4–1 1/2 hrs.
		Grill: 1–1 1/4 hours
Whole Roaster	5–7 lbs.	Roast: 2–2 1/4 hrs.
		Grill: 1 1/2–2 1/2 hrs.
Breast halves, boneless	4–6 oz.	Roast: 20–25 mins.
		Grill: 12–15 mins.
		Fry: 10–15 mins.
Breast halves, with bone	5–8 oz.	Roast: 30–40 mins.
		Grill: 20–30 mins.
		Fry: 20–30 mins.
Drumsticks	4 oz.	Roast: 35–45 mins.
		Grill: 15–25 mins.
		Fry: 20–25 mins.
Whole Legs, Thighs	4–8 oz.	Roast: 40–50 mins.
		Grill: 20–30 mins
		Fry: 20–30 mins.
Wings	2–3 oz.	Roast: 25–40 mins.
		Grill: 15–25 mins.
		Fry: 15–25 mins.
Rock Cornish Hens	1–2 lbs.	Roast: 50–60 mins.
		Grill: 45–55 mins.

Don't Fowl Up

Never eat raw poultry or try to cook poultry rare. Cooked chicken should be tender when pricked with a fork, white and opaque, not pink, and juices should run clear when the meat is cut, without any tinge of red or pink. When eating meat on the bone, as with fried chicken, there is occasionally some dark purple discoloration around the bone or a slight bit of red at the bony tip of a drumstick. This is acceptable (it is just blood leaching out of the bone) if the meat is completely opaque and not itself red.

If you have served meat that is in any way red or pink and with cloudy pink or red juices, put the meat back in the frying pan or the oven, or even the microwave, and cook further. An unplanned trip to the kitchen might be embarrassing at a dinner party, but it's sure a lot better than a trip to the hospital.

Don't Fowl Up

Never partially cook chicken and store to finish later. The heat may simply start cultivating bacteria that will be thriving too strongly to be fully destroyed by the briefer cooking time when you go to finish the chicken.

Storing Cooked Chicken

Rotisserie chicken should be purchased hot and used within two hours if eaten that day, or stored in the refrigerator for no longer than three to four days.

Leftover cooked chicken should be covered and stored in the refrigerator for up to three to four days. Remove any stuffing from roast chicken immediately after cooking and, when storing, place stuffing in a separate container from chicken to discourage bacteria.

The Least You Need to Know

➤ Potentially harmful bacteria such as salmonella and campylobacter can be already present in chicken or transmitted by improper handling by the processor.

➤ It's important for the consumer to keep raw chicken juices away from all other foods and to cook the meat to a high enough internal temperature (180°) to kill the bacteria.

➤ The safest way to quickly thaw frozen chicken (besides defrosting in the microwave) is to put the plastic-wrapped bird in a basin of cold water for several hours. Don't be tempted to put hot water on it, or you may thaw the outside and encourage the growth of bacteria while the inside is still frozen solid.

➤ Chicken should be cooked till the juices run clear, not pink or cloudy, and there's no trace or pinkness or redness in the meat.

➤ If you cut into chicken at the table and find it's undercooked, put it back in the pan or the oven or even zap it in the microwave until there's no trace of redness.

Chapter 4

Someone's Gotta Do It: Jointing and Carving

In This Chapter

➤ Tools for the job

➤ How to cut up a whole raw chicken, step by step

➤ Boning breasts

➤ Carving a whole roast chicken

The most economical way to buy chicken is whole, but assuming you want to do something other than roast it, it needs to be cut into parts. A whole raw or whole roast chicken sitting on the counter can be very intimidating if you don't know where to cut into it, but here, as always, knowledge is power, so sharpen your knife and let's get in there. It's really very easy.

Tools for the Job

You can bone a chicken with only a knife, and the best size and shape for the job is a chef's knife, the heavy-handled wide blade that professional cooks use for most chopping and cutting. An 8-inch knife is a good length for chicken (and most other general kitchen jobs) and the edge must be very sharp. A dull knife means you have to use more force, and that's very dangerous if you should slip. Be sure you have a knife with a rigid blade. A flexible blade won't give you enough control.

Poultry shears are a more specialized tool, but a worthy investment if you cut up much chicken. With large, heavy-duty blades on a spring mechanism, poultry shears have the strength and sharpness to cut right through bone, making it a breeze to separate the backbone from the breast, a job that requires a little more skill when using a knife. The blades of good poultry shears separate for cleaning, so that you can ensure no raw chicken bits remain caught in the crevices.

The Full Monty: How to Cut Up a Whole Raw Chicken

If you're using poultry shears, you'll still need a knife for some steps, such as separating the leg from the body, but you can do the job with only a sturdy knife. Begin using poultry shears in step 5—they make cutting up the wings, breast, and backbone a breeze. Have a clean work surface with plenty of light so you see what you're cutting, and have a bowl or plate ready to receive the finished pieces as you work.

When you're done, save any waste bits such as wing tips and backbones for stock, or discard them, and scrub the countertop or cutting board with dishwashing detergent and a clean dishcloth.

1. Place the chicken breast-side up on your work surface. Reach into the cavity and remove the package of giblets, if you haven't done so already. Pick up the loose skin between the thigh and breast and with the tip of your sharp knife, pierce the skin and then cut the skin open all around both thigh joints.

Step 1: Slicing open skin around thigh joint.

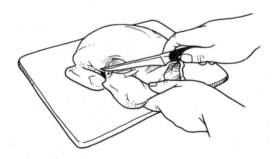

2. Grasp both legs and bend them back away from you until you feel the joints pop out. You should see the ball at the top of the thighbone pop through the meat. Lift the entire chicken by one leg and detach the leg by cutting in a straight line right below the ball of the thighbone. Since you've popped the thigh out of the socket, you don't need to actually cut through bone, but you may need to wiggle the knife around to find your way through the popped joint. Repeat on other side.

Step 2: Grasping both legs, with bird breast-side up, and bending back till thigh joints pop out of socket.

Lifting chicken by one leg and detaching leg by cutting below the ball of the thighbone you've just popped out.

3. Take a drumstick in your hand so that the crook of the joint forms a V, with the base of the V resting on the counter. Put your knife in the crook of the V and push straight down. If you look carefully at the inner part of the joint, there's a little white streak of fat that's directly over the joint. Cut there. If you encounter a lot of resistance, you've hit the bone, so jiggle the knife to find the softer center of the joint, then cut clean through. Repeat with other leg. You now have four finished pieces: two drumsticks and two thighs. Set these aside.

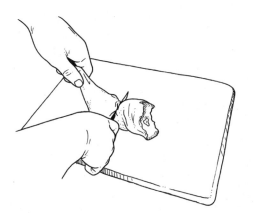

Step 3: Jointing leg by cutting through joint between thigh and drumstick.

25

4. Grasp the bird by the wing and place your knife in the inside of the joint closest to the breast and cut straight through the base of the wing, wiggling the knife to find the joint. This is a tighter joint than the thigh, so jiggle the knife to find the cartilaginous part and try to cut through there rather than forcing the knife through the bone.

Step 4: Detaching wing by holding body up by wing and jiggling knife through the flesh till it can slip through the cartilage of the joint.

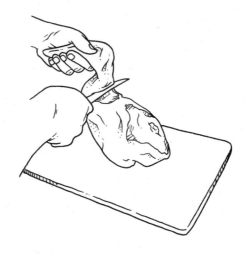

5. Cut off the bony wing tip at the far end of the wing and discard or save for stock. You may now joint the wings if you like, although you may want to keep them whole for baking or fricasseeing. To joint, as with the legs, rest the V of the detached wing on the counter and cut straight down through the crook of the joint.

Step 5: Detach and discard wing tip.

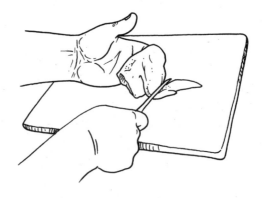

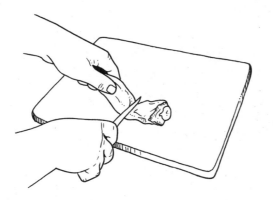

Disjoint wing by cutting through central joint.

6. With the breast side up, look inside the chicken's cavity. You can see the ribs and the long backbone in the bottom, the ribs rising to meet the breast meat. Insert your knife into the cavity to the right of the backbone and cut straight down through the rib bones just where they meet the breast meat. Repeat on the left side of the backbone. This will detach the back from the breast but the back piece may still be attached at the neck end. Flip the whole backbone and ribs out and away from the breast, cracking through those bones, and cut it off. This back piece, wing tips, and giblets may all be saved for stock.

Step 6: Lay bird breast-side up on counter, slip knife inside cavity, and cut straight down on one side of the backbone.

Cut through back on other side of backbone.

27

Use knife to cut through rest of the back to separate from breast at neck of bird.

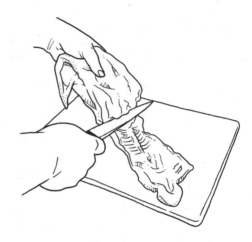

7. With the skin side of the whole breast facing down on the work surface, lay the knife down the middle of the inside of the breast, and cut the breast in half longways, right up the middle of the breastbone, through the hard bone and the long piece of cartilage. You should now have two halves of breast.

Step 7: Split the breast by cutting through the middle of the bone with skin-side down.

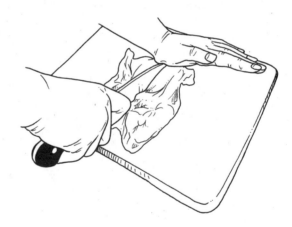

8. If you want to bone these breast pieces, insert the tip of your knife between the remainder of the ribs and the breast meat, and slice the meat off the bone. You should have eight or ten pieces, depending on if you jointed the wings: two drumsticks, two thighs, two breasts, and two or four wing pieces.

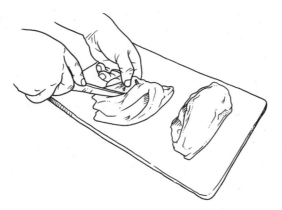

Step 8: Fillet breasts if desired by slicing meat off bone.

Boning Breasts

To bone the breasts, remove legs and wings as described above. You can cut the backbone off the breast piece, split the breast, and then bone the two breast pieces. But you can also skip step 7, separating the back, altogether and cut the breasts directly off the carcass.

Instead of cutting off the back and cutting the breast in half, place the whole breast facing up on the work surface and use a sharp knife to release the meat from either side of the chicken, cutting alongside the breastbone and rib cage.

Pay special attention to the section around the wishbone, which is the top of the breast on the neck end. Either cut off the whole wishbone before starting to cut the breast meat off, or cut right through the wishbone and use your fingers to remove the two tiny slivers of wishbone from the cut breasts.

If you're cutting up a large chicken for frying, and it has particularly large breast pieces, you can cut the breasts, on the bone, in half crosswise through the bone. (Poultry shears will break right through the hard part of the breastbone.) This will give you four medium sized breast pieces, which is easier to cook through evenly.

Carving Roast Chicken

While jointing is done to a whole raw chicken, carving is done to a whole, cooked, usually roast, chicken. The knowledge of the chicken's structure that you gain while jointing a raw chicken will stand

Feathered Facts

You can tell how young a chicken is by the amount of cartilage on the tips of the bones. A younger chicken will have much more cartilage, whereas older birds will have much more bone, making their joints harder to cut through. If the chicken is young, the end of the breastbone will be almost all cartilage. If the breastbone is very bony, it's an older bird and should be cooked long and slow for maximum tenderness.

Feathered Facts

At the end of the backbone is a bit of fat with some small vertebrae and hardly any meat in it. It has a triangular shape, and is colloquially known as "the Pope's nose" (although in Ireland they call it "the Parson's nose"). It's not useful for much, though you might want to toss it in your stock. Leave it on when you roast a whole bird so that the extra fat will melt into the pan for basting. Some people like to nibble on the crisp skin of the Pope's nose after roasting.

Roost Rap

A chicken's oysters are the two tender, bite-size pockets of meat on either side of the backbone, just by where you removed the legs. Don't confuse them with prairie oysters, which are the testicles of steers enjoyed deep-fried by some Midwesterners. On a chicken, they are just pockets of meat on the backbone.

you well for the times when you're carving a whole roasted chicken. The legs and wings are removed from a cooked bird in a similar manner, but the cooked breast is sliced differently.

Proper carving of poultry was once considered a specialized skill and many a man who couldn't find his way to the kitchen was nonetheless ready to sharpen a knife and step up to the head of the table to carve for guests. Carving tends to take place in the kitchen these days, instead of being a show at the dinner table, but you still need the same basic skills, or your beautifully roasted, golden-brown bird could turn into a pile of shredded chicken.

When the roast chicken is removed from the oven, allow it to rest for ten minutes or so, to cool slightly and allow the meat to settle. The cooling allows the hot juices to distribute themselves more evenly throughout the meat, and for the hot chicken to firm up just slightly, making it easier to cut.

It's good to have a sharp carving knife, which has a long, thin, flexible blade, and a carving fork, which has only two prongs and won't tear up the meat, but you can manage with any sharp knife and a big fork.

You can cut the chicken directly in the roasting pan, if it's a shallow one, and transfer the meat to a warmed serving platter, or transfer the chicken to a cutting board and transfer the meat from there to a platter.

1. To start, push the legs back and cut them off with the tip of a sharp knife. If you've roasted your chicken well, they should be tender enough to nearly pull off. Either cut through the joint of the thigh and drumstick, or serve the legs whole.

2. Next, carve the breast, leaving the wings on to provide support. Using a large fork or carving fork, stab one side of the breast to hold the chicken steady while you carve the other side. Cut off the outer, fat, rounded side of the breast by cutting down and away from the chicken at a 60° angle. Continue slicing like this, following the contours of the breast, until you hit bone and can't cut any more clean slices. Then you can use the carving fork to pull off any more pieces of breast meat.

3. Repeat with the other breast, balancing with your carving fork in the rib cage of the carved side.

4. Cut off the wings and joint them if you like, and add to the serving platter. For roast chicken, you don't have to remove the wing tips.

5. Last, turn the chicken over and pull out the oysters, the two soft little pockets of meat found on either side of the backbones, near the leg joints. Serve the carved chicken right away while it's still hot and moist.

This same method works for all poultry, though turkeys will require some further slicing of the legs and thighs to create manageable portions.

Don't Fowl Up

While a warmed platter might seem unnecessarily fussy, the point is to keep the hot meat from hitting a chilly plate. The shock of the cold will make the meat's juices seize up, and your meat will not be at its best when served.

Don't Fowl Up

It's easier to carve a cooked chicken breast, if the wishbone has been removed. You want to do this before roasting: Put your fingers into the neck end of the raw chicken and you'll be able to feel the wishbone at the front of the breastbone. Using a sharp knife, cut it out. If you've already roasted the chicken, you won't be able to feel the wishbone, so you'll have to cut around it.

The Least You Need to Know

➤ A good quality sharp knife is necessary to joint (or cut into pieces) a raw chicken. Poultry shears are a specialized tool which make the job even easier by crunching right through bones.

➤ Keep your knife very sharp for cutting chicken; a dull knife makes you use too much force to cut through the joints and is thus more dangerous.

➤ Carving is what you do with a whole roasted chicken. The legs and wings are removed in a way similar to that of a raw chicken, but the breast is sliced at a 60° angle.

Chapter 5

Marinating: A Little Effort, A Lotta Flavor

> **In This Chapter**
>
> ➤ What marinating really does—and how it works
>
> ➤ Basic marinades
>
> ➤ Dry rubs and how to use them
>
> ➤ Brining—the pro's secret

Food purists feel that mass production has resulted in the lessening of the "chicken" flavor in chicken. No matter, you can fight back with marinades that imbue the meat with tasty juices. For grilling, for roasting, even frying, marinating adds new depth of flavor.

What Marinating Really Does—and How It Works

The accepted wisdom about marinades is that they tenderize the meat and add flavor. But what do they really do?

The connective tissue in meat is made of collagen, which has long protein strands lying coiled within each individual cell. When you cook meat, the heat converts some of the collagen to gelatin (which is why hot cooked meat is easier to chew, and why cold meat is firmer than hot).

Acids also start converting the collagen to gelatin. When any type of meat is soaked in acids such as vinegar or lemon juice, the acids gradually enter the cells of the meat and

Feathered Facts

Meats can also be tenderized by enzymes that rapidly break down the proteins in connective tissue. Many of these are found in fruit. One of the most potent is the enzyme papain, found in papaya. Papain is the base of nearly all commercial powdered meat tenderizers, but you have to be careful not to overdo it with chicken's delicate white meat. A brief marinade that includes fresh papaya juice or flesh can add a tangy flavor in thirty minutes, but excessive soaking will result in a mushy quality. Even a tough old stewing hen is better served by long, slow cooking than a too potent tenderizing marinade.

Wing Tips

The chemical reaction between acid and protein that occurs during marination is more effective at room temperature. If you're going to marinate chicken a short time, such as an hour or two, then you're safe to leave it out on the counter. If you want to marinate it longer, however, it's best to put it in the refrigerator to slow the potential growth of bacteria.

denature the protein, i.e., cause the long protein strands to relax and unwind. The longer the meat remains in an acid environment, the more the proteins will unwind.

Unlike beef, chicken is made up of relatively short protein strands that are already quite tender, so attempting to tenderize chicken further could bring mushy results. Any chicken that's going to be stewed, roasted long and slow, boiled, or cooked in liquid any way, will enjoy the tenderizing benefits of heat. The flavor benefits of a marinade may be lost in the cooking process, so in these cases, a marinade is a waste.

That is not to say that chicken should not be marinated. If you're going to saute, grill, broil, or fry, chicken benefits greatly from being marinated for extra flavor.

Chicken must be marinated long enough to actually make a difference. All the meat must be in contact with marinade, and if you're talking about an entire chicken, that could be a huge bowl of liquid. To get around this, put the chicken to be marinated in a plastic bag with an airtight seal, such as those with zipper locks. This means that with a relatively small amount of marinade, you can coat an entire chicken, particularly if you turn the package from time to time to move the marinade around.

Removing the skin from chicken pieces makes an enormous difference in the quality of the flavor that the chicken absorbs. Skin on, the marinade will permeate the skin but will take much longer to go into the meat. Skin off and the outer layers of meat can be pleasantly permeated with flavor with a much briefer soaking time.

It's difficult to make a marinade permeate to the absolute inner parts of a cut of meat. Lengthening the marinating time would help but then you run the risk of drying out the meat by replacing all the cells' water with acid. Some cooks like to make several stabs with a knife into the inner parts of the chicken piece, assuming that this will allow the marinade to seep up into the meat, but actually, this only creates a channel for more of the inner moisture to seep out as the acids permeate the cells. Plan on your marinade only flavoring about the outer half-inch of flesh or cut the meat into smaller pieces and soak for a shorter amount of time.

Don't Fowl Up

Chicken with the skin on, either whole or in parts, can be left marinating for up to 24 hours. Chicken with the skin off should not be marinated longer than about 2 1/2 hours, or the meat will begin to "cook" in the acid. As the acid moves into the cells, some of the water in the cells is expelled. When the flesh becomes whitish in the marinade, this is probably starting to occur and you're ready to start cooking right away. If you continue marinating, you may let the marinade acids replace all the moisture in your chicken, and the cooked product will be unpleasantly dry.

Basic Marinades

A marinade need only consist of an acid but for flavor's sake, most of them contain an acid, an oil, and one or more flavorings such as herbs or spices. In general, the leaner a meat is, the more oil you want to use proportionately in your marinade. Extra virgin olive oil tastes best and, because it contains emulsifiers, seems to help penetrate the meat. The acid can come from many sources: vinegar, wine, lemon, lime, or other fruit juices, yogurt or buttermilk, and tomatoes.

Feathered Facts

Delicate, short-strand proteins can actually be "cooked" in an acidic marinade. This is what happens when you make seviche, in which fish or scallops are marinated in lemon or lime juice until their proteins have been "denatured," or unwound, with the collagen breaking down into more tender gelatin. But don't try this with chicken. The proteins in fish are far more suitable for seviche, and chicken is more prone to carry dangerous bacteria which require cooking over heat to destroy them.

Garlic is a tasty addition, either crushed or slivered, and fresh herbs are delicious, especially stronger flavored ones such as rosemary, tarragon, or thyme. Soy sauce and sesame oil are perfect for chicken, and there's a whole range of additions that can give your chicken a regional flavor, from curry powder and minced cilantro for an Indian touch to balsamic vinegar and fresh mint for a more Mediterranean feel.

Below are some starter marinades, but feel free to experiment with all sorts of ingredients. Once you get used to marinating chicken, you can start modifying to add a little extra garlic or a little less soy sauce, etc., as your taste dictates. Each of the recipes below makes approximately 3/4 cup, enough to marinate one 2- to 4-pound broiler-fryer, either whole or jointed.

Roost Rap

A clove is one section off a whole head of garlic—it could be a pretty potent mistake to confuse them! (See illustration.)

Head and clove of garlic (the clove is the small one).

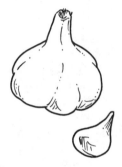

Super-Simple Marinade

Makes about 3/4 cup, to marinate a 2–4-pound chicken

1/2 cup extra virgin olive oil

1/3 cup lemon juice

2–3 cloves garlic, finely chopped

1/2 teaspoon salt

1/4 teaspoon freshly ground black pepper (or more to taste)

1. Mix all the ingredients together in a bowl.
2. Place the chicken parts in a gallon-size zipper-lock plastic bag, pour the marinade over the chicken, and seal the bag.
3. Turn the bag several times to coat well, and marinate for 1–2 hours at room temperature, or up to 24 hours in the refrigerator.

Don't Fowl Up

When you're marinating in a zipper-lock plastic bag, you may want to set the bag in a bowl or on a plate in case of leaks.

Basic Asian Marinade

The cornstarch in this recipe helps make the sauce a little thicker and enables it to cling to the chicken better.

Makes about 3/4 cup, to marinate a 2–4-pound chicken

1/2 cup soy sauce

3 tablespoons cider vinegar or rice wine or dry sherry

2 tablespoons sesame oil

1 tablespoon minced fresh ginger

2–3 cloves garlic, minced

1 teaspoon cornstarch

1. Mix all the ingredients together in a bowl and whisk well with a fork.
2. Place the chicken parts in a gallon-size zipper-lock plastic bag, pour the marinade over the chicken, and seal the bag.
3. Turn the bag several times to coat well, and marinate for 1–2 hours at room temperature, or up to 24 hours in the refrigerator.

Don't Fowl Up

Never put a marinade in which raw meat soaked onto the cooked meat. If you want to use the marinade as a sauce, bring it to a rolling boil for three to five minutes to kill off all bacteria, and do not return it to the same dish or container.

Basic Indian Marinade

Yogurt in the marinade makes an excellent tenderizer and helps add a velvety texture to the chicken. This is a good marinade for grilling and broiling, and the yogurt makes a coating that helps keep skinless chicken from burning.

Makes about 3/4 cup, to marinate a 2–4-pound chicken

1/2 cup plain yogurt	1 teaspoon curry powder
3 tablespoons lemon juice	1/2 teaspoon chili powder
3 tablespoons extra virgin olive oil	1/2 teaspoon cumin
2–3 cloves garlic, minced	2 tablespoons chopped fresh cilantro

1. Mix all the ingredients together in a bowl.
2. Place the chicken parts in a gallon-size zipper-lock plastic bag, pour the marinade over the chicken, and seal the bag.
3. Turn the bag several times to coat well, and marinate for 1–2 hours at room temperature, or up to 24 hours in the refrigerator.

Basic Italian Marinade

The balsamic vinegar and addition of herbs distinguishes this Italian-accented marinade. It's great for chicken you're going to grill or bake.

Makes about 3/4 cup, for a 2–4-pound chicken

1/2 cup extra virgin olive oil

3 tablespoons lemon juice

3 tablespoons balsamic vinegar

1 tablespoon chopped fresh rosemary, oregano, or basil or 1 teaspoon dried rosemary, oregano, or basil

1. Mix all the ingredients together in a bowl.
2. Place the chicken parts in a gallon-size zipper-lock plastic bag, pour the marinade over the chicken, and seal the bag.
3. Turn the bag several times to coat well, and marinate for 1–2 hours at room temperature, or up to 24 hours in the refrigerator.

Don't Fowl Up

Never marinate meat in an aluminum pan, which can react with the acids in the marinade. Although stainless steel is nonreactive, it's best to marinate in glass or ceramics, or in a disposable zipper-lock plastic bag. Plastic bowls or containers are fine too, but sometimes the scent of a strong marinade will linger unpleasantly in plastic. If you don't have zipper-lock plastic bags, use a shallow dish and turn the pieces frequently in the marinade. Cover with plastic wrap during marination time.

Dry Rubs

Dry rubs are a form of marinating that involves no liquid, or only enough to form a thick paste. A mixture of dried herbs and spices is rubbed into the chicken either skinned or not, and left to sit for a time while the spices permeate the meat. Dry rubs range from mild herbs such as dried basil that add a pleasant hint of flavor to potent concoctions including strong spices and zesty citrus peel that can turn a simple roast chicken into a gourmet event. Like wet marinades, dry rubs and pastes can be created to your taste, but here are a few to get your imagination going. Each recipe makes enough for a 2- to 4-pound chicken, whole or jointed.

Basic Barbecue Dry Rub

Makes a generous 1/4 cup, for a 2–4-pound chicken

3 tablespoons paprika	1 teaspoon dry mustard
2 tablespoons brown sugar	1 teaspoon chili powder
1 teaspoon salt	1 teaspoon cumin
1 teaspoon freshly ground black pepper	1/2 teaspoon ground allspice

1. Mix all ingredients together and rub all over the skin of a jointed or whole chicken.

2. Allow to sit at room temperature for at least 20 minutes before roasting, grilling, baking, or broiling, or refrigerate up to 4 hours.

Spicy Cajun Dry Rub

Similar to the spices rubbed on "blackened" fish and chicken dishes, this Louisiana-inspired rub is best used on whole chickens before roasting. If you don't love hot food, you may want to cut down on the cayenne to suit your heat resistance.

Makes 1/4 cup, for a 2–4-pound chicken

2 tablespoons paprika	1 teaspoon garlic powder
1 tablespoon chili powder	1/2 teaspoon celery salt
1 tablespoon dried oregano	1/2 teaspoon salt
1 teaspoon cumin	1/2 teaspoon freshly ground black pepper
1 teaspoon cayenne	

1. Mix all ingredients together and rub all over the skin of an entire chicken.

2. Allow to sit at room temperature for at least 20 minutes before roasting, or refrigerate up to 4 hours.

Chinese Chicken Dry Rub

Five-spice powder is a distinctive blend of Chinese flavors, with a strong hint of anise, that makes this rub taste extra special. You'll find it in the spice sections of many grocery stores, or check in an Asian market or gourmet shop.

Makes 1/4 cup, for a 2–4-pound chicken

2 tablespoons dry mustard	1 teaspoon grated orange zest
2 tablespoons brown sugar	1 teaspoon soy sauce
1 1/2 tablespoons five-spice powder	1 teaspoon sesame oil

1. Mix all ingredients together and rub all over the skin of a jointed or whole chicken.

2. Allow to sit at room temperature for at least 20 minutes before roasting, grilling, baking, or broiling, or refrigerate up to 4 hours.

Don't Fowl Up

Orange zest is the fragrant orange-colored part of the rind, full of pungent oils that help impart the essence of orange to other foods. You can grate it off an orange or peel it off and chop it finely. However you remove it, be sure to avoid the white part underneath, known as the pith. It can add a bitter flavor.

Don't Fowl Up

If your spices and herbs have been sitting on the shelf for years, it's time to throw them out and buy more. Paprika in particular loses its flavor quickly, so many people are unfamiliar with the rich, slightly smoky flavor that fresh paprika has to offer. Chili powder, cayenne, cumin, basil, parsley, oregano—they all become tired and stale over time, particularly if stored where light can reach them. If your spices don't smell fresh and strong, the food you cook with them simply won't taste as good.

Brining: The Pro's Secret

Soaking chicken in saltwater might sound like a cheap industrial trick to increase the weight of a commercial bird—and sometimes it is. But practiced at home with clean salted water, brining is a fabulous way to increase the moisture and improve both the texture and flavor of chicken.

An old farmwife trick, a salty bath draws blood out of the meat and puts moisture in, leaving the meat milky white. Furthermore, the salt that seeps into the cells makes the meat taste pleasantly seasoned all the way in toward the bone.

Wing Tips

If you're in a hurry but you still want the benefits of brining, double the salt and halve the time. The resulting chicken won't be quite as plump and juicy as it can be with longer soaking, but it will still have improved taste and texture.

The reason that salt water seasons the meat and makes it juicy instead of drying it out and making it salty, as you might expect it to, is because of the coiled strands of meat protein. As the salty water seeps into the meat cells, the salt denatures the strands of protein, making them more sticky and viscous and causing them to attract and retain water molecules.

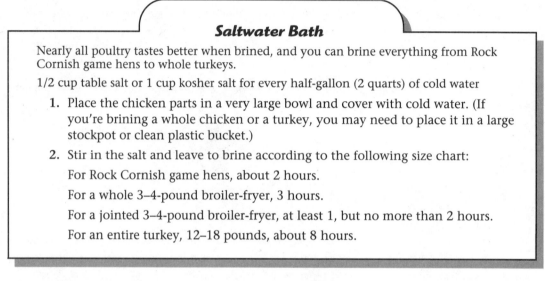

Saltwater Bath

Nearly all poultry tastes better when brined, and you can brine everything from Rock Cornish game hens to whole turkeys.

1/2 cup table salt or 1 cup kosher salt for every half-gallon (2 quarts) of cold water

1. Place the chicken parts in a very large bowl and cover with cold water. (If you're brining a whole chicken or a turkey, you may need to place it in a large stockpot or clean plastic bucket.)

2. Stir in the salt and leave to brine according to the following size chart:

    For Rock Cornish game hens, about 2 hours.

    For a whole 3–4-pound broiler-fryer, 3 hours.

    For a jointed 3–4-pound broiler-fryer, at least 1, but no more than 2 hours.

    For an entire turkey, 12–18 pounds, about 8 hours.

Don't Fowl Up

Always use very cold water for brining poultry. It may seem as if warm water would speed up the process, but not only do you run the risk of encouraging bacterial growth, you'll also damage the texture of the meat with warm water.

The Least You Need to Know

➤ Marinating chicken in a mixture including an acid, an oil, and a seasoning (such as lemon juice, olive oil, and garlic) can imbue the flesh with flavor and make the meat more tender.

➤ Dry rubs are a sort of dry marinade made of spices and flavorings mixed together and rubbed all over the raw chicken. The bird is then left for a while before cooking to allow the flavors to penetrate the meat.

➤ Brining is the secret to plumper, moister, more flavorful birds.

➤ Any kind of poultry, from Rock Cornish game hens to turkeys, can benefit from a soaking for several hours in salt water (1/2 cup salt to two quarts water).

Part 2
Chicken Wrangling: Major Cooking Methods

Chicken is an amazingly versatile food that suits nearly every type of cooking method you can imagine. From making stock to roasting, frying and sauteing to stewing and fricasseeing, across the spectrum from steaming to grilling, each method brings out certain favorable characteristics, and as you get to know chickens, you can decide what cooking method will best suit the bird in your fridge.

Chapter 6

Chicken Stock: Good for What Ails You

Chicken stock is a vital ingredient in restaurant kitchens, where it's used in soups, sauces, stews, and gravies, even to blanch vegetables and cook rice. Using chicken stock instead of water adds extra body and flavor to nearly any finished dish, and it's a basic requirement for plenty of soups that don't even call for chicken in any other form. Once you get into the habit of making and using your own stock, you may find it hard to do without.

Stock Secrets: Tips for Making Good Stock

The best and most flavorful stock is made from a whole raw chicken, simmered very gently with a few aromatic vegetables such as onions and celery, and then, after several hours, gently strained and cooled and placed in the refrigerator, where overnight it turns into a sort of soft, intensely flavored chicken jelly.

When you don't have the time or inclination for this kind of ultimate stock, though, there's also quick and easy stock, with a few raw chicken pieces (or unused parts such as the backbone) tossed in cold water and bubbled on the back of the stove for an hour. You won't get a blissfully rich chicken broth this way, but you will get a good, functional stock that has more body and flavor (and far less salt) than a stock cube dissolved in hot water.

The quick and simple kind of stock has few hard and fast rules beyond the fact that you must always start with cold water. You can use onions and celery if you like, and a few whole peppercorns and a bay leaf for added flavor, and then throw in whatever raw pieces you have.

After you've jointed a whole chicken (see p. 24), use the leftover back and ribs and the wing tips. If you're making Buffalo Wings and trimming all the tips off a couple pounds of wings (see p. 128), put the tips in a saucepan to make stock, or store them in a plastic bag in the freezer till you've collected enough to make stock. Get into the habit of never throwing away a piece of raw chicken, and you'll always have fresh stock on hand.

One Last Peep: Stock from Cooked Chicken

Stock made with cooked chicken is a different matter—it can be a good way to make a quick soup and get a last bit of use out of a roasted chicken (or turkey) carcass, but it tastes completely different. It won't have the fresh flavor of stock made with raw chicken. Some people don't like the taste of stock made from cooked chicken, and if you find you agree, you might do as well to simply discard your roast chicken carcasses without trying to get one more use out of them.

If you do want to make stock with it, though, place the remains of the roast bird, along with any loose bones such as those from the drumsticks, in a pot and cover with 1 to 1 1/2 quarts of cold water. Add a quartered onion with the skin on, one to two stalks of celery, halved, and a carrot, halved. Simmer gently for one to two hours and strain out and discard all the solids.

Ultimate Stock

For your best soups, nothing will do but the very rich kind of stock, starting with a whole chicken and fresh, aromatic vegetables. There are a lot of steps you can take to make perfect stock, and you'll have to decide which ones are worth your while. You can break all the rules and still have usable stock, but for stock perfection, always follow:

The Rules of Stock

1. Don't boil your stock. Hard boiling is the main thing standing between you and clear but intensely flavored, fresh-tasting stock. Boiling makes stock cloudy and muddies the flavor. It emulsifies the fat and can extract unpleasant flavor from the bones.

2. Instead, always simmer your stock very gently, with only a few bubbles rising, and don't let it reach a hard, rolling boil.

3. It helps to blanch the bones before beginning. This Japanese approach to stock starts with a quick dip in boiling water to remove the impurities from the surface of the bones and dramatically lessen the amount of gray scum that usually must be skimmed from the surface of the stock. If you prefer not to blanch, then skim frequently while simmering. Any scum that rises to the top should be removed, not stirred in.

4. Even after blanching, always use cold water when you actually make the stock. You want to gradually increase the heat of the bones, vegetables, and water all together to leach the maximum flavor out of the stock ingredients.

5. Use very low heat and raise the stock to a very slow simmer, then lower the heat to make sure the stock won't boil. The surface of the liquid should tremble gently, but bubbles shouldn't rise.

6. Use a tall, narrow stockpot when possible and don't cover it or stir. The shape of a stockpot is designed for slow evaporation. You want the flavors to gradually concentrate, and if the lid is on, nothing can evaporate.

7. Don't stir up the bones or break up the bits of vegetable, or the stock will be cloudy. Just let the simmering water slowly extract the flavor.

8. Salt is your decision. Some schools of thought hold that the merest hint of salt in stock is an abomination and destroys the pure chicken flavor, but others think that a little salt at the stock stage lays down a more solid flavor base for later. If you're watching the salt content in your diet, leave it out altogether. If using, a teaspoon of salt to 1 1/2 quarts of cold water is a good amount for stock.

Feathered Facts

Colonial Americans used onion skins to dye wool. The papery skins when boiled create a deep, muted yellow. If you don't peel the onions for your stock but add them cut into quarters with the skins still on, they'll add a lovely rich color to the stock.

Feathered Facts

Chicken stock didn't get the name Jewish Penicillin for nothing. Those who flout their grandmothers' advice to drink chicken soup for the common cold are really missing out. Science still isn't quite sure why, but research has shown that hot chicken soup actually brings relief. If your nose is stuffy, shake a few flakes of dried red chili or a pinch of powdered cayenne into your bowl of soup. The chili heat will bring relief.

Don't Fowl Up

Don't use starchy vegetables such as potatoes and turnips in your stock. They make good soup additions, but they'll cloud your stock and mask the pure chicken flavor. For flavor reasons, don't use any cabbage or vegetables from the cabbage family: cauliflower, broccoli, broccoli rabe. Standard stock vegetables are carrots, onions, and celery, though some favor leeks. These vegetables offer a pure, unintrusive flavor that won't overpower your stock.

In the Stocks

Type I: Quick Basic Stock

This is a practical stock for using up the raw carcass of a chicken you may have just jointed and boned for dinner, or any leftover pieces such as wing tips. The recipe calls for all the bones except for the thigh and drumstick bones, which are still inside the thighs and drumsticks as it is unlikely you would have boned those parts of the bird.

Feel free to use all the giblets except for the liver; include the neck, the back, the ribs, and the wings or wing tips—everything you just cut off the chicken as well as any raw bits of meat attached. If you make a lot of Buffalo Wings, collect the trimmed wing tips in the freezer and make this stock when you have amassed about two cups of wing tips.

Don't Fowl Up

If you're not using your stock right away, cool it and store it in the refrigerator as quickly as possible. If it's a warm day, you may consider dipping the pot holding the stock in a cold water bath in your sink. Letting warm stock sit out on the counter is just asking for stray bacteria to make a home there. Also, don't cover hot stock and put it in the refrigerator. The air space between the surface and the lid can stay hot for a long time even as the stock cools, permitting further bacterial growth.

Quick Basic Stock

Makes 1–1 1/2 quarts of stock

1 chicken carcass, including giblets (except liver) and wing tips

1 medium carrot, cut into 2-inch lengths

1 stalk of celery, cut into 2-inch lengths

1 sprig fresh parsley

1 bay leaf

1 teaspoon salt

1/2 teaspoon whole black peppercorns

1. Place all ingredients in a pot and cover with 1 1/2–2 quarts of water.

2. Place over low heat and bring slowly to a simmer. The heat should be low enough that it takes 15–20 minutes to come to a simmer. As soon as you see bubbles start to rise, adjust heat so that the stock does not begin to boil, then let simmer over this very low heat for an hour. Do not cover, and check occasionally to make sure it's not boiling.

3. After an hour, use a slotted spoon to remove and discard the chicken and the vegetables. If desired, continue to simmer the stock over low heat for another hour. This will evaporate some of the water and concentrate the flavor of the stock, but you can skip this step.

4. Strain the stock through a fine-mesh strainer, cool, and refrigerate in a covered container. (Don't cover hot stock. Let it cool for awhile first or bacteria may grow.) When the stock has cooled in the refrigerator, the fat will harden into a solid layer on the top. Skim off the fat and discard. Store the stock for no longer than a week in the refrigerator or for up to three months in the freezer.

Type II: Elaborate Stock

This is a much richer stock, starting with a whole bird and ending up with an intensely flavored stock that's the essence of chicken. You can leave the chicken whole, but jointing it will allow more flavor to seep out of the bones. In either case, all the meat and skin stay on the bones as you cook it so that all their flavor goes into the stock. Add all the giblets (neck, heart, gizzard) as well, except the liver.

The gourmet way of making this Elaborate Stock involves straining out all the solids, including all the chicken, and discarding them, leaving nothing but a pure, intensely flavored stock. Any cook with the slightest thought of frugality, however, may feel that she's just thrown away the soup!

Feathered Facts

Chris McGowan, a paleontologist at the Royal Museum in Toronto, Ontario, has come up with a novel way to explore the possible links between modern birds and dinosaurs. With the bones of three whole chickens (which you can save from making stock) and some help from an adult, a child can build an incredible scale model of a brontosaurus, following the instructions found in *Make Your Own Dinosaur Out of Chicken Bones* (HarperPerennial, 1997).

Instead, pull the chicken meat off the bones, and discard the bones and skin, reserving the meat for whatever soup you make, but note that much of the meat's flavor will be gone, and the texture may be a bit mushy due to the long cooking. It's suitable for soup (when added toward the end of cooking to keep it from cooking down further and into shreds), but don't expect to use it for chicken salad.

Do discard the cooked-out vegetables and flavorings, and start with fresh vegetables to make the best soup possible.

This is such a concentrated stock that you may want to make it for immediate use in a soup, perhaps reserving a cup or two of the stock to use in a special sauce or gravy.

If you make a large quantity of stock using the Elaborate recipe, you may find you have plenty extra to store. A good way to always have stock on hand is to freeze the stock in ice cube trays, then put the frozen cubes in a plastic bag and store in the freezer. You'll always have stock for a sauce or you can melt a handful of cubes to whip up a quick bowl soup.

Elaborate Stock

Makes 3–4 quarts of stock

1   4–5-pound stewing hen or a large broiler-fryer, jointed (or left whole)
2   stalks celery, cut in 2-inch pieces
2   large carrots, cut in 2-inch pieces
1   large onion, unpeeled and quartered
1   sprig fresh parsley
1   sprig fresh thyme (optional)
1   teaspoon peppercorns
1   teaspoon salt
2   bay leaves

1. Bring 4 quarts of water to a boil in a large stockpot. Immerse all the chicken pieces in the water and bring it back to a boil. Boil for 1 minute, then drain in a strainer and rinse the chicken pieces under cold water.

2. Rinse the pot with cold water and return the chicken pieces to it. Add all remaining ingredients and cover with 4 1/2 quarts of cold water.

continued

3. Slowly bring to a very gentle simmer over medium-low heat. Simmer slowly for 3–4 hours, checking occasionally to make sure it's not boiling. If it begins to boil, reduce heat promptly.

4. Strain it through a fine-mesh strainer, discarding all the solids except for some of the meat, which you may wish to reserve for soup. If making soup with the stock, you can proceed now without cooling stock first. Cool the stock on the counter for an hour or two, and then refrigerate in several covered containers. (Don't cover hot stock. Let it cool uncovered at first or bacteria may grow.)

5. When the stock has cooled in the refrigerator, the fat will harden into a solid layer on the top. Skim off the fat and discard. Store the stock for no longer than a week in the refrigerator and up to three months in the freezer.

The Least You Need to Know

➤ A quick, light chicken stock can be made simply by simmering a few raw pieces of meat, such as the back off a jointed chicken, in some water.

➤ A richer, more concentrated, and far more intensely flavored stock is made with a whole raw chicken, which is slow cooked in water with aromatic vegetables, such as onions and celery.

➤ However stock is made, always start with cold water to leach the most flavor possible out of the bones.

➤ For best results, don't ever let the stock boil, but adjust heat so that it simmers very gently.

Chapter 7

Roasting: The Ultimate Test

In This Chapter

➤ What's so great about roast chicken?

➤ Tips for better roasting

➤ A foolproof roast chicken recipe and variations

Roasting is a method of cooking a whole chicken, uncovered, with dry heat. Cooking a jointed chicken is usually called baking, though the same oven and the same heat is used, but to roast, no liquid is added to the pan other than the chicken's own melting fat, which is then used to baste the bird. The skin is richly browned, and the fat keeps the meat moist.

Roast chicken is the benchmark of chicken cooking and it takes a little bit of effort to get it just right. But a few simple techniques will ensure that you pass muster with a golden-skinned bird that's tender, juicy, and cooked through.

What's So Great About Roast Chicken?

You may have noticed in restaurant reviews that the critic will frequently comment on the roast chicken. In a fine restaurant, it would seem that there are much more fancy dishes to discuss than a simple roasted bird. But that one dish is considered a testing point for even the greatest chefs, and the reference is something of a code in the food world: If the roast chicken is just right, then the chef is skillful. If the roast chicken isn't good, nothing else will be too great either.

Why is this humble dish the benchmark of a cook's talent? Possibly because when the ingredients are few, technique is all. Every turn of the basting spoon, every moment in the oven, it all shows in the finished dish. There are differing thoughts on basting and heat, oven position and quantities of seasoning, but the result must be the same.

Removing leg from roast chicken.

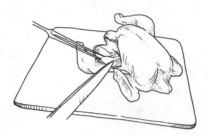

Slicing breast meat.

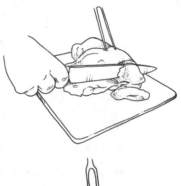

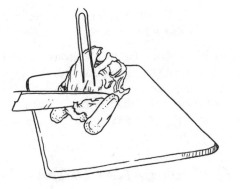

Slice off the wings.

Purely perfect roast chicken is not stuffed, but allows the meat to shine through above all else. It should be juicy, with a crisp golden-brown skin, the meat so tender that it yields to the fork like butter, and the flavor must be above all chicken-y, accented with a whisper of salt and butter.

Once this technique has been mastered, there's a world of fabulous things to do to roast chicken, but let's walk before we fly.

Tips for Better Roasting

Although roasting chickens can be five to six pounds, and capons even larger, for simple roasting it's best to start with a smaller bird such as a 3-pound broiler-fryer. When you're an expert, then you can transfer your knowledge to a more stately bird.

A 3-pound chicken will take just over an hour to roast, although with slow cooking techniques, it can be slowly roasted and basted for twice that long, resulting in a meltingly tender bird with a perfectly caramelized exterior.

The difference lies in your approach to oven temperature. The high-heat method starts with the oven at 450° to 500°. The prepared chicken is placed into this searingly hot oven, the bird's temperature is rapidly increased and the skin is swiftly browned, then the heat is lowered after ten to fifteen minutes and the roasting is continued at the more usual temperature of 325° to 375°. Roasting at higher temperatures requires a lot of watching, because the fat tends to sizzle and spit a great deal, but the result is beautifully roasted, crisp-skinned chicken in a relatively short amount of time.

The opposite extreme is the slow-oven, long-basting method, which starts with a seasoned chicken in a very low oven, 250° to 300°. The chicken is basted frequently to keep it from drying out during the long cooking. This is a high-maintenance way to roast chicken, but the result is deliciously tender chicken practically falling off the bone. If deliciously crisp skin is your favorite part, or you don't have a lot of time, go for the high-heat method. But if you have a quiet afternoon in which to baste your chicken, try the low and slow way—it makes meltingly moist, flavorful meat.

For roasting, buy the best chicken you can find. If you have access to free-range, organic chickens, splurge on one for your roast chicken.

Cook chicken in a roasting pan with low sides. High-sided roasters prevent heat from evenly reaching the whole chicken. If your pan is too big and deep, you end up steaming your chicken more than roasting it. You may want to set the chicken on a roasting rack, which raises it from the pan juices and lets the heat reach it evenly on all sides.

Roost Rap

To truss a chicken is to tie the legs and wings with one long piece of clean cotton string (or special linen trussing string, available at cookware shops). The traditional truss is an elaborate web of loops and knots, designed to hold the chicken's exterior parts close to the body so that the cooked bird is in a neat, tidy package.

Wing Tips

If you don't have a roasting rack, cut peeled onions into rings 1 1/2 to 2 inches thick and lay four to six of these thick rings at least an inch apart under the raw chicken. They act as a stand-in roasting rack, raising the chicken from the pan juices so that it doesn't steam or boil in its own juice. When you're done, you have roasted onions deeply infused with the pan juices.

To Truss or Not to Truss?

Trussing a chicken by tying the legs and wings with string was intended to hold the bird in a neat shape while roasting, so that those parts couldn't flop open in the oven. It's a fussy procedure that not many cooks bother with these days. The extra step adds preparation time, and tying the chicken into such a dense little package actually makes it take longer to roast.

The best advice is to dispense with trussing altogether, unless it's absolutely necessary, as with a chicken (or turkey) brimming with stuffing. In this case, tying the legs together helps hold the stuffing in while the bird roasts. But go for the simple way: Use a short, clean length of twine and simply tie the drumsticks together at the tips. Cut off the loose ends, and trim off the string altogether before carving and serving.

On the Rack

Cookware shops carry cone-shaped wire roasters that let you roast the chicken standing upright, on the theory that this will let the fat drain out of the bird. If you've already got one, they're fine and work quite well, but they're not necessary.

If you're roasting correctly, the fat will drain out anyway as it melts in the heat, and you'll spoon it back over the skin to baste and keep the skin brown, but it won't soak back into the meat. A flat or V-shaped roasting rack is good and useful; you just want something to hold the chicken up out of the pan juices to keep it, essentially, from boiling in its own liquid.

The best way to keep the breast meat moist is to roast the chicken lying on its breast and sides, instead of its back, for part of the cooking. This way the fat and juices from the dark meat on the legs and back drips down through the breast. Start with the chicken's back facing up. Then turn it onto one side, and then the other every fifteen to twenty minutes. Before the end of cooking, the chicken is turned on its back, breast up, and the roasting is finished in the traditional position so that the breast is beautifully browned. It sounds unorthodox, but it works wonderfully. (It's also great with turkey.)

Frequent basting is crucial to well-roasted chicken. Those turkey basters with a rubber suction bulb work well for sucking up pan juices if you have a small roasting pan, but if you don't own a bulb baster and you do have room to slide in a large spoon on either side of the chicken, a spoon is just as good. The chicken roasts undisturbed for an initial twenty to thirty minutes to start the juices flowing, then you have to baste.

If you're roasting long and slow, open the oven every 10 minutes (told you it was high-maintenance) and spoon the pan juices and fat over the chicken. For the higher heat roasting, baste every twelve to fifteen minutes. You may need to use a potholder to tip the roasting pan up a bit and pool the juices to one side of the pan so you can spoon them up easily.

Don't Fowl Up

Remember to always look inside the chicken's cavity and remove the package of giblets or the neck or anything else you see lurking in there! It also helps to give the chicken a rinse with cool water inside and out, to ensure the skin is clean and ready to eat.

A Foolproof Roast Chicken Recipe and Variation

This is easy-to-roast-for-dinner chicken that is elegant enough to serve to guests. The first, higher-heat method is for young, small birds. If you have an older, bigger bird, use the slow-roast variation below. The lemon and onion inside add a delicate bit of perfume to chicken that is moist and tender, with a buttery and crisp crust. Eat as soon as possible after it emerges from the oven, while the skin is still crisp. It is delicious cold, too—leftovers make marvelous chicken sandwiches: Serve the meat on white bread with a touch of mayonnaise, and a sprinkle of salt.

Wing Tips

If the pan juices start to spatter, carefully pour a cup of water directly into the roasting pan.

Foolproof Roast Chicken

Serves 4

1 3–4-pound broiler-fryer

Salt and pepper

1 lemon, halved

1 medium onion, quartered

2 tablespoons softened butter

1. Preheat oven to 450°. Remove the giblets and rinse the chicken inside and out. Pat it dry with paper towels and sprinkle with salt and pepper inside and out. Rub all over with softened butter and place the lemon halves and onion quarters in the cavity.

2. Place the chicken breast side down on a rack in a roasting pan. Place in the preheated oven and roast at 450° for 30 minutes. After 20 minutes, baste once.

3. After 30 minutes, lower the heat to 350° and flip the chicken over so it's breast-side up. Cook for another hour, basting every 10–15 minutes, or until the legs move easily, the juices run clear, and there's no hint of pink in the meat.

Don't Fowl Up

If it's rare, beware. Never serve chicken that's even slightly pink. Use the tip of a sharp knife to poke the thigh of a roast chicken and look at the color of the juices that leak out. They should be clear with some hint of oily yellow fat. If they're cloudy and red or pink, it's not done yet, so pop your bird back in the oven and roast some more.

Low and Slow Roast Variation

Preheat oven to 250°. Follow directions above for preparing chicken, place in oven, and cook for 3–3 1/2 hours.

Start basting after 30 minutes, when the juices have started to flow, and baste every 10–15 minutes after that, until chicken is dark golden brown and almost falling off the bone.

Don't Fowl Up

Don't neglect your basting. Basting is the key to low and slow roasting and if you forget to, you will have tough, dry chicken. If you're two hours into cooking and you realize you haven't basted for the last hour, flip the breast over so it faces down, letting the fat run downward through the white breast meat, and baste vigilantly for the remaining time. Turn the breast up again about twenty minutes before you remove it from the oven.

The Least You Need to Know

➤ Roasting is a dry heat method of cooking a whole chicken in a low-sided pan in the oven. No liquid is added, so the skin gets crisp and brown as it cooks.

➤ Roast chicken is the height of chicken cooking and the technique is worth mastering. The quality of their roast chicken is a code among the chefs of the world for the quality of all their cooking.

➤ The two main methods of roasting chicken are quickly at a very high temperature, highlighting the very crisp skin, or long and slow at a low temperature, highlighting the meltingly tender meat nearly falling off the bone.

➤ Whatever method you choose, never neglect the basting, or spooning of fat and pan juices over the roasting bird, every ten to fifteen minutes while it roasts. This keeps the meat moist.

Chapter 8

Frying: Everyone's Got a Theory

In This Chapter

➤ Favorite fried chicken

➤ Tips for better frying

➤ Recipe for Mom's fried chicken

One of the tastiest ways to make chicken is also one of the more tricky. Frying chicken can be a messy procedure but if you follow some basic ground rules, you can make mother-approved fried chicken with a minimum of fuss.

Favorite Fried Chicken

The reason people tend to think that their own mothers' fried chicken is best is probably because it is. So many travesties in the name of fried chicken are served in restaurants and diners, tarted up with unnecessary sauces and excess flavorings in the crust, that homemade is almost always better. Restaurants tend to think they can make better fried chicken because they have access to deep-fat fryers and can drop a piece of chicken coated in batter into a great deal of hot oil.

Real fried chicken, however, is not deep-fried. It's fried in shallow oil, making the crust toothsome, without that firm, thick crust that deep-frying can create.

Because fried chicken is such a production, involving jointing and brining, shaking up the flour coating, and resulting in the smell of frying oil in your kitchen for a day or two after, you may want to heat up two skillets and fry more than one chicken. Cooking two broiler-fryers will mean plenty of fried chicken for four to six people with leftover pieces to go into the refrigerator for the next day.

Tips for Better Frying

Everyone has his or her own theory as to the best way to fry chicken. Some people swear that it should only be turned once, others consider dipping the pieces in beaten egg to be vital before dredging them in flour. Some like cracker crumbs and cornmeal in the crust and others can't imagine chicken without the traditional Southern touch of milk gravy made with some of the fat and brown bits left in the pan.

The easiest fried chicken, the kind that purists love, is dredged lightly in flour and shallow-fried. Skin can be removed if you're trying to cut calories, but the end result won't be nearly the same. Fried chicken has to have the skin on to achieve the best possible crust.

For best results, fry the chicken in a high-sided cast-iron skillet (or any other wide frying pan with a lid). If you don't have a lid, improvise with another piece of cookware that will lie over the surface of the frying pan, such as a metal cookie sheet or the lid to your wok.

With most other fried foods, each food needs plenty of room in the pan, but chicken takes well to crowding. As long as each piece is lying on the bottom of the pan, the pieces can jostle each other without affecting the cooking.

Roost Rap

Dredging is a term that refers to any sort of food being coated in flour prior to cooking. To dredge chicken, you can either roll the chicken in flour in a bowl or plate, or put the flour in a bag and toss the chicken in it. (Always discard the flour in which you've dredged raw chicken.)

Roost Rap

A warm oven means that the oven is heated at the lowest temperature, usually 180° on the dial, to keep food hot until ready to serve. If chicken is left on the counter to cool while you finish making the rest of dinner, it will become tough. This is fine when you're raiding the fridge for that last drumstick, but fresh-fried chicken should be served warm, tender, and crisp.

Know Your Oil

Peanut oil is a good frying oil because it can withstand high temperatures well, but any vegetable oil, such as corn oil, is fine. Traditional Southern fried chicken is cooked in hydrogenated shortening, the kind that comes in a can, but science is finding that the trans-fatty acids in this kind of oil are even worse for your heart than might have been assumed, so if you're going to fry, it may be best to use an oil that's in a liquid, not solid, form. Don't fry chicken in olive oil, which imparts a heavy flavor.

The oil should be heated to about 350°, not hot enough to smoke, but hot enough that a cube of bread or a tiny pinch of flour sizzles when dropped in. If the oil is not hot enough to make the chicken sizzle when you put it in the pan, the chicken will be heavy with oil and the crust won't be properly crisp. You want the oil hot enough to seal the flour crust around the chicken, but not so hot that it browns too quickly and burns. The chicken is going to be cooking for about forty minutes, so it's not like rapid deep-frying and the temperature should be monitored.

The Big Cover-Up

After it's placed in the hot oil, the chicken is browned on both sides and then covered with a lid to continue cooking. This step is necessary so that the chicken cooks all the way through to the bone. If you skip this part and assume the chicken is done because the outside is nicely browned, you may end up with underdone meat near the bone— it's not safe because of possible bacteria, and it's also unappetizing.

The lid is placed slightly askew so that steam can escape while the chicken cooks. If you put the lid on tightly, the crust will be mushy and soft, and it may fall off the chicken entirely. After you remove the lid, you increase the heat slightly and fry the chicken until the crust is completely crisp again. Remove to a warm, paper towel lined platter or serving dish. The paper towels will soak up excess oil on the surface of the crust.

Wing Tips

Jointed chicken for frying will particularly benefit from the brining process. Let the chicken parts soak in saltwater for a couple of hours before cooking. It will draw the blood out from the bones and leave you with pristine fried chicken.

Fried chicken should still be warm when served, despite the legendary status of cold fried chicken left in the fridge. That's delicious, but it's a completely different thing from the perfectly tender meat with a crisp crust that you'll take out of the hot oil. So if you need to let the chicken sit for awhile as you prepare the rest of a meal, for best results put it in a warm oven set to the lowest temperature.

Recipe for Mom's Fried Chicken

This is the simplest way to fry chicken. There are all sorts of things you can add into the flour, such as celery salt and cayenne, but purists prefer their fried chicken to taste of nothing but chicken.

To serve 4

1 2–3-pound broiler-fryer

1 cup all-purpose flour

1 tablespoon paprika

1 1/2 teaspoon salt

1/2 teaspoon black pepper

Vegetable oil for frying

1. Remove the giblets and save them for stock (p. 137). Joint the chicken into 8 pieces as described on p. 24. If desired, leave the pieces to soak for 2 hours in a

continued

saltwater solution. (If you do brine the chicken, rinse in cool water when finished.)

2. When ready to fry, pour oil into a heavy skillet till the oil is 1/2-inch deep, and begin heating over medium heat to about 350°, or until a tiny pinch of flour or a cube of bread will sizzle when dropped into the oil. It should not be hot enough to smoke. If it is smoking, remove pan from heat and cool for a few moments.

3. Combine all dry ingredients in a paper bag such as a brown lunch bag or a plastic zipper-lock bag. Drop in four chicken pieces at a time and shake until well coated with flour. Slip the floured chicken into the hot oil and repeat with the remaining pieces. All eight pieces should fit into the hot oil, even if they're crowded.

4. Increase the heat slightly to keep the oil hot enough to sizzle. After 5 minutes, turn all the chicken pieces and brown on the other side. Lower the heat and cover with the lid slightly askew so that steam can escape, and cook for 25–30 minutes.

5. Remove cover and increase the heat slightly. Turn the chicken pieces again and fry for another 5–10 minutes to crisp up the crust. Both sides should be a rich, golden brown. Remove to a paper-towel lined platter and place the platter in a warm oven (180°) until ready to serve.

The Least You Need to Know

➤ For the best results, fried chicken should be shallow fried in about 1/2 inch of oil, not deep fried.

➤ Peanut oil works well for frying, because it can withstand high temperatures, but never make fried chicken in olive oil, which imparts a heavy taste.

➤ Brown the chicken on both sides for a few moments, then cover the pan with the lid slightly askew for twenty-five minutes so it cooks through to the bone. Remove the lid and crisp up the skin before serving.

➤ If your fried chicken has to wait to be served, put the platter in the oven at a very low heat to keep it warm and keep the crust crisp and dry until serving.

Chapter 9

A Hot Pan, A Little Butter: Sauteing

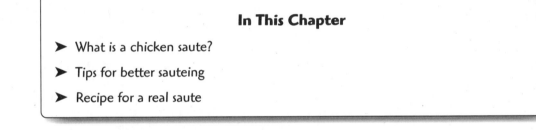

In This Chapter

➤ What is a chicken saute?

➤ Tips for better sauteing

➤ Recipe for a real saute

A quick-cooking method with very little fat, sauteing leaves chicken tender and juicy, and with a little help, the bird almost makes its own sauce.

What Is a Chicken Saute?

The term saute is now used loosely to describe almost any sort of pan-frying, but the word is a French one that is derived from the verb *"sauter,"* meaning "to leap."

In cooking, the term specifically means to rapidly cook meat or vegetables in a small amount of butter and maybe a touch of oil over a high temperature while skillfully jerking the pan back and forth so that the food literally leaps in the pan. (We'll be doing a modified version of this to ensure that your chicken stays in the pan.) Rather than the more sedate exercise of pan-frying, sauteing is much more akin to the Asian technique of stir-frying.

The result is a fresh-tasting, swiftly cooked food that retains almost all of its natural juices. Classic French sauteed chicken is then coated with a small amount of sauce made from deglazing the pan with stock or wine.

Roost Rap

To deglaze is to swirl a liquid such as wine, stock, water, or cream in a hot pan in which meat has been cooked. The liquid dislodges the browned bits and fats left clinging to the pan. The liquid used to deglaze is then rapidly boiled and used as a sauce, sometimes with other additions, so that all the meat's flavor can go into the dish.

Feathered Facts

At this moment, there are more than 7 billion chickens in the world.

Tips for Better Sauteing

Although any light skillet will do, the classic saute pan is slope-sided to help you shake and toss the ingredients without flipping them out of the pan.

More important than the pan, though, is the use of real butter. A tablespoon of butter to a tablespoon of extra virgin olive oil will give the right proportions in terms of flavor. The butter is not absolutely necessary—it just adds a little oomph to your sauce when you deglaze the pan, but if you're watching fat, use a nonstick skillet and only a teaspoon or two of oil. (Don't leave it out entirely, though, or the chicken will taste dry and tough—just that touch of oil makes a real difference.)

The heat must be high enough to cook the chicken quickly but not so high that it burns the butter. If the butter starts to burn or blacken, throw it out, wipe out the pan with a paper towel, and start again.

The chicken pieces to be sauteed must be patted dry with a paper towel to remove all the surface moisture possible. And so must the pan. Wet chicken will not brown properly. Because of the quick-cooking properties of sauteing, chicken with the skin removed works very well with this method. The skin, if it is left on, will brown rather than crisp when sauteed.

If you like, you may simply remove the sauteed chicken to a plate and eat immediately. But the quick browning of the saute process lends itself particularly well to deglazing, so even if you just use a splash of water, you can easily make a swift sauce to accent the cooked chicken.

Recipe for a Real Saute

Here's a quick and classic saute using only chicken breasts for speed and ease. The deglazing sauce is quick and tasty, with white wine and a hint of butter, but you can leave the butter out if you're watching fat.

To serve 4

4 boneless chicken breasts		To deglaze (optional):
1 tablespoon olive oil		1/2 cup white wine
1 tablespoon butter		1 tablespoon butter
Salt and pepper		1 tablespoon chopped fresh parsley

1. Remove skin if desired and pat the chicken breasts dry with a paper towel. Heat the saute pan over medium-high heat for 1–2 minutes.

2. Add the olive oil and swirl to coat the pan. Heat for a few moments, then drop in the butter. The butter will foam up in the hot oil, but as soon as the foam subsides, lay the four chicken breasts in the pan and sprinkle lightly with salt and pepper.

3. Let cook for 3–4 minutes, then slip a spatula under the breasts and loosen the browning chicken where it may have stuck to the pan. You don't want it to weld to the bottom in the heat here.

4. Turn each breast over, sprinkle very lightly with salt and pepper, and reduce the heat a little. Cover loosely and cook for 10–12 minutes, shaking the pan now and then to make sure the chicken isn't sticking. Remove to a warm serving platter and place in a warm oven if not ready to serve immediately.

5. Keeping the pan over the heat, pour in the white wine and swirl around the pan. Stir with a wooden spoon to loosen any brown bits and increase the heat so that the wine boils. Boil for 1–2 minutes until half of the wine has evaporated, then lower the heat and add the butter.

6. Remove from heat right away and taste to see if the sauce needs any salt and pepper. Drop in the parsley, stir, and pour over the sauteed chicken breasts. Serve immediately.

The Least You Need to Know

➤ Sauteing is a method of quickly cooking chicken in a little oil over a medium-high heat. The name comes from the French verb *"sauter,"* meaning "to leap."

➤ A mix of half olive oil, half butter, will add a little extra flavor to the chicken.

➤ Deglaze the pan with wine, water, or cream to release any browned bits stuck to the bottom and make a quick sauce, to be poured over the chicken and served immediately.

Chapter 10

A Chicken in Every Pot: Stewing

In This Chapter

➤ What's the point of stewing?

➤ Making a better stew

➤ Recipe for chicken stew

Stewing is a long, slow process of cooking a meat with vegetables and liquid and sometimes a starch until the whole melange is soft enough to be eaten with a spoon.

What's the Point of Stewing?

Stews have fallen by the wayside in modern times because they need a lot of time to sit on the back of the stove and, well, stew. Busy cooks looking for a fifteen-minute dish to whip up for dinner don't want something that takes anywhere from two to four hours to be ready. (Even if during most of that time, you don't need to be anywhere near the kitchen.)

But that's a shame, because stews are one of life's great comfort foods, with all the elements of a square meal cooked down into a bowl of well-blended flavors. Stews are a cousin to soups, but they imply a heartier sense of well-being, with so much solid food included that they don't need to be rationed out with extra stock. Stews are solid food for prosperous times.

When it comes to certain types of chicken, stews are the only option. Anything labeled "stewing hen" or any chicken over about six pounds (unless it's a capon) needs to be cooked slowly in liquid or it will be tough and stringy and unpleasantly rubbery.

Gently cooked into submission, however, an old bird is extremely flavorful, tasting more "chicken-y" than younger birds. Size signifies age, and an older bird has had much longer to develop flavor than a broiler-fryer rushed to market after four weeks. Stewing breaks down the collagen in the toughened connective tissues so that the meat is melting and tender. If you fried a stewing hen, you wouldn't even be able to chew it. It is possible to work the other way around: You can use a younger bird in a stew. If you do use a younger bird such as a broiler-fryer, decrease the cooking time somewhat and keep a close eye on it in the second hour. Because the meat of a young bird is so much more tender, it's likely to fall apart instead of becoming moist and succulent.

An added benefit of the stewing process is that stewed food cooks together long enough that the flavors have time to "marry," as cooks say about a dish where one flavor complements another so completely that they are hardly distinguishable. But these days, who has enough time to cook so that flavors even have time to exchange a first kiss?

Fortunately, stews are very forgiving, so that if you do have time to cook one over a lazy weekend, it will sit peacefully in the refrigerator for days until you pull it out and pop it in the microwave for dinner, from which it will emerge fragrant and comforting and possibly even tastier than it was the day you made it. If you have an electric slow cooker such as a Crock Pot, you can put your tough old bird and a savory selection of vegetables in it before you leave for work and come home to a rich hot pot of stew that night. On a chilly winter night, it's well worth the extra bit of time; it certainly doesn't require any more effort.

Making a Better Stew

A chicken stew is cooked in liquid from the start of its cooking and the ingredients are not browned in oil prior to stewing. In the strictest sense, if you fry or saute first, the stew becomes a fricassee, but many cooks prefer to brown the meat or vegetables first. If you use a slow cooker, however, browning adds an extra step and makes an extra pan to wash. The stew recipe below is formulated without browning, so that all the ingredients cook in liquid. The result is light in color and delicately flavored.

Always start with cold water or liquid and bring all the ingredients to the same temperature together. If you add hot or boiling water to cold raw chicken, the chicken will seize up and it won't release its flavor as succulently as it will if you cajole and cosset it with slow heating and long cooking.

A stew can't be rushed. The essence of it is that all the ingredients gently exchange flavors, and if you rush, your results simply won't be as good. For this reason, as with making stock, simmer stew instead of boiling it. Boiling will draw unpleasant flavors out of the bones and turn the vegetables to mush.

Use a large, heavy-bottomed pot, such as a Dutch oven with a lid. A heavy pot will lessen the chance that your stew will burn and will distribute the heat more evenly so that you don't get "hot spots" where the stew is burning on one side of the pot and hardly even bubbling on another.

Recipe for Chicken Stew with White Wine

This is an easy chicken stew enlivened by the addition of white wine. The flavors are very simple and a nice accompaniment would be a green salad dressed with a strong dressing. Because the meat is not browned first in this recipe, you may want to pull the skin off the chicken pieces.

This recipe is perfect for cooking in a slow cooker such as a Crock Pot. Layer the chicken pieces and vegetables in the slow cooker, then sprinkle on the herbs, salt, and pepper. Pour the wine over all, cover, and cook on high for eight to ten hours.

Serves 6

1 4–6-pound stewing hen, cut into 8 pieces (see p. 24)

6 medium potatoes

1 medium onion, sliced

1 stalk celery, chopped

1 carrot, peeled and sliced

1 sprig fresh parsley

1 sprig fresh thyme or 1 teaspoon dried thyme

2 teaspoons salt

1/2 teaspoon black pepper

1 bottle dry white wine

1. Combine all ingredients in a large Dutch oven or stewpot. Add enough water to just cover the top of the chicken, probably about 1 1/2 quarts. Bring to a boil and reduce heat.

2. Cover and let simmer for 2 1/2–3 1/2 hours, until the chicken parts are tender when poked with a fork and the liquid has started to thicken. The vegetables will be soft and almost translucent, and the potatoes may have fallen apart. Taste and add salt and pepper as needed. Store covered in the refrigerator for three to four days, or in the freezer for up to three months. This stew tastes even better the next day.

The Least You Need to Know

➤ To stew meat and vegetables is to cook them in liquid over a low heat for a long time, till the whole dish is thick, the meat is tender, and the flavors have blended together.

➤ Use a large, older bird such as a stewing hen for long, slow cooking in a stew.

➤ If you use a smaller, younger bird, such as a 3-pound broiler-fryer, reduce cooking time so that the meat doesn't fall apart into shreds.

➤ Many stews benefit from being served the following day, giving the flavors more time to blend.

Chapter 11

MR FRICASSEE

The Dish with the Funny Name: Fricassee

In This Chapter

➤ Fricka-who?

➤ Tips for better fricassees

➤ A classic fricassee: Coq au Vin

Everyone has heard of chicken fricassee but not everyone knows what it is. It's just a cooking technique that's easy to master—easier than saying "chicken fricassee" three times fast.

Fricka-who?

The word fricassee is derived from an old French verb *"fricasser,"* meaning "to cut up and cook in sauce." That pretty much sums it up, except that anything cut up and cooked in sauce might be a stew, and a fricassee has shades of meaning beyond stew. A fricassee is a jointed fowl (or sometimes sliced meat or game) which is first sauteed in butter and then stewed in liquid, and usually enriched with a roux, or cream, or egg yolks.

A fricassee can be "white," with the chicken sauteed in butter till the flesh turns white but does not brown. This type of fricassee is usually cooked with white wine. Other fricassees are "brown," with the chicken browned in butter and cooked with red wine.

But these definitions are loose, and fricassees can contain all variations of ingredients. The important point is the cooking method, which must involve first a saute with no liquid added, and then a stewing period, usually with wine.

Roost Rap

A roux is a mixture of butter and flour used to thicken sauces and stews.

Tips for Better Fricassees

Read the chapter on sauteing (p. 67) for tips that will help with the saute portion of the fricassee process.

Make sure you fry the chicken in butter, or butter enriched with a little extra virgin olive oil, rather than in margarine or vegetable oil. There is a subtle but distinct difference in taste, and you'll be able to tell that the butter-based fricassee has a richer flavor.

Use a heavy Dutch oven or stewpot to saute the chicken and then later to stew. If you saute in a separate pan from the one you plan to stew in, you'll leave behind all the browned bits that will enrich the fricassee.

No Spring Chicken

Don't use too young or too small of a chicken. Look for a 3- to 4-pound broiler-fryer or even a slightly larger bird. Little broiler-fryers from 2 to 2 1/2 pounds have flesh that's too delicate to withstand the sauteing and stewing. The meat will fall apart and become stringy and dry. A big stewing hen is perfect for a fricassee.

Like a stew, a fricassee may actually taste better the next day, and fortunately, this sort of dish stands up well to reheating. By letting your cooled fricassee sit, tightly covered, in the refrigerator overnight, you give the flavors a chance to blend and deepen, especially in a wine-based sauce.

A Classic Fricassee: Fricassee of Chicken with White Wine and Mushrooms

This easy recipe shows all the possibilities of a rich-tasting fricassee without too much extra effort. If you want to make a more authentic fricassee, saute the mushrooms separately and add them just before serving. This helps the mushrooms keep a stronger flavor, but they're still delicious cooked along with the chicken. This dish stores well and can be reheated the next day. Serve with buttered noodles or potatoes and garnish with chopped fresh parsley.

Fricassee of Chicken with White Wine and Mushrooms

Serves 6

1 4-pound broiler-fryer

2 tablespoons olive oil

2 tablespoons butter

2 medium onions, thinly sliced

1/2 pound mushrooms

2 cups chicken stock

1 cup dry white wine

1 bay leaf

1/2 teaspoon dried thyme

1 teaspoon salt

1/2 teaspoon black pepper

1 tablespoon butter, softened

2 tablespoons flour

1. Joint the chicken into 8 pieces (see p. 24). Pat the pieces dry with a paper towel. Heat a Dutch oven or heavy stewpot over medium-high heat for 1–2 minutes.

2. Add the olive oil and heat for a minute, then drop in the butter. The butter will foam up in the hot oil, but as soon as the foam subsides, lay the chicken pieces in the pan.

3. Let cook for 3–4 minutes. When the flesh has turned white and taken on a slight yellow color from the butter, turn each piece over and cook 3–4 minutes. The chicken will not be cooked through but the exterior should be all white and not show raw spots.

4. Remove the cooked chicken to a plate, increase the heat slightly, and place the onions and mushrooms in the pot. Cook 5–7 minutes, till onions start to brown lightly, then return the chicken to the pan.

5. Add chicken stock, wine, bay leaf, thyme, salt, and pepper. Bring to a simmer, reduce heat, cover, and simmer gently for 25–30 minutes. Remove cover and simmer gently for another 10 minutes to evaporate some of the cooking liquid.

6. On a small plate, blend the softened butter and flour with a fork until combined. Stir this roux into the hot fricassee, and stir to blend. Simmer 6–8 minutes, till sauce thickens. Serve immediately or store overnight in the refrigerator and reheat to serve the next day. The fricassee keeps well in the refrigerator for three to four days, or in the freezer for up to three months.

The Least You Need to Know

➤ The word fricassee derives from an old French word, *"fricasser,"* meaning "to cut up and cook in sauce."

➤ Today, fricassee usually applies to chicken, and the method is defined by the chicken being sauteed in butter before being stewed in liquid.

➤ As a finishing touch, the sauce of a fricassee is usually thickened with butter and flour, cream, or egg yolks.

➤ Saute the chicken in the same pan in which you plan to stew it, so that all the browned bits from sauteing go into the sauce.

➤ For a "white" fricassee, the chicken is cooked in butter but not browned before being stewed with white wine or chicken stock.

➤ For a "brown" fricassee, the chicken is browned in butter and stewed in red wine for a deeply flavored, rich sauce, as in the classic French dish, Coq au Vin, or "chicken cooked in wine."

Chapter 12

Let the Water Smile: Poaching

> ### In This Chapter
>
> ➤ Clucking good poached chicken
>
> ➤ Tips for better poaching
>
> ➤ A proper poached chicken recipe

It's not boiling, it's poaching, and there's a world of difference in the way the chicken ends up tasting.

Clucking Good Poached Chicken

Any time chicken needs to be precooked for a recipe, such as chicken salad or chicken pot pie, poaching is the way to go. Chicken is cooked delicately and slowly in water that's moving so gently it's not even simmering, and the result is meat that is moist, velvety, and slightly custardy in texture. You don't even need to use it in another dish—poached chicken is ideal sandwich meat! Chicken breasts work well with this method, but entire chickens can also be poached with excellent results.

The water shouldn't boil when you poach. You want to see the barest hint of motion beneath the surface of the water, but no actual bubbles should break onto the surface as they do when simmering.

The shortest amount of time at the lowest temperature that will let you cook the meat completely will provide you with the tenderest, juiciest chicken. A whole chicken kept just under boiling will take about one hour to cook through. It's better to let the time go longer and keep the heat low, rather than increasing the heat to shorten the time.

Tips for Better Poaching

Keep a close eye on the water the whole time, and lower the heat or even remove the pan from the burner if it begins to bubble. The key to velvety chicken is that the water jiggles just beneath a simmer, keeping the meat from toughening up.

If you're using a whole chicken, leave the skin on and don't disjoint. If you have breasts on the bone, leave the skin on these, too, but only cook for about thirty minutes. After the chicken has cooked and cooled, you can remove the skin and bones and just use the tender meat.

Feathered Facts

Poaching is different from, not to mention better than, boiling because the temperature of the water is kept deliberately low to prevent the meat from toughening. Even simmering is too hot for poaching chicken. The water should be *"souriant"* or "smiling," as the French say.

Boneless, skinless breasts can be poached as well. Put them in a small saucepan and just cover them with salted water. Poach for about fifteen minutes.

Don't use a lid on the pot you're cooking in, or the water will be more inclined to boil.

Salt the water so that the salt goes into the cooking chicken. Saltless water will result in bland chicken, even if the texture is great.

You can flavor the poaching water with the addition of a few herbs or spices. Try a bay leaf, some peppercorns, a clove or two of garlic, a sprig of parsley, half an onion, some allspice berries, or a dusting of nutmeg. Don't go heavy on the spices because poached chicken has a concentrated flavor. You just want to hint at the spice.

After the chicken has finished poaching, remove from the water. It will continue cooking for a short time after it's removed. Don't let it cool in the water or it will become bland and overcooked.

After the chicken has cooled slightly, pull off the skin, and remove the tender meat from the bones in big chunks. Don't try to break it up any more than necessary.

For a really tender texture, put the meat you've pulled off the bones in a bowl and add a little bit of the cooking liquid. Let it finish cooling overnight in the refrigerator. This will result in a slightly gelatinous finish to the chicken that makes perfectly moist sandwich meat.

The poaching liquid will be much thinner and less hearty than a properly made chicken stock, but you can certainly use it in soups, stews, or sauces.

A Proper Poached Chicken Recipe

This is as easy as it gets. The ingredients are a whole chicken (not jointed), salt, and water. Everything is riding on the technique, so make sure the water never boils.

Serves 4–6

1 2 1/2–3 1/2-pound broiler-fryer   1 bay leaf

1 teaspoon salt   1 sprig fresh parsley (optional)

1. Rinse the chicken under cool running water and remove giblets (save them for stock). Place chicken in a cooking pot and add water to cover. Add salt, bay leaf, and parsley, if using.

2. Bring to a simmer over medium heat and reduce heat immediately to low. Keep the water just under a simmer for about an hour.

3. Lift the chicken out of the cooking liquid with a large slotted spoon and a fork (reserving the liquid till you ascertain if the chicken is done and to put some on the meat, if desired) and let chicken cool till you can touch it.

4. Discard the skin and remove the meat from the bones. Use it right away, or follow the instructions in step 5 to make the meat's texture more velvety.

5. If desired, put the boneless meat in a glass or stoneware bowl (not metal). Add a little bit of the poaching liquid, about 1/2 cup, to the bowl of meat, and let it cool in the liquid in the fridge overnight. Store in the refrigerator for up to four days. Poached chicken can be stored in the freezer for up to three months, but you'll lose the distinctively tender texture and just have cooked chicken.

Don't Fowl Up

If you start to pull the cooked chicken off the bones and it's not done (if there's any hint of pink or red), put it back in the cooking water and continue to poach.

The Least You Need to Know

➤ Poaching is a method of cooking a whole chicken (or breasts, if you like) in water kept just under simmering, so that bubbles don't actually break on the surface.

➤ The relatively low heat of poaching makes the meat tender and delicate.

➤ Cooling the meat in a little of the poaching liquid in the refrigerator makes it almost custardy.

➤ When the chicken is cool enough to handle, start tearing the meat off the bones. If there's any sign of red or pink, put it back in the poaching water and continue cooking.

Chapter 13

Steaming: Moist and Velvety Chicken

In This Chapter

➤ The Chinese secret: Steaming

➤ Tips for better steaming

➤ A sensational steamed chicken recipe

There's more to steaming than chicken and water, and the results can be quite impressive.

The Chinese Secret: Steaming

Steaming is an underrated method of cooking chicken, which can yield delicious results. Chinese cooking utilizes steaming a great deal, because it leaves foods moist and tender and tasting very much of themselves. The steam heat forces the meat to cook in its own natural juices, and it drives any seasonings used on the chicken deep into the meat. It is also favored as one of the cooking methods lowest in fat.

In the American kitchen, a steamer usually means the small, round metal rack with hinged wings that open out to hold the food. The metal rack is set in a pan holding a small amount of water, and the food is set on the opened wings. It's a perfectly good way to steam, but most of these steamers won't hold much food. Some woks come equipped with a metal rack that clips over the edge for steaming, but they can give a slightly metallic taste to the food being steamed.

The traditional Chinese method involves a basket with stackable trays of woven bamboo. This is balanced over a wok or large saucepan with boiling water in it. The different layers will allow you to steam all parts of your meal over the same boiling water, and the trays can hold enough to feed a family of six or even more if necessary. One of the big benefits of these steamers is that the lid is also made of bamboo, which lets the steam escape instead of condensing on the lid. When water condenses on the metal lid of a regular saucepan, it can drip back onto the food being cooked, making it more prone to be water-logged and tasteless.

The Chinese method allows plenty of room for improvisation even without a set of bamboo steamers. You can stand a footed stoneware dish in a small amount of boiling water, or cross a pair of wooden chopsticks in the bottom and balance a heatproof bowl on them over a small amount of boiling water.

A particularly flavorful method involves a tightly covered dish set into the boiling water, so that the heat of the steam cooks through the dish without any water coming into contact with the surface of the food.

Bamboo steamers wear out over time, so most of them are reasonably priced at cookware shops. Used frequently, they impart a very vague but pleasant woody flavor to the food being cooked, for an authentic Asian touch to your dish. To clean, scrub any food that might have stuck to the bamboo with a stiff brush and hot water. If the food was greasy, use hot soapy water, but otherwise don't overload your steamer with soap, which may cling to the bamboo.

But how does all this relate to chicken? The white meat of chicken is one of the meats that benefits most from steaming. This moist heat method is inappropriate for red meats, and even works less well with the dark meat on chicken. But for white meat, steaming brings out all the delicate flavor, and imbues the chicken with moisture, not to mention being one of the lowest calorie ways to cook, with absolutely no added fat.

Feathered Facts

Steaming cooks meat faster than direct heat because its high temperature can permeate the meat more efficiently.

Wing Tips

A boneless chicken breast will cook in less than ten minutes in a steamer. After you remove the chicken, let it sit uncut for two to three minutes, and any slight pinkness on the interior will gently finish cooking in the chicken's own steam.

Don't Fowl Up

Because steam cooks food with such a high, penetrating heat, you need to keep a close eye on it. One minute your chicken breast will be just cooked and moist, next minute it will be overcooked, with the interior becoming dry and the exterior becoming overly damp from condensed steam. After five minutes, check the chicken breast frequently. If you remove it and find it's still pink inside, either place it back in the steamer or pop it in the microwave for a minute or two.

Tips for Better Steaming

Don't put too much water in the bottom of the saucepan or wok. It may boil up and get into your steamer. If you're using a wok, two inches is plenty, and if you're using a regular saucepan, one inch or less will work. Keep an eye on the water level and top it up as necessary. Don't let your pan boil dry.

Try to avoid steaming dark meat for best results. Boneless, skinless breasts are easiest and taste best.

Add extra flavor to steamed chicken by adding a little wine or vinegar to the water being boiled. Salt and pepper the chicken before cooking, and rub on a pinch of dried herbs or spices (try sage or cumin) if you like. Try rubbing them with a touch of toasted sesame oil for a real Asian flavor. A bed of fresh herbs such as rosemary or thyme directly under the chicken in the steamer will impart the herbal flavor to the meat as it cooks, and you can also lay sliced onions or garlic over the chicken.

A Sensational Steamed Chicken Recipe

A quick marinade coats the chicken in flavors that the steam will drive into the heart of the chicken breast. Fresh ginger adds a lively flavor. Cornstarch helps make a light glaze on the outside. Rice and broccoli make a healthy and delicious accompaniment, and the broccoli can be steamed in the upper tray if you're using a stacked bamboo steamer.

Serves 4

1/4 cup dry sherry or Chinese rice wine

2 tablespoons grated fresh ginger

2 cloves garlic, minced

1 bunch scallions, cleaned, roots removed, and green stalks chopped into 3-inch lengths

1 teaspoon cornstarch

1 teaspoon salt

4 boneless, skinless chicken breasts

1. Mix the sherry, ginger, garlic, cornstarch, and salt in a medium bowl and combine well. Add chicken breasts and stir, turning in the marinade, to coat well. Let marinate for 20 minutes.

2. Bring a small amount of water to a boil in a wok or saucepan. Place steamer over boiling water and lay chicken breasts in steamer, still coated with any bits of ginger or garlic that may have clung to them in the marinade. Blanket the chicken breasts with a layer of chopped green onions.

3. Cover the steamer and let steam for 8–10 minutes or until juices run clear when prodded with a fork. Remove breasts from steamer and serve immediately. Steamed breasts are best eaten right away, but leftovers, which are great for sandwiches, can be stored in the refrigerator for up to four days, or frozen up to three months if necessary.

The Least You Need to Know

➤ Steaming cooks foods quickly as the water boiling under the steamer basket turns into very hot, penetrating steam.

➤ Food can be steamed in metal steamers with hinged wings that open out to hold the food in the bottom of a saucepan, in stackable Chinese bamboo trays, or on a heatproof dish set on top of a pair of crossed wooden chopsticks over boiling water.

➤ Boneless, skinless chicken breasts are best to use when steaming chicken, and you can add extra flavor by rubbing them with a spice or herb before steaming, by marinating, or by laying them on a bed of fresh herbs in the steamer.

Chapter 14

The Art of Grilling

In This Chapter

➤ An American art form

➤ Tips for great grilling

➤ Great grill recipes

Chicken on the grill, because it's cooked over an open flame, has the tendency to look done on the outside while the meat is still pink, so make sure it cooks through and the meat is heated to the correct temperature.

An American Art Form

Americans love to cook out over a backyard barbecue, and what do we like to cook? Meat—either hamburger, steak, or best of all, chicken. Chicken on the grill is not only delicious, the smoky undertones complementing the delicate chicken flavor, but also extremely versatile. You can go upscale gourmet, such as the whole butterflied chicken with a chili marinade on page 91, or make the standard Fourth of July fare of drumsticks dabbed with a barbecue sauce, either store-bought or homemade. The deliciously smoky flavor imparted by an open flame, be it charcoal or gas, can't be duplicated any other way, although the increasing use of grill pans means we can all try to duplicate that grilled taste in the kitchen when it's raining outside.

Chicken on the grill, like every other meat, is prey to the twin gremlins of a burned exterior and an underdone interior. Some cooks try to combat this by partially cooking the chicken before putting it on the grill, either in the microwave or by steaming or boiling, though the results are not as richly smoky as chicken cooked completely over the grill.

Wing Tips

Chicken with the bone in requires approximately thirty minutes to cook through on the grill.

But chicken can be well-finished without precooking. The problem is that too many backyard barbecuers arrange their chicken parts over direct heat. Even if you cover the grill to try to cook through to the bone, a chicken piece over direct heat is going to burn before the interior of the meat can reach a safe temperature of 180°. Instead you have to shuffle your chicken around, moving over and away from the hottest parts as necessary, to get that juicy interior and just-charred skin.

Tips for Better Grilling

Don't build too hot a fire for grilling chicken. Very hot coals are good for quickly searing a rare steak, but chicken needs a fire that's had time to burn down and mellow. The coals should be glowing, with white ash around the outside. This type of fire is hotter than the first flush of heat when the coals are still flaming, but you have better control because the heat is even.

Don't Fowl Up

Let the coals burn at least fifteen minutes before putting food on the grill. This lets them burn down evenly and burns off any chemical flavors that may be left from the lighter fluid.

Bank the coals on the outer sides of the grill for cooking large pieces, such as a whole chicken or breasts with the bone in. Put the meat to be cooked in the center of the grill so that the heat is thrown toward it from the coals banked on either side. For cooking individual chicken pieces, gather the coals toward the center of the grill and arrange the pieces around the other edges of the grill rack. This arrangement gives you more control, so you can move pieces that are starting to burn away from the fire, and shuffle the more raw pieces in toward the center.

Don't baste the meat with any sauce containing sugar until the last fifteen minutes of cooking. This means nearly every barbecue sauce, including homemade ones that are ketchup-based. The sugar in the sauce will singe and char very quickly. You want to give the chicken time to cook through before dabbing with barbecue sauce right at the end of cooking time.

Don't Fowl Up

Use a light hand when basting chicken with oil- or butter-based sauces. If you dab too heavily, the fats will drip through onto the coals and flame up, leaving greasy black marks on the chicken.

As a rule of thumb, dark meat pieces such as the legs and thighs will bear up better against the grill's heat. The breasts will be prone to dry out more quickly. Try searing the outside of breasts over direct heat, then moving to the outer edges of the grill (or toward the center if the coals are banked around the edge of the grill pan) to let them finish cooking more slowly.

Skinless chicken pieces will dry out much more quickly than those with the skin on. The fat layers in the skin form a natural protection against the direct heat of the grill and will help seal in moisture.

Feathered Facts

During the summer, the Weber grill company has a team of home economists who will answer your questions about outdoor grilling. Call weekdays on their toll-free number, 1-800-GRILL-OUT (474-5568).

Chicken is very susceptible to the flavorful smoke that is emitted from burning aromatic woods such as mesquite and hickory. Aromatic wood chips are a reasonably priced way to add flavor on the grill. The chips should be soaked in water at least an hour (and as long as overnight) before being tossed on the hot coals. Soaking ensures that the wood chips will smoke instead of burn.

Great Grilling Recipes

Recipe for Best Barbecued Thighs

The dark meat of chicken thighs stands up well to the high heat of the grill. Top them with a store-bought barbecue sauce that's been thinned out and doctored up with some extra hot sauce, vinegar, and Worcestershire sauce. You can bone the thighs for additional speed of cooking and ease of eating. A quick dry rub adds extra zip.

Serves 4

1 1/2 pounds chicken thighs, skins on	1 cup bottled barbecue sauce
1 teaspoon cayenne	2 tablespoons red wine vinegar
1 teaspoon black pepper	1 tablespoon Worcestershire sauce
1 teaspoon salt	1 tablespoon hot sauce (or more to taste)

1. Put the chicken on a plate and sprinkle with cayenne, black pepper, and salt. Rub into each side of the skin of the thighs and let sit for about an hour.

2. In a small bowl, mix barbecue sauce with vinegar, Worcestershire, and hot sauce.

3. Prepare a medium-hot fire. Let it burn down till the coals are covered in white ash, and bank the coals in the center of the grill pan.

4. Arrange the chicken pieces around the outer edges of the grill rack and cook for 20 minutes, turning every 5 minutes, and moving underdone pieces toward the hot center of the grill and more cooked pieces to the outer edges, away from the heat. After 20 minutes, dab each thigh with barbecue sauce. Cook, basting with sauce and turning occasionally, for another 5–10 minutes. Serve immediately.

Don't Fowl Up

If your chicken pieces are too dark to go back on the grill but still red or pink on the inside, put them in the microwave for a few moments to finish cooking. Next time you're grilling, keep the pieces over indirect heat longer.

Butterflied Chicken with Chili

It's difficult to cook a whole chicken over the grill unless you butterfly it. This is done by splitting the entire chicken up the back and pressing it open with the flat of your hand. The result is almost like a sheet of chicken that you can lay directly on the grill.

A hot chili pepper marinade adds zest to this dish, but tone down—or even leave out— the chili flakes if you like a milder flavor. It's easiest to marinate the butterflied chicken in a zipper lock plastic bag.

Butterflied Chicken with Chili

Serves 4–6

1 2 1/2–3-pound broiler-fryer	2 cloves garlic, minced
1/2 cup olive oil	1 teaspoon salt
1/4 cup lemon juice	Freshly ground black pepper
1 tablespoon red chili flakes	

1. Butterfly the chicken by slicing directly up the back with a poultry shears, as shown. (If you're using a knife, it's easier to cut to one side of the backbone.) Open the split chicken up and lay it breast-side up on a flat surface and press down with the heel of your hand. You should hear some of the rib bones cracking as you force the chicken to lie flat.

   You'll need (a slightly unusual requirement for preparing chicken!) a brick, a big rock, or a cast-iron skillet to keep your chicken flat on the grill.

2. Rinse the butterflied chicken and pat dry with a paper towel.

3. Place the remaining ingredients in a gallon-size zipper-lock plastic bag and seal. Shake to mix, then fold the chicken again as if you hadn't cut it and fit it into the bag. (If your chicken is too big or you don't have a zipper-lock bag, mix the marinade ingredients in a glass casserole and turn the chicken in it frequently.) Let the chicken marinate for about an hour.

4. Prepare a medium fire. Let it burn down till the coals are covered in white ash, and spread the coals flat across the bottom of the grill pan.

continues

continued

5. Lay the flattened chicken breast-side down on the grill rack. Place a sheet of aluminum foil over the chicken and weight the chicken down with a brick, a rock, or a cast-iron skillet. If you don't do this, your flattened chicken will curl back up in the heat. (You can also wrap the aluminum foil around your brick, rock, or skillet—the point is to keep any dirt or cinders off the actual chicken.)

6. Grill the chicken with the grill cover down for 20 minutes. Remove your weight and foil, and turn the chicken over so the breast is facing up. Replace the foil and the weight to keep the chicken pressed flat, and grill for another 20 minutes with the grill cover up. Remove and serve immediately on a large platter. The chicken doesn't have to be carved specifically—the pieces can just be pulled off the carcass with the help of a knife and fork.

Don't Fowl Up

Watch for flame-ups as you grill the butterflied chicken by lifting the lid and checking occasionally. If a lot of oil or fat is dripping off your chicken and catching fire, spritz the coals with some water in a spray bottle. Otherwise your chicken will have overly blackened skin that's far less tasty.

The Least You Need to Know

➤ America loves to grill and chicken is one of our favorite meats for it, from simple barbecued chicken with a store-bought sauce to upscale gourmet, such as a whole chicken split open (or, "butterflied") with a chili marinade.

➤ Let the coals burn for about fifteen minutes, till white ash is showing around the edges, so they give off an even heat.

➤ For cooking chicken pieces, create indirect heat by banking the coals around the outer edges of the grill pan and putting the chicken pieces in the center of the grill rack.

➤ Alternately, make a heap of hot coals in the center of the grill pan and lay the pieces around the edges of the grill rack. Move the pieces closer to and away from the heat so they cook through without burning the outsides black.

➤ If the outsides are charred very dark but the chicken is still pink or red near the bone, place the pieces in the microwave for a few moments to finish cooking.

Part 3

Chicken by the Part: I Saw a Sale on Drumsticks for 39¢ a Pound! Or, What to Make When There's Nothing to Cook but Chicken Thighs

Chicken can be bought in almost any form, from whole birds to individual joints to ground meat. Chicken also comes in varying quantities, from 10-pound "family-packs" of drumsticks to a pint-sized tub of livers to one breast cut into strips. Sometimes you're shopping for a specific cut for a recipe, but other times, the frugal cook keeps an eye open for super-bargains on chicken and buys whatever's on sale. As a rule, breasts are the most expensive. Wings, once sold off cheap for stock, now tend to be surprisingly expensive when bought in large packs. Whole chickens are usually a good buy and occasionally sold packaged in sets of two, at a slightly lower price per pound than that of single birds. The best buys of all can often be large packs of whole legs, as well as packs of thighs and drumsticks. You can cook them all for a large family dinner, or separate the pack and freeze some for later use.

But in whatever form you find your chicken, it helps to know how to cook according to the individual piece, in a way that takes advantage of that joint's virtues and keeps everyone from growing weary of seeing drumsticks yet again. But first and foremost, there's the unjointed chicken and a whole range of fabulous roast chickens to explore.

Whole Chicken

A whole chicken can be cooked in one piece or jointed. When baked whole, it's called "roasted," while "baked" usually implies jointed chicken cooked in the oven. The whole chicken is usually roasted, although it can also be pot-roasted, a moister method involving chicken in a covered pot on top of the stove or in the oven, or stewed whole in liquid. But however you are cooking it, there's a world of possibilities.

Roast Chicken Variations: Anything Goes

The two basic methods of roasting whole chickens, fast and slow, are outlined in detail in Chapter 7, p. 55. But whichever method you prefer, you can vary the flavorings and additions for a substantially different dish every time.

You can put a few aromatics, such as onion or lemon or rosemary, in the cavity of the bird or slide it under the skin by slipping your fingers between the skin and flesh starting at the neck. Work your fingers gently down, separating the skin from the

Wing Tips

If fresh rosemary is not available, you may substitute a generous table-spoon of whole dried rosemary. Rub it between your fingers to release the fragrance and smooth it under and over the skin with the olive oil.

breast. You can rub flavorings, such as soy sauce, honey, mustard, or orange marmalade, under the skin and over it, so that the whole bird is permeated with flavor. A good rubbing with olive oil and butter, salt, and pepper will ensure a beautifully browned, flavorful chicken every time, and you can also try molasses, orange juice, hot sauce, or sherry.

Fruity flavors, such as apricot and lemon, can make a lighter-tasting, more refreshing dish for summer, and a wintertime chicken begs for sliced carrots, onions, and potatoes surrounding it in the pan, to roast alongside the bird for a spectacular one roasting-pan dinner. Once you get your roasting technique down pat, let your imagination take over. Practically anything goes with roast chicken.

Classic Italian Roast Chicken

The classic Italian trio of olive oil, rosemary, and garlic make this dish a favorite at any time of year. The pungent scents of roasting garlic and rosemary mingling with slowly roasting chicken perfume a kitchen like nothing else. A small broiler-fryer makes this dish more succulent, though it works equally well with a larger roasting bird. You can also roast this bird at high heat, following the instructions on p. 57.

1 3–4-pound broiler-fryer

3–4 sprigs fresh rosemary

1 head plump garlic cloves, unpeeled and separated

1 lemon, cut in half

2 tablespoons extra virgin olive oil

Salt and freshly ground black pepper

1. Preheat oven to 300°. Remove the giblets and rinse the chicken inside and out. Pat it dry with a paper towel.

2. Peel two of the garlic cloves, slice thinly, and slip the garlic slices under the skin of the breast. Slide a sprig of rosemary under the skin on each side of the breast. Place the remaining rosemary, the unpeeled garlic cloves, and the lemon halves in the cavity of the chicken.

3. Using your hands, rub the chicken all over with olive oil, salt, and pepper. Lay it breast-side down in a roasting pan and place in the oven.

4. After 20–30 minutes, enough juices should have emerged that you can begin to baste. Tip the pan gently to one side to pool the juices and spoon them over the chicken. Baste every 15 minutes or so for 1 1/2 hours.

5. Then turn the chicken breast up, and cook for another 30 minutes to an hour, basting every 10 minutes, until the legs move easily and the juices run clear.

Flying the Coop: New Ideas for Roast Chicken

The variations on roast chicken that follow should help get your creative juices flowing. Before you try any of these variations, remove the giblets, rinse the bird, and pat it dry with a paper towel before following the instructions and roasting fast or slow as you like, unless otherwise noted. Look on p. 57 for tips on roasting methods.

Roast Chicken with Pesto

In the blender or food processor, mix 1/2 cup fresh basil leaves with 1 clove garlic, 2 tablespoons olive oil, and 1 tablespoon pine nuts or walnuts. Rub this under the skin of the chicken. Rub the outside of the chicken with olive oil, salt, and pepper and then roast it.

Quick Italian Chicken

Rub the bird inside and out with 1/4 cup of good quality bottled Italian salad dressing and leave to marinate in the refrigerator for two to three hours. Roast, basting with additional dressing.

Bacon Roast Chicken

Rub 1 tablespoon of butter, 1/2 teaspoon of salt, and some freshly ground black pepper over the outside of the chicken and put 1 large onion, peeled and quartered, inside the cavity. Drape 4 slices of hickory-smoked bacon (pick the fattiest strips from the pack) over the outside and roast. The bacon bastes the chicken as it cooks, so you can baste less frequently.

Chinese Spice Chicken

Rub 1 teaspoon of Chinese five-spice powder and 2 tablespoons of dark sesame oil over the outside of the chicken. Roast for 45 minutes at 450°, then reduce heat to 350° and roast for an hour, basting with 1/4 cup soy sauce blended with 2 tablespoons honey, 1 teaspoon cider vinegar, 1/2 teaspoon red chili flakes, and one finely minced clove of garlic.

Honey Mustard Chicken

Rub olive oil all over the outside of the chicken. Roast for 45 minutes at 450°, then reduce heat to 350° and cook for another hour, basting with a blend of 1/4 cup honey, 1/2 cup Dijon mustard, and 2 tablespoons orange juice.

Herb and Butter Roast Chicken

Blend 4 tablespoons softened butter with 1 tablespoon chopped fresh parsley, 1 tablespoon chopped fresh oregano (or 1/2 tablespoon dried) and 1 tablespoon chopped fresh tarragon (or 2 teaspoons dried). Smooth this mixture under the skin of the breast and legs. Rub the outside of the bird with 2 tablespoons butter, salt, and pepper. Roast.

Orange Roasted Chicken

Quarter a whole orange and stuff it in the cavity. Rub olive oil all over the outside of the chicken. Roast for 45 minutes at 450°, then reduce heat to 350° and cook for another hour, basting with 1/4 cup soy sauce, 1/4 cup orange juice, 2 tablespoons cider vinegar, and 1 tablespoon orange marmalade.

Kosher Salt-Roasted Chicken

Kosher salt-roasted chicken is a remarkable way to cook chicken that keeps it incredibly moist and tender. It's an elaborate procedure, and not something you'll want to do very often, but it will amaze and delight both children and guests, so you may want to save it as a party piece.

You'll need a 3-pound box of kosher salt and a small deep roasting pan or Dutch oven. Preheat oven to 450°. Wash a 3–4-pound chicken and pat very dry. Pour about a third of the salt into the roasting pan, nestle the chicken on top, and cover thickly with the rest of the salt. Sprinkle with about 1/2 cup of cold water, distributing evenly over the surface so that the water can form a crust with the salt. Roast for one hour. When done, let chicken rest for fifteen minutes, then break off the crust of salt and brush away all salt from the surface. The chicken won't be overly salty, just well-seasoned on the skin.

Wing Tips

If you don't have a Dutch oven, brown the chicken and onions in a large skillet and transfer it to a heavy, lidded casserole or baking dish. Make the gravy in the skillet, pour it over the chicken, and follow baking instructions.

Out of the Oven: Whole Chicken in the Pot

As delicious as a whole roast chicken is, sometimes it requires a little more attention than the busy cook can spare. One of the easiest ways to deal with chicken is to cook it whole on top of the stove or in a slow cooker, such as a Crock Pot. When you do this, you don't have to joint the bird, and once you've done a little preliminary work assembling ingredients, the chicken can be left to cook by itself for several hours or even all day. Chicken cooked this way is extremely tender. It needs to be highly seasoned as it's set to cook or it can turn out tasteless, so don't be shy with seasonings.

Oven-Braised Chicken
in Milk Gravy

Rich and flavorful, this dish makes its own gravy as it cooks. You need a large Dutch oven to protect the bird during long, slow cooking. The result is a tender chicken in a thick, milky gravy that's delicious served over rice, noodles, or mashed potatoes.

Serves 4

1/3 cup all-purpose flour	1 3–4-pound broiler-fryer
2 teaspoons salt	1/3 cup vegetable oil
1 teaspoon freshly ground black pepper	1 medium onion, diced
1 teaspoon paprika	3 cups milk
1/4 teaspoon nutmeg	1/2 cup heavy cream or half-and-half

1. Preheat oven to 350°. Mix the flour with the salt, pepper, paprika, and nutmeg on a dinner plate. Remove the giblets, rinse the chicken, and lightly dry it with a paper towel, then lay the dampish bird in the flour and pat the flour all over it. Set aside the extra flour.

2. Heat the oil in the Dutch oven over medium heat. Put the chicken in breast-side down and brown, being careful not to burn it, then turn on its back and brown, and flip so that each side is touching the hot oil, 7–8 minutes altogether. When the whole bird is nicely colored, remove to a clean dish and set aside.

3. Add the onions to the hot oil in the pan, lower heat to medium-low, and cook till golden and translucent, 7–9 minutes.

4. Add the remaining seasoned flour left from coating the chicken to the onions and stir well. Slowly blend in the milk, stirring constantly to prevent lumps from forming. Add the cream and turn off the heat.

5. Put the chicken back in the Dutch oven, breast-side down, cover the pot, and place in the oven. Bake for 1 1/2–2 hours, turning the bird breast-side up after 45 minutes, till the chicken is tender and the gravy has cooked down to a thick and creamy consistency.

Don't Fowl Up

Take extra care not to burn the chicken or the flour as you brown it in the hot oil. If the pan is too hot and the flour burns, you'll suffuse the entire dish with that taste, since that same flour thickens the gravy. Keep the heat at medium to brown the chicken.

Mushroom and Herb Slow-Cooked Chicken

Because you cook this chicken in a slow cooker or Crock Pot, it is never browned and the sauce is somewhat pale. The addition of a few tablespoons of tomato paste and some wine adds depth, and the chicken cooks for so long that it's infused with flavor. You can set it to cook in the morning, let it stew all day, and have a whole meal ready when you come home from work. Make sure you buy a smallish chicken that will fit in a Crock Pot. The cream smoothes and enriches the sauce, but you can leave it out and still have a delicious stew.

Serves 4

1 2 1/2–3-pound broiler fryer

2 medium onions, coarsely chopped

2 stalks celery, chopped

1 carrot, finely diced

2 cloves garlic

1 1/2 cups chicken broth

1 1/2 cups dry white wine

1/2 pound fresh white mushrooms, sliced, or 1 8-oz. can mushrooms, drained

4 tablespoons tomato paste

1 teaspoon dried parsley

3/4 teaspoon whole dried thyme

1/2 teaspoon dried rosemary

1 teaspoon salt

Freshly ground black pepper

1/2 cup heavy cream (optional)

1. Put the chicken in the Crock Pot. Cover it with the onions, celery, carrot, mushrooms, and garlic.

2. In a bowl, whisk the chicken broth with the wine, tomato paste, parsley, wine, rosemary, salt, and pepper. Pour this over the chicken and vegetables.

3. Put the heat setting on low and leave for 7–9 hours. Just before serving, add the half cup of cream, if using, increase heat to high, and let cook for half an hour. Taste and adjust seasonings and serve.

Note: If you want to make this on top of the stove, lightly brown the chicken and vegetables in step 1 in a large Dutch oven or stewpot, using two tablespoons cooking oil. Add the remaining ingredients, except cream, and simmer, covered, for 1 1/2 to 2 hours. (You may need to add a little extra wine or chicken stock if it looks too dry. If you don't have chicken stock, you can use one cup hot water mixed with one chicken bouillon cube.) Add cream before serving and simmer uncovered for another ten minutes to thicken slightly.

Cooking Jointed Chicken

Jointing a whole chicken opens it up to a whole range of cooking possibilities, from fried to stewed, baked or sauteed with an easy sauce. Although you can do anything to a package of individual pieces, such as two pounds of thighs, that you can do to a jointed chicken, it's much more economical to joint your own chicken and cook it rather than buying, say, a whole package of breasts.

Oven-Barbecued Chicken

Using a bottled barbecue sauce makes this the easiest weeknight supper imaginable. Chicken barbecued in the oven is much tangier than chicken cooked with barbecue sauce on the grill, where the smoky flavor tends to predominate. Because the sauce really shines here, make sure you buy a good quality barbecue sauce (or make your own if you're feeling ambitious). It's very tasty served with rice and beans.

Serves 4–6

1 3–4-pound broiler-fryer, jointed into 8 pieces (p. 24)

1 16-ounce bottle barbecue sauce

1. Preheat the oven to 350°. Lightly grease a 9 x 13-inch glass baking dish.

2. Put the chicken pieces in the pan. Pour half the sauce over, stirring the chicken pieces around to make them well-coated. Arrange them skin-side down, not touching.

3. Place in the oven and bake for 35 minutes, then pour on remaining sauce and turn them over skin-side up.

4. Bake another 35 minutes, till chicken is tender and sauce is thick.

Don't Fowl Up

Use a glass baking dish for barbecued chicken so the acidic barbecue sauce doesn't react with metal to leave a metallic undertaste. Lightly oiling the pan ensures that the sauce, which usually contains sugar, won't stick and burn. If the pan seems overly dry and the sauce is scorching, pour in 1/4 to 1/2 cup of water.

Country Captain

Country Captain is a classic Southern recipe, one that Southerners reserve for special dinner parties and luncheons. No one is quite sure how this slightly sweet, curried chicken dish with its elaborate finish of currants and raisins became so deeply ingrained in Southern cuisine, but it's a specialty that crops up throughout the South, sometimes attributed to a long-ago South Carolina sea captain. For a Sunday lunch that conjures up a real Southern party, serve Country Captain over steaming hot white rice with sweetened iced tea, long-cooked green beans, dinner rolls, and a green salad.

Serves 6

1 4–5-pound chicken	2 cloves garlic, minced
1/2 cup all-purpose flour	1 tablespoon curry powder
1 teaspoon salt	1/2 teaspoon whole dried thyme
1/2 teaspoon white pepper	1 28-ounce can whole tomatoes (with their juice)
5 tablespoons butter or margarine	1/2 cup currants
1 medium onion, diced	1/2 cup blanched, slivered almonds
2 green bell peppers, seeded and chopped	

1. Joint the chicken into 8 pieces (p. 24), rinse, and pat dry with a paper towel. Mix the flour with the salt and pepper, and dredge the chicken in this flour mixture. (To dredge is to dust a food with a dry seasoning such as flour or spices.)

   You may split each breast in half sideways (so you have four breast pieces), which will leave you with ten pieces when jointing a whole chicken and also makes the pieces of a more even size for cooking. This also works well for fried chicken, so that the breast fries faster and doesn't dry out during cooking.

2. Heat butter or margarine in a large heavy skillet over medium-high heat. Add the chicken and brown it well on both sides, about 10 minutes altogether. Remove chicken to a platter and set it aside.

3. Add the onions, pepper, and garlic to the butter left in the pan and cook 5 minutes, stirring occasionally, until softened. Stir in the curry powder and thyme and cook for an additional 2–3 minutes.

4. Return the chicken to the pan and add the tomatoes and their juice. Break up the tomatoes with a spoon. Cover the pan and simmer over medium-low heat for 30–40 minutes, until the chicken is tender and the sauce is thickened.

5. While chicken is cooking, heat a dry skillet over medium heat until hot. Toss in the almonds and shake them in the dry pan until they start to brown and you smell the almond scent, which will only take about a minute. Remove immediately from pan (if you let them stay in the hot pan, they'll scorch).

6. Stir the currants into the chicken and cook for 2–3 minutes. Spoon hot cooked white rice onto a large serving platter and arrange the chicken pieces on it. Pour the sauce over the platter and sprinkle the toasted almonds over everything. Serve immediately.

The Least You Need to Know

➤ Cooking a whole chicken is a good way to feed a family, with a variety of pieces available.

➤ Chicken can be cooked whole by roasting, or by stewing it whole either on top of the stove or in a slow cooker.

➤ When the whole chicken is jointed, it can be cooked by any method—baking being the one that requires the least effort from the cook.

Chapter 16

Breasts: Endless Possibilities

> **In This Chapter**
>
> ➤ Breast benefits
>
> ➤ Quick on the draw: Dinner in fifteen minutes
>
> ➤ White meat for me: Deliciously simple recipes

They may be a little more expensive, but chicken breasts are the perfect food for health-conscious people on the go.

Breast Benefits

If you're trying to feed a family of six, packages of chicken breasts are probably not your best bet for an economical supper, but chicken breasts do have their up side. All white meat, they take to all sorts of cooking methods and nearly any flavor, making them unparalleled in versatility. Being all white, they're also the lowest in calories, with about forty-three calories per ounce (dark meat is about fifty).

Buying chicken breasts can be accomplished sensibly. Don't get the little strips and squares marketed under names such as "tenders" or "nuggets." You can do that yourself to boneless, skinless breasts. Breasts on the bone are sometimes more reasonably priced that boneless, and it's a few quick knife strokes to take the meat off the bone and pull off the skin (see p. 29). But a package of boneless breasts in the refrigerator can mean no waste and a quick, easy meal. Sometimes you have to weigh up other factors besides cost. A whole chicken may have been only 68¢ a pound while breasts may be $2.39 or more a pound.

But if you can't face dealing with a whole chicken and you don't mind sauteing a quick cutlet, which is the better bargain for you? Chicken breasts can sometimes be a minor luxury, a cheap way to pay for convenience and a shortcut to simplify your cooking—and your life.

Wing Tips

Make simply cooked chicken breasts look prettier and more elaborate on the plate by cutting them shortways into five slices, then fanning them out on a bed of greens, pasta, rice, or potatoes.

Roost Rap

Fresh cilantro, also known as coriander, is sometimes called Chinese parsley and is usually available in supermarkets. It looks like big lacy leaves of flat parsley but is easily distinguished by its sharp, pungent scent. It's an indispensable ingredient of Asian and Mexican cuisine.

Quick on the Draw: Dinner in Fifteen Minutes

If you have two boneless breasts in the refrigerator and a few basic ingredients, you can have an impressive and well-balanced dinner ready for two people in less than fifteen minutes. The clock is ticking: Ready, set . . . go!

1. Scrub two baking potatoes, prick them with a fork, and put in the microwave for ten minutes.

2. Heat a little butter and oil in a frying pan over medium-high heat and lay in the two boneless, skinless breasts, sprinkling lightly with salt and pepper.

3. While they cook, rinse and dry some lettuce and tear it into bite-size pieces onto two dinner plates, adding a few slices of cucumber for texture. Flip the chicken breasts and check the potatoes to make sure they're not overcooking. Pour your favorite bottled dressing on the lettuce.

4. Put the potatoes on the plates, split them and add a bit of butter and sour cream, if desired.

5. Lay the sizzling hot breasts on the plate and pour a splash of white wine into the pan. Swirl it around and then pour over each chicken breast. For a festive touch, sprinkle with chopped fresh parsley or grate on a sprinkle of Parmesan cheese.

Voilà—dinner is served. Pour a glass of Chardonnay and you're entertaining!

White Meat for Me: Deliciously Simple Recipes

Teriyaki Chicken

The real Japanese method of making this dish involves cooking the chicken first before adding teriyaki sauce, unlike the American method of marinating the raw chicken in the sauce. In the Japanese way, the flavors of chicken and teriyaki remain more distinct.

The traditional Japanese garnish is sansho pepper, which is best replicated in American kitchens with a few grinds of black pepper. Making your own teriyaki sauce—out of soy sauce, mirin wine, saki, and sugar—might make you feel more authentic, but a bottled teriyaki sauce will contain the same ingredients.

Serves 4

4 boneless, skinless chicken breasts

2 tablespoons vegetable oil

2/3 cup bottled teriyaki sauce

Freshly ground black pepper

2 tablespoons chopped fresh cilantro, optional

1. Heat the oil over medium-high heat in a skillet. When the oil is hot but not smoking, put in the chicken breasts and cook for 5 minutes, then turn and cook 5 minutes on the other side, until browned.

2. Remove the chicken breasts from the pan and add the teriyaki sauce to the pan. Bring the liquid to a boil and let it reduce and thicken for 3–4 minutes.

3. Return the chicken to the pan and turn to coat well in the thickened teriyaki sauce. Let the sauce continue to reduce until it begins to cling to the chicken.

4. Remove the breasts to a platter and cut into slices. Garnish with black pepper and chopped cilantro and serve with hot white rice and steamed vegetables.

For extra flavor, you can cook the chicken breasts on an outdoor grill or in a stove-top grill pan and then add them to a skillet of reduced teriyaki sauce.

Don't Fowl Up

When just-cooked or -sauteed chicken is going to sit for any length of time while you prepare a sauce to serve over it, keep it warm in a very low oven on an ovenproof platter. Turn the oven to the lowest heat, usually 180°. If the chicken needs to be kept warm for five to ten minutes, you can place it in the oven uncovered. If you're going to hold it longer (though no longer than thirty minutes, by which time your meat will be starting to become tough and over-cooked), cover it with aluminum foil.

Crispy Dijon Cutlets

Fancy enough for dinner parties, Crispy Dijon Cutlets are also simple to prepare for a family supper. The cornmeal in the breading adds an extra bit of crunch and the oven-frying technique keeps the fat content low.

Although beating the breasts into very thin cutlets called paillards (pronounced pay-YARR—with just a hint of a "d" sound at the end—it's the French term for a boneless chicken breast pounded into a flat cutlet that's of a uniform thinness, both for attractiveness on the plate and ease of cooking) helps them cook quickly and evenly, you could also use this oven-fried technique for bone-in breasts and other chicken joints—just lengthen the cooking time till the meat is tender.

Beat chicken breasts thin by trimming each one of all bones, fat and skin. Place each breast between two sheets of plastic wrap and, starting at the center, hit it with a meat mallet or a flat-bottomed pan, working your way outward. Hit firmly and steadily, being careful not to tear the meat. (If you don't have a meat mallet, use the palm of your hand.) Beating the breasts makes them cook more quickly and evenly.

Serves 6

6 boneless, skinless chicken breasts, beaten into thin cutlets, 1/4-inch thick

1/4 cup Dijon mustard

1 1/2 cups dried bread crumbs

1 tablespoon cornmeal

1/2 teaspoon salt

1/2 teaspoon freshly ground black pepper

1. Preheat oven to 400°. Lightly grease a metal baking sheet that has sides.
2. On a dinner plate, blend the bread crumbs with the cornmeal, salt, and pepper.
3. Spread the Dijon mustard liberally over the six flattened chicken breasts. Dip each side of the mustard-coated chicken in the bread crumbs and lay the breasts on the baking sheet.
4. Bake for 30 minutes until golden brown and crispy.

Chicken Parmesan

The addition of a little marinara sauce and cheese elevates the simplest ingredients to a higher plane, and chicken benefits particularly from this treatment. Chicken Parmesan is delicious served directly on a plate with a discreet side of spaghetti noodles and a green salad, or it makes a terrific lunch or supper encased in chewy Italian bread for a Chicken Parmesan hero. Some Chicken Parmesan recipes call for the breasts to be breaded and fried before baking in the sauce. Eliminating this step not only speeds preparation but cuts the calories. Using bottled marinara sauce makes it even faster.

Serves 6

6 boneless, skinless chicken breasts, flattened to an even thickness of 1/2 inch

Salt and freshly ground black pepper

3 tablespoons olive oil

continues

continued

1 32-ounce jar marinara sauce (or 4 cups of your own homemade sauce)

1 cup grated mozzarella cheese

1/4 cup grated Parmesan cheese

1. Preheat oven to 350°. Heat the olive oil in a skillet over medium heat.

2. Sprinkle salt and pepper on each chicken breast. Brown them for 5–6 minutes on each side and place the breasts in a 9 x 9-inch glass baking dish.

3. Spoon the marinara over the breasts and place a mound of mozzarella cheese over each breast. Sprinkle the whole dish with Parmesan and bake for 20 minutes, until sauce is bubbling and cheese is melted.

Cajun-Seared Chicken Breasts

Chef Paul Prudhomme swept across the American food landscape in the 1980s with his method of "blackening" fish and meats—coating them with a breathtakingly hot blend of Cajun spices, then quickly searing, or actually blackening, the outside over a very high heat while leaving the insides juicy. It's a hard technique to duplicate exactly in the home kitchen without a big restaurant stove, but a well-heated cast-iron skillet or stove-top grill pan will help you replicate the blackened effect. This milder spice blend can be modified with less cayenne for delicate palates. Dirty Rice (see p. 138) and a salad make admirable accompaniments.

Serves 4

4 boneless, skinless chicken breasts, beaten
to 1/4-inch thickness

Cajun-Spice Blend:

1 teaspoon salt

1 teaspoon paprika

1 teaspoon cayenne

1/2 teaspoon garlic powder

1/2 teaspoon black pepper

1/2 teaspoon dried mustard

1/2 teaspoon whole dried thyme

1/2 teaspoon whole dried oregano

4 tablespoons (1/2 stick) butter, melted

1. Blend all the spices in a small bowl and dredge the chicken pieces, patting the spices on to make sure they stick in a thick layer.

2. Heat a cast-iron skillet or stove-top grill pan over high heat for at least 5 minutes and up to 10 minutes, until it's very hot.

3. Lay the coated chicken breasts directly onto the hot surface. They will smoke a great deal. Cook for about 3–4 minutes, turn, and cook for another 3–4 minutes. Remove to a warm serving plate. Drizzle the seared chicken breasts with the melted butter and serve. (The insides of the breasts should be all white when cooked through, with no pink at all. If you find your blackened breast is pink inside, put it back in the pan at a lower heat for a few minutes, till it's all white throughout.)

Don't Fowl Up

You must use a cast-iron skillet for blackening. A nonstick skillet or a thinner metal one can't take the heat necessary for this technique. If you have an extractor hood or fan over your stove, you'll need to turn it on for blackening, and you may want to open the windows. The high heat and the cayenne pepper can make fumes that will leave you coughing as you cook. And don't be surprised if you accidentally set off your fire alarm, if you don't have a fan. But don't worry—just exercise special care while blackening. The fumes will clear and leave you with deliciously flavorful chicken.

The Least You Need to Know

➤ Buying breasts isn't the cheapest way to get chicken, but it can't be beaten for ease and convenience.

➤ You can have dinner on the table in fifteen minutes by serving microwaved baked potatoes, a green salad, and quickly sauteed chicken breasts.

➤ Beating chicken breasts out to a uniform thinness with a meat mallet or the palm of your hand makes cooking even faster.

Chapter 17

Thighs: The Underrated Part

> ## In This Chapter
>
> ➤ Why thighs?
>
> ➤ Boning a chicken thigh
>
> ➤ Shaping up your thighs: Recipes to bring out the best

Chicken thighs used to be the piece that came attached to the drumstick when you bought a package of legs, but more and more, thighs are available on their own—on the bone and off.

You've Got Chicken Legs: The Underrated Thigh

The thigh is the dark-meat lover's secret. It's the most flavor-packed part of the bird, but it remains so underrated that it's available at a fraction of the price of most other chicken parts. Much of chicken pricing is all about demand, and most people eye a package of thighs and wonder what to do with it as they reach past it to buy a package of breast meat.

Once you come around to the thigh, though, it may well become your favorite piece of chicken. Thighs are no secret in Asian cooking where they're always preferred for braising, particularly in classic dishes, such as Chicken in Black Bean Sauce, where they're cooked long and slow with fermented black beans for a distinctive, earthy flavor. Tender and meaty, thighs are surprisingly versatile. If they're boneless, you can stuff them with garlic, a sprig of rosemary or tarragon, a wedge of orange or lemon, or perhaps something more adventurous, such as sugarcane or a dab of goat cheese or even a piece of a truffle, and bake, grill, or saute. You can also spoon in a traditional bread stuffing and roast them like a panful of tiny stuffed chickens.

Thighs are terrific with a tangy or fruity sauce, from orange to cherries to apricots, and they're also perfect for earthier flavors such as mushrooms and red wine. Their slightly thicker layer of fat makes them a bit greasier than other parts, but because of that, they take well to long, slow cooking, unlike chicken breasts, which are prone to dry out. This also makes them less likely to burn and consequently, they're more forgiving on top of the stove, in the oven, and on the grill.

Boning a Chicken Thigh

Boning thighs is a bit of extra work, but boned thighs can be a much cheaper (though slightly higher fat) substitute for breast meat in most dishes. Boned and skinned, you can do practically anything to them that you can do to breast meat, including stuffing.

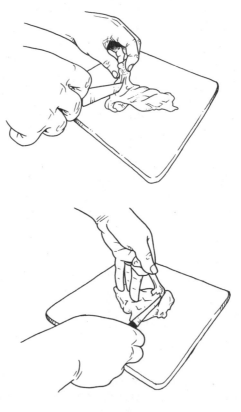

Slice open the underside of the thigh to expose the bone and use the tip of the knife to scrape the meat away from the bone.

Cut the joint of the thighbone out of the meat and discard the bone.

Thighs have a single bone through the middle, and the meat is attached, as it is in the drumsticks, by tendons. To remove the thigh bone, slice down the center of the piece to reach the bone, using a small sharp knife. Cut the meat away from the bone, digging in just under the flesh to cut each tendon's connection to the bone. Using your fingers, pull the meat away from the bone. Cut the bone off and discard or use for stock. You need to work gently, using your knife as necessary, to keep from mauling the flesh or turning it inside out.

You can leave the skin on; if you're frying or sauteing, the skin will help make a crisper crust. But for most presentations, pulling the skin off will cut the calories somewhat without affecting the moistness of the thigh meat. Usually the thigh skin will pull off very easily, but you may want to use the knife to cut away hanging pieces of yellow fat.

Shaping Up Your Thighs: Recipes to Bring Out the Best

Fruity and sharp flavors accent the moistness and the richness of the thigh's dark meat. Thighs are excellent for baking because they're the least likely to dry out in the oven. Boned and stuffed with a flavorful dressing, they're so good you may never go back to breasts.

Orange Marmalade Chicken Thighs

Dark chicken meat and orange are as good together as the traditional pairing of duck and orange. The edge of citrus flavor plays up the richness of the meat, making this a warm and hearty dish for a cold night.

The blend of marmalade and wine is as easy as it can be—the cooking method and presentation make the whole more than the sum of its parts. Have everything else ready to serve before cooking the chicken so the skin will be crispy as you pour on the warm sauce and bring it to the table.

You can substitute any kind of chunky fruit preserves (not jelly) for the marmalade. Try apricot jam or bing cherry preserves. Blueberry preserves taste great but your chicken will be a little blue. Stay away from grape and strawberry, which are too sweet, but raspberry is good if you also add a couple tablespoons of lemon juice to perk up the sauce.

Serves 4

2 pounds chicken thighs, boned (about 8 pieces), skin on

Salt and freshly ground black pepper

2 tablespoons olive oil

1/4 cup white wine

1/2 cup orange marmalade

1. Rinse the chicken and pat dry. Sprinkle each thigh with salt and pepper.
2. Heat the olive oil in a nonstick skillet over medium-high heat and put the breasts in skin-side down. Brown well, 5–6 minutes. Turn and brown well on the other side, 5–6 minutes. Remove to a warm platter.
3. Pour the white wine into the pan and swirl it around, stirring with a wooden spoon to scrape up any browned bits. Stir in the orange marmalade, bring the sauce to a boil, and turn off the heat.
4. To serve, slice each thigh into four pieces on the diagonal. Fan the slices out on four individual serving plates and spoon some sauce over each. Serve immediately.

Lime-Grilled Thighs

A sharp, citrus-y marinade permeates the meat of chicken thighs before they're grilled, for a smoky, pungent flavor that's perfect for a summer evening. Try it with a creamy potato salad on the side, corn on the cob, and fresh sliced tomatoes.

Serves 4

2 pounds chicken thighs (about 8 pieces), bone in, skin on

1/2 cup lime juice (juice of 3–4 limes)

1 teaspoon grated lime zest

1/4 cup chopped fresh cilantro

1/2 cup olive oil

1 teaspoon cayenne

1/2 teaspoon salt

1. Rinse chicken thighs and pat dry. Whisk together remaining ingredients in a medium bowl. Place thighs in the bowl, turning well to coat. Leave to marinate for 30–45 minutes, but not much longer or the lime juice will start to break down the fiber of the chicken.

2. Prepare a medium-hot fire on an outdoor grill. Arrange the thighs on the grill skin-side down and cook 8–10 minutes. Turn and cook 8–10 minutes more, basting frequently with the remaining marinade.

Note: If you don't want to grill, bake these thighs in a 350° oven for 30 to 35 minutes.

Don't Fowl Up

Limes won't juice as easily as lemons. To ensure that you get the most out of each, use the flat of your hand to roll the whole lime back and forth—hard!—on the countertop before squeezing.

The zest is the green outer skin of the lime (or the yellow part of a lemon), full of aromatic oils that impart a potent flavor to food. Zesting is grating or peeling the outer edge with a grater, vegetable peeler, or knife. When zesting, be sure not to grate or peel off the pith, the soft inner white coating just under the zest. It has a bitter flavor that it's best to avoid.

Southern Thighs with Cornbread-Pecan Stuffing

Cornbread stuffing is a traditional Southern favorite, and you don't have to bake a panful to make this dish. Supermarkets carry dry cornbread crumbs for stuffing, and if you use a flavorful chicken broth, you'll hardly know the difference. Pecans are another Southern favorite, but you can change the character of this stuffing by substituting walnuts, hazelnuts, or cashews. Serve with all the trimmings: mashed potatoes, cooked carrots, a green salad, and perhaps a dollop of cranberry sauce.

Serves 4–6

2 pounds (about 8 pieces) boneless chicken thighs, with skin

2 tablespoons butter

1/2 cup finely chopped onion

1/4 cup finely chopped celery

1/4 cup chopped pecans

1/2 cup packaged cornbread stuffing

1/2 teaspoon dried sage

1/2 cup chicken stock

1. Preheat oven to 350°. Lightly butter a 9 x 13-inch glass dish. Rinse and pat dry chicken thighs.

2. Heat the butter in a skillet over medium heat and saute the onions and celery until softened but not browned, 5–6 minutes. Stir in the pecans, cornbread crumbs, and sage and pour on the chicken stock, stirring to combine well.

3. Lay the thighs out skin side down and spoon a few tablespoons of stuffing into the middle each thigh and wrap the meat over around it. (You can secure them with wooden toothpicks, but it's easier to just wrap the meat around the stuffing in a free-form way and lay it gently in the pan.) Lay each thigh in the pan skin-side up, and sprinkle with salt and pepper.

4. Place in the oven and bake 45–50 minutes, until thighs are browned and tender.

Ginger-Glazed Thighs

Grated fresh ginger is rubbed under the skin and added to soy sauce and honey for an aromatic glaze that plays well off the dark thigh meat. Baking at a high temperature helps drain the fat from under the skin and the absence of fat in the glaze makes this a healthful main dish, with a simple accompaniment such as plain white rice and a cucumber salad.

Ginger-Glazed Thighs are also good on the grill. Prepare as for the oven but arrange over a medium-hot fire and grill eight to ten minutes, baste with the soy glaze, then turn and grill another eight to ten minutes, basting frequently.

Serves 4–6

2 pounds chicken thighs (about 8 pieces), bone in, skin on

1 teaspoon salt

1/2 teaspoon freshly ground black pepper

4 teaspoons grated fresh ginger

3 tablespoons honey

2 tablespoons soy sauce

1 teaspoon cornstarch

1. Preheat oven to 425°. Rinse the thighs and pat dry with a paper towel.

2. Combine salt, pepper, and 2 teaspoons of the grated ginger and rub a little under the skin of each thigh. Place each piece in a roasting pan, well spaced, and roast for 35–40 minutes.

3. Whisk honey, soy sauce, and cornstarch with remaining ginger. Tip the baking pan to one side and spoon out any fat that has run out. Spoon the glaze over each thigh and bake another 10 minutes.

Tomato-Baked Thighs
with White Wine

The tomatoes and wine provide a slightly acidic sauce that is enriched with the smoky taste of bacon and a sprinkle of Parmesan cheese. If you strip the skin off, you can cut the calories for a quite low-fat dish, but leaving it on adds moisture during baking.

Serves 4–6

2 pounds chicken thighs (about 8 pieces) on the bone, with skin

Salt and freshly ground black pepper

2 tablespoons olive oil

3 slices bacon, diced

1 large onion, thinly sliced

4 cloves garlic, minced

1 28-ounce can whole tomatoes, with their juice

1/2 cup dry white wine

2 bay leaves

1 teaspoon whole dried oregano

1/4 cup Parmesan cheese

1. Preheat oven to 400°. Wash the thighs and pat them dry. Sprinkle with salt and pepper.
2. Heat the olive oil in a heavy skillet over medium-high heat and add the thighs. Brown well on each side, about 10 minutes. Remove to a 9 x 9-inch glass baking dish and set aside.
3. Add the bacon, onion, and garlic to the oil remaining in the pan. Saute over medium heat till the onion is translucent and the bacon begins to brown slightly. Pour in the tomatoes and their juice and break up the tomatoes with a spoon. Stir in the wine, bay leaves, and oregano, and pour this mixture over the chicken in the baking dish.
4. Sprinkle the pan with Parmesan cheese. Bake 50 minutes or until thighs are tender and sauce has cooked down and thickened.

The Least You Need to Know

➤ Chicken thighs, which are all dark meat, are a particularly moist piece of the bird.

➤ Cook thighs on the bone, or remove the bone yourself using the tip of a sharp knife to cut the tendons holding the meat to the bone.

➤ Boned and skinned, you can use a chicken thigh for any recipe where you'd use a chicken breast, but thighs go especially well with fruity sauces.

Chapter 18

I Get a Drumstick!
The Favorite Part

> **In This Chapter**
>
> ➤ The original finger food
>
> ➤ Boning drumsticks
>
> ➤ Kiddie food: Recipes to get the fun back into drumsticks

Why pretend? Drumsticks were never intended for a knife and fork. Even if the sauce is sticky, just lick your fingers.

The Original Finger Food

Drumsticks have passed into caricature as the leftover piece of chicken that you pull out of the refrigerator while rummaging for a snack in the middle of the night. This probably came into being because drumsticks are such an easily recognizable chicken part—movie and TV directors know that practically anything else actors might pull out of a fridge would look funny. As if there would be drumsticks left over in a platter of fried chicken!

Drumsticks are one of the few foods that come with a natural handle, something obvious to hold onto while you eat the meat. But there's good meat on them—dark meat that stays moist and flavorful while drumsticks are fried, baked, or roasted. Because of the slightly higher fat content as well as the tendons of the leg, drumsticks are one of the least satisfying pieces to stew or braise because then the tendons are less likely to break down and the meat can look stringy. The meat on a drumstick cries out to be baked, broiled, or fried, resulting in tender, moist meat that can then be accented with a sauce or dipped into one.

Boning Drumsticks

Boning drumsticks is a little more complicated than boning thighs and actually involves cutting through the bone, but boned drumsticks make an unusual stuffed chicken dish that's surprisingly good. It's not something you'll want to do very often, but once in a while, it makes this most casual piece of chicken into something far more elegant.

Use a paper towel if necessary to help you pull the slippery skin off the bottom of the drumstick.

Pare around the top of the bone at the narrow end, cutting the tendons' connection to the bone, and gradually work the meat down toward the thicker end, cutting tendons as necessary and turning it inside out as you go.

Cut around the top of the drumstick, through the flesh and any attaching tendons.

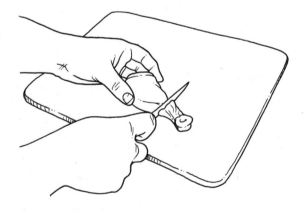

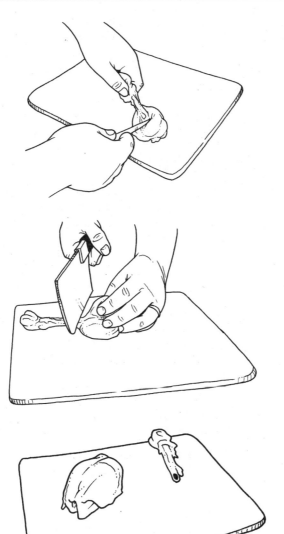

Scrape flesh down toward fat end of the drumstick.

With meat turned inside out over fat end of drumstick, use a cleaver to chop off the bone, leaving a knuckle of bone and cartilage inside the drumstick to hold it together.

Turn the meat right-side out, leaving a little "sock" of boned drumstick.

Pull the meat as far as you can off the end of the bone and chop off the bone using a cleaver or the heel of a strong knife. Leave the cartilaginous knuckle of bone up under the meat (otherwise, you get a "tube" instead of a "sock"), and fold the meat back right side out (see illustration).

Kiddie Food: Recipes to Get the Fun Back into Drumsticks

Except for the stuffed drumsticks below, none of these recipes requires a knife and fork, and they're equally tasty fresh from the oven or grill, or cooled and served later. Drumsticks make perfect picnic fare, because they're easy to transport and make fabulous finger food.

The recipes below all call for two pounds of drumsticks, which is about ten pieces, and they're calculated to serve four or five people, assuming two drumsticks per person with maybe one or two pieces leftover for anyone who's still hungry. However, the marinades and dips will accommodate a few extra drumsticks in each recipe. You may want to double the recipe if you're planning a picnic, since drumsticks are among the best chicken parts for transport. Picnickers tend to be a little hungrier than dining-room diners!

Don't Fowl Up

If you're picnicking with your drumsticks, be safe with them as with all picnic food, and don't leave them sitting in the hot sun, lest you encourage bacteria to grow. To be safest, transport your drumsticks in the cooler with your other perishable foods, such as mayonnaise and potato salad.

Devilled Drumsticks

Drumsticks are roasted in a tangy coating of breadcrumbs and mustard spiked with lemon juice and a little parsley for color. This zesty coating provides the drumsticks with all the flavor they need and the final product travels well. Along with potato chips, devilled eggs, carrot and celery sticks, and chocolate cupcakes, these drumsticks make a meal that requires hardly any implements other than paper plates and napkins. Sling a jug of homemade lemonade in your picnic basket and you're ready to hit the beach.

Serves 4–5

continues

continued

1/4 cup melted butter

2 tablespoons Dijon mustard

2 tablespoons lemon juice

2 tablespoons fresh parsley, chopped

1 teaspoon salt

1 teaspoon paprika

1/2 teaspoon cayenne

1/2 teaspoon black pepper

Pinch of nutmeg

2 pounds (about 10) drumsticks

3 cups dry breadcrumbs

1. Preheat oven to 350°. Combine all of the ingredients except for the drumsticks and breadcrumbs in a large bowl and mix well.

2. Rinse the drumsticks and pat dry. Toss the drumsticks in the mixture until they are well coated, then roll them in the breadcrumbs until completely covered.

3. Lay the drumsticks on a lightly greased cookie sheet and bake for 1 hour. They should be tender and deep golden brown with a crispy skin.

Cumin-Browned Drumsticks

The yogurt acts as a natural tenderizer and the cornmeal makes the crust extra crispy. Pungent scents of cumin and chile powder add an exotic hint of Indian cooking to these drumsticks, and a cool yogurt-dressed cucumber salad and some plain white rice make a good accompaniment.

Serves 4–5

1/2 cup plain yogurt

1/4 cup lime juice

2 tablespoons cumin

2 pounds (about 10) drumsticks

1 cup coarse ground cornmeal

1 teaspoon oregano

1 teaspoon salt

1/2 teaspoon chili powder

1/2 teaspoon black pepper

Oil for frying

1. Combine the yogurt, lime juice, and 1 tablespoon of cumin in a large bowl and mix well. Rinse drumsticks and pat dry. Toss drumsticks in the mixture to coat well.

2. In another bowl, combine the remaining dry ingredients and roll the chicken in this mixture to cover completely. Heat 1/2 an inch of oil in a large skillet over medium heat.

3. Carefully place the drumsticks in the oil and cook for 10 minutes. Turn the chicken, reduce the heat to low and cover the pan, leaving the lid slightly askew so steam can escape. Cook for 10 minutes.

4. Remove the lid and turn the heat back up to medium-high, and cook for another 5 minutes to crisp up the crust. Remove the drumsticks and drain on a paper towel. Serve hot or cold.

Grilled Drumsticks in Garlic Marinade

Like an intense Italian salad dressing, this garlic-filled marinade permeates the dark meat of drumsticks with flavor. These drumsticks can also be cooked on an outdoor grill instead of broiling. Cook for 20 minutes over a medium-hot fire, turning frequently to avoid burning and basting with any remaining marinade. These drumsticks taste best hot.

Serves 4–5

1/2 cup extra virgin olive oil	1 teaspoon salt
1/4 cup red wine vinegar	1/2 teaspoon dried thyme leaves
4 cloves garlic, minced	1/2 teaspoon black pepper
1 teaspoon dried rosemary	2 pounds (about 10) drumsticks

1. Combine all the ingredients, including the chicken, in a large zipper-lock bag and shake well. Let the drumsticks marinate in the bag for at least an hour, or preferably overnight, in the refrigerator.
2. Remove the drumsticks from bag and place under a broiler for 20–25 minutes turning every 5 minutes until cooked through. Serve hot.

Wild Rice-Stuffed Drumsticks in Sour Cherry Sauce

This is an elaborate and delicious dish, ideal for a special evening. Boned drumsticks are stuffed with a wild rice and walnut stuffing, then baked till golden brown and topped with a sophisticated and tangy sauce of cherries. Serve it to that special someone with scalloped potatoes, a green salad, and a glass of white wine. For a summer evening, substitute potato salad.

Serves 4–5

1/2 cup wild rice	1/2 teaspoon black pepper
1/2 cup white long grain rice	2 pounds (about 10) drumsticks, boned
1/4 cup walnuts, chopped	1 16-ounce can sour cherries, drained
2 tablespoon chopped green onions	1/2 cup white wine
2 tablespoons chopped fresh parsley	1 teaspoon cornstarch
1/2 teaspoon salt	1 teaspoon orange zest

1. Cook wild rice according to package directions, but add 1 cup extra water and after 15 minutes, add the white rice. When cooked, cool to room temperature. Stir in walnuts, green onions, parsley, salt, and pepper.
2. Preheat oven to 350°. Rinse drumsticks and pat dry. Using a spoon and your fingers, stuff 3–4 tablespoons rice mixture into each boned drumstick.
3. Lay the stuffed drumsticks in a lightly greased 9 x 13-inch glass baking pan and bake for 1 hour, turning after 30 minutes, until drumsticks are golden brown.
4. Place cherries in a small saucepan. Whisk the cornstarch into the wine with a fork and add to the cherries along with the orange zest. Bring to a boil and cook for about a minute, until sauce thicken slightly. Pour over the drumsticks and serve immediately.

Don't Fowl Up

A jelly roll pan is a metal baking sheet with four raised edges, while a cookie sheet is technically a flat metal sheet with only one raised side that acts as a sort of handle. When cooking chicken on a baking sheet, always use the jelly roll pan with sides so the fat doesn't drip off and cause a grease fire on the floor of your oven.

Crispy Pecan Drumsticks with Creamy Honey-Mustard Dip

Drumsticks become dippable in this terrific oven-fried dish. Rolled in a coating of bread crumbs and chopped pecans, the crisp baked chicken is served with a creamy honey-mustard dip that accentuates the sweetness of the nuts.

Serves 4–5

For drumsticks:

3 pounds (about 15) drumsticks
1 cup shelled pecans
1 cup plain, dry bread crumbs
1 teaspoon salt
1/2 teaspoon black pepper
1/2 teaspoon paprika
1/4 teaspoon cayenne
2 eggs, beaten

For dipping sauce:

1/2 cup Dijon mustard
1/2 cup sour cream
3 tablespoons honey
1/2 teaspoon Worcestershire sauce

1. Preheat oven to 450°. Rinse and dry drumsticks. Lightly grease a jelly roll pan.
2. In a food processor or blender, coarsely grind the pecans with 1/4 cup of the bread crumbs. In a bowl, blend this mixture with the remaining breadcrumbs with the salt, pepper, paprika, and cayenne.
3. Dip each drumstick in beaten egg, then in crumb mixture, and lay on baking sheet. Bake 30–35 minutes, turning the pieces after 5 minutes, until golden brown.
4. While chicken is cooking, blend mustard, sour cream, honey, and Worcestershire. Serve on the side for dipping.

The Least You Need to Know

➤ Drumsticks are dark meat, moist and full of flavor, but the tendons that attach the meat to the bone make them better suited to baking, broiling, or frying than to stewing or braising, which accentuates their potential stringiness.

➤ One of nature's perfect finger foods, with a natural handle, drumsticks are ideal for picnics, especially when you take along a dipping sauce.

➤ If you are picnicking, treat drumsticks with care like all perishable picnic foods, such as mayonnaise and potato salad.

Chapter 19

Wings: Beyond Buffalo

In This Chapter

➤ When wings were waste

➤ Mini-wings: Making drummettes

➤ Wild ways with wings

Wings are a favorite cocktail snack and finger food. They show up at children's parties, weddings, and church suppers—and there's a lot more to do with them than Buffaloing.

When Wings Were Waste

Wings, if sold at all, were once sold as leftover parts that the frugal cook might use for stock. They were nearly all skin, too fatty, and the little meat they contained was considered veiny and unappetizing. It was hard to find any use for them beyond enriching a broth. Until sometime in the early 1960s in a bar in Buffalo, New York . . . .

Buffalo wings spread like wildfire across America's culinary consciousness, cropping up in cookbooks starting early in the 1970s and penetrating deep into the cooking of the heartland. There's barely a mother in America who hasn't at some time fried up a big batch of wings and doused them in the obligatory hot sauce, and the poultry produc- ers sat up and took note. Wings became one of the most sought after chicken parts after breasts, and prices increased accordingly. Even today, when that early frenzy surrounding Buffalo Wings might have been presumed to have died down a bit, prices stabilized at their high levels and stayed that way. The thing is, wings in their many forms are just so darn good, nobody cares.

Here's a question: Why *are* wings so good? The answer isn't surprising, on the theory that anything that tastes that good has to be bad for you. Wings are the fattest part of the chicken, with a far higher skin to meat ratio than any other part of the bird. One wing has eighty-two calories. A pound of wings is anywhere from eight to ten wings, depending on size, and if you're chatting with friends and washing your wings down with beer, one person can eat a pound of wings pretty easily. Add to that the butter in the traditional Buffalo sauce and the usual accompaniment of blue cheese dip, and your fat intake goes through the roof. So by all means enjoy the occasional wingfest, but remember that just because chicken is a healthier meat than many, not all of it is low in fat.

It's hard to pinpoint the exact moment of creation for Buffalo Wings, but the story that has gained the most credence, at least the one that gets repeated over and over in cookbook lore, is that Teresa Bellissimo in the Anchor Bar in Buffalo served up spicy, deep-fried wings late one night when her son, Dominic, and his buddies wanted a late-night snack. There are various embellishments, including that Teresa was trying to find something to do with a mistaken extra delivery of wings, or the detail that the hungry friends, all Catholic, were waiting till after midnight on Friday for a meaty snack, but in any case, all signs point to The Anchor Bar.

Trimming and Jointing

Packaged wings can be bought fresh or frozen and they come in three different ways: whole, with all three limbs intact including the wing tip; trimmed, with wing tip removed but with the joint intact; and "drummettes," the first joint only. (The third way is by far the most expensive.)

If you buy them whole, trim off the short, pointy wing tip and save it for stock. Then you have a trimmed wing, which must be split at the joint, leaving you with the two recognizable pieces that mean "chicken wings" to most of us.

You'll often see huge packages of frozen trimmed wings, from five to ten pounds, and people who wouldn't consider buying a package of icy frozen chicken breasts will buy frozen wings. These bags usually contain little balls of frost that gradually melt to reveal wings, and the quality is not necessarily the best. Despite the heavy dousing of sauce most wings receive, the meat underneath should be the tastiest and freshest you can find. Fresh wings are nearly always available in the chicken section of the super-market, so try to forego the frozen ones.

A Different Drummer: Making Drummettes

The first joint of the wing, the one attached to the body, not the one attached to the wing tip, can be made into a miniature drumstick. It's good for cocktail parties if you have a whole bag of wings, and it makes a nice extra part for when you're frying a whole chicken.

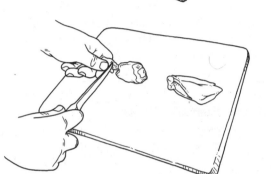

Separate the two parts of the wing.

Use the tip of the knife to scrape the flesh of the drumstick-shaped piece (the single-boned piece of the wing, attached directly to the body) down toward the fatter end.

The finished drummette.

The meat of the wing is attached at either end of the wing bone by tendons. With a small sharp paring knife, cut in a circle around the end of the bone opposite where it was attached to the chicken's body. Use the point of the knife to loosen the meat. Using your fingers, pull the meat down the bone toward the opposite end. The meat will hang in a little mass as it does on the fat end of a drumstick (see illustration). Cooked, it looks like a tiny drumstick.

129

Wing Tips

If you're not making stock right away, save the trimmed wing tips in a sealed plastic bag in the freezer.

Wild Ways with Wings

Wings lend themselves to a surprising number of cuisines and in a number of different forms. Frugal Chinese chefs were serving them up braised and stewed long before American bar patrons were dunking them into blue cheese dip. Some dishes call for partially deboned wings, but for the average cook, that's far too much work. If you're grilling wings or frying them—as for normal fried chicken—you may want to just trim the tips off and leave the wings attached at the first joint for a more substantial piece of chicken. For most of the zesty-sauced dishes below, however, the fully jointed wing is preferable.

Classic Buffalo Wings

The recipe that started the craze. Restaurants guard their recipes jealously and insist they won't give them out, but it's astonishingly simple to make restaurant-style wings at home. Here's the amazing special sauce for those few members of the free world who still don't know: Hot sauce and butter. That's all there is to it.

The blue cheese dip is a different matter, though, and opinion varies wildly. Here's a very simple one to complement the very simple wings, but you may want to dress it up with a squeeze of lemon juice, some minced garlic, and chopped fresh parsley. Easier yet, use a good commercial blue cheese dip, preferably one from the refrigerator case at the grocery store.

Serves 4–6 as an appetizer, 2–3 as a main course

1 cup mayonnaise

2 ounces blue cheese

3 stalks celery

1/2 cup bottled hot sauce for mildly spicy wings or 3/4 cup or more to taste for hot wings

3 pounds whole chicken wings

Oil for deep frying

4 ounces (1 stick) butter

1. Cut each stalk of celery in half lengthwise and then cut the lengths into 3-inch sections.

2. Crumble the blue cheese into the mayonnaise and blend them together well with a fork or whisk. Set the dressing and the celery sticks aside until ready to serve.

3. Joint the wings as described on p. 128 and discard the tips or save them for stock. In a deep, heavy saucepan, heat 3 inches of oil to 375°, then put in small batches of the jointed wings (8–10 wings at a time). Cook each batch for about 10–15 minutes, until golden brown.

4. While wings are frying, prepare the sauce by melting the butter and whisking in the hot sauce. When all the wings are done, toss them in the hot sauce and serve with celery and blue cheese on the side.

Don't Fowl Up

Deep-frying can be a messy procedure and even though it results in golden, crispy wings, baking can produce an even tastier result. Long, slow baking makes wings a deep mahogany brown, melting much more of the fat out of the skin and leaving the wing chewier and more caramelized on the surface. What's more, baking requires less fuss and attention to the cooking process than frying.

Lay the wings in a single layer on a lightly greased cookie sheet, leaving plenty of room between wings, and put them into a preheated 350° oven for 35 to 40 minutes or until deep golden brown. Turn them halfway through the baking and follow the instructions above when they are cooked.

Even better, joint the wings as usual and cook them on the outdoor grill for fifteen minutes before tossing with the sauce.

Asian-Spiced Wings

These wings are dark, spicy, and slightly sticky, perfect for cocktail parties. The sauce cooks on the wings as they bake, so they're not overly crisp on the outside. But the coating permeates deep into each wing. For a different main dish, cut off the wing tips but leave the other two pieces joined and serve the wings on a bed of steamed white rice with steamed broccoli on the side.

Serves 4–6 as an appetizer, 2–3 as a main course

1/4 cup dark soy sauce

1/2 cup hoisin sauce

1/2 teaspoon cayenne

1 tablespoon dark sesame oil (optional)

3 pounds whole chicken wings

1/2 cup chopped scallions

1. In a large bowl combine the soy sauce, hoisin sauce, cayenne, and sesame oil if using and mix well, then set aside.

2. Joint the wings as described on p. 128 and discard the tips (or save them for stock). Put the wing pieces into the marinade and stir well to coat them with the mixture. Set aside to marinate for about 30 minutes.

3. Preheat oven to 350°. Spread the wing pieces out on a greased cookie sheet and bake for 35–40 minutes, turning two or three times during the cooking to avoid burning. Serve with chopped scallions sprinkled over all for garnish.

Jamaican Wings

Inspired by the flavors of Jamaican jerk chicken, the addition of soy sauce makes these wings mellower than the aggressive bite of real jerked meat.

Habaneros are fiercely hot South American chilis. Small and round, they come in a range of bright colors from red to yellow to green, and they impart a distinct citrus flavor along with their heat. It's hard to replace that flavor, but if you can't find habaneros, use red chili flakes or any fresh chili.

Serves 4–6 as an appetizer, 2–3 as a main course

3 pounds whole chicken wings	2 tablespoons lime juice
1 medium onion, finely chopped	1/2 teaspoon dried thyme leaves
2–3 cloves garlic, minced	1/2 teaspoon allspice
1 habanero chile, finely chopped	1 cup canned whole tomatoes
1/4 cup soy sauce	1/2 teaspoon salt

1. Joint the wings as described on p. 128, rinse and pat dry.

2. Put remaining ingredients in a blender and process until smooth. Place jerk marinade in a bowl or zipper-lock plastic bag, add the wings, and toss to coat. Marinate for 20–30 minutes.

3. Lift wings out of the marinade and cook either by grilling over a medium fire for 8–10 minutes, turning and moving often to prevent burning, or broil for 8–10 minutes, turning once.

Maple-Glazed Wings

Make sure you use real maple syrup and not "pancake syrup," which usually contains no more than 2 percent maple syrup, if any. These wings are deliciously sticky and sweet with a bit of a zingy nip from the mustard.

Serves 4–6 as an appetizer, 2–3 as a main course

3 pounds whole chicken wings	2 tablespoons lemon juice
1/2 cup maple syrup	1 teaspoon freshly ground black pepper
1/4 cup spicy brown mustard	1/4 teaspoon nutmeg

1. Preheat oven to 350°. Joint wings as described on p. 128, rinse, and dry with a paper towel.

2. Blend remaining ingredients well in a medium bowl and add wings, tossing well to coat.

3. Pour wings into a 9 x 13-inch glass baking dish and bake for 35–40 minutes, turning occasionally, until wings are crisp and golden.

Rosemary-Garlic Roasted Wings

These wings are unusual in being equally good served at room temperature as they are hot. A long soak in an herby, garlicky marinade followed by extra long baking time cooks out a lot of the fat and reduces each wing to a delicious little strip of crisp skin and meat. You can cook them longer than some of the recipes above because there's no sugar in the marinade that might burn, so by the time they're finished cooking, they should be practically frying in a pool of chicken grease in the bottom of the pan. Lift the wings out and drain on a paper towel, leaving the fat and excess marinade behind.

Serves 4–6 as an appetizer, 2–3 as a main course

3 pounds whole chicken wings

5 cloves garlic, minced

1/2 cup olive oil

1/4 cup lemon juice

2 teaspoons dried rosemary

1 teaspoon salt

1/2 teaspoon freshly ground black pepper

1. Joint wings as described on p. 128, rinse, and dry with a paper towel.

2. Combine the rest of the ingredients in a medium bowl or zipper-lock plastic bag. Add chicken wings and toss well to coat. Marinate for at least an hour, and up to overnight.

3. Preheat oven to 350°. Remove the wings from the marinade and lay them out in a 9 x 13-inch glass casserole or on a jelly roll pan. Bake the wings for 40–50 minutes, until they're extremely crisp and mahogany brown (keeping an eye on them to make sure they're not actually burning). Serve hot or at room temperature.

The Least You Need to Know

➤ Chicken wings, once the most disposable of chicken parts, became one of the more expensive after the craze for Buffalo Wings started to sweep the country in the 1970s.

➤ The most economical way to buy wings is to get whole ones and joint them yourself.

➤ For party food, the single-boned piece of the wing can be trimmed into a miniature "drummette."

➤ Big bags of frozen wings might look tempting, but buy the freshest ones you can find. Despite all the sauce you'll probably add, the frozen wings have the least flavor of any frozen chicken part.

GIBLET LOVER'S FAN CLUB

Chapter 20

Gaga for Giblets— Gizzards, Hearts, Livers, Necks

In This Chapter

➤ Don't throw it away!

➤ Cleaning organ meat

➤ Better than you'd think: Tasty recipes for chicken innards

Giblets are actually one of the tastiest parts of chicken—that's if you know what to do with them.

Don't Throw It Away!

Many a novice cook has been startled and astonished to discover, sometimes after cooking (Oops!), that the inner cavity of a whole chicken usually contains a paper-wrapped package of giblets and neck. Some cooks routinely pull them out and throw them away without a second thought, while others sometimes flour and fry the livers as a little treat for themselves.

What this bag actually contains, if you bother to open it, is a gizzard, a heart, a neck, and a liver. Only the gizzard, heart, and liver are technically considered giblets, but the neck is almost always lumped in with the designation, partly because the neck plays a crucial part in making giblet gravy.

The gizzard is an organ that only birds have. It is part of their digestive system and, fried or roasted, is delightfully chewy. The heart is similarly chewy, though slightly more tender, and the neck is covered in tender strips of dark meat that wily cooks will roast and eat in secret, lest anyone ask them to share the treat. The chicken liver is far more familiar to most diners, appearing in a variety of pates and appetizers, but what to do when you only have one or two?

The easy answer is to flour it, fry it, and eat it right away. You can also save the livers in a sealed plastic tub in the freezer, sorting out the hearts and gizzards into their own tubs. Then, when you've collected enough, you can use the livers for a number of dishes and serve the other giblets up fried or in that Cajun classic, Dirty Rice.

You may have never developed a taste for chicken giblets, but once you start experimenting with these versatile tidbits, you may be surprised. Chicken liver tastes far less "liver-ish" than calves liver. It has a lighter, more delicate flavor that is nicely accented by bacon. It's even good for you. The liver, although high in cholesterol, is low in saturated fat and rich in iron, vitamin A, the B vitamins, and folic acid (which is necessary for everyone but particularly important for pregnant women). So don't just pull the giblet package out of the chicken and throw it away—store it in the freezer while you consider your options. Indeed, chicken livers are considered the secret ingredient in classic Italian ragus. Next thing you know, you may be at the supermarket buying individual packages of chicken giblets.

Cleaning Organ Meat

All giblets should be well rinsed before cooking. Using a sharp paring knife or a small kitchen scissors, trim off any hard bits of gristle. Livers should be well-trimmed of any signs of yellow fat, any bit of gristle, and particularly anything that is greenish, leaving only the dark reddish-brown lobes of the liver.

Better Than You'd Think: Tasty Recipes for Chicken Innards

There are several classic styles of cooking chicken giblets, with livers playing a starring role in some.

Giblet Gravy

One of the most basic recipes for giblets and the neck is a giblet stock to use for gravy. You make a giblet stock while your chicken is roasting, and then use that for a gravy to serve over the finished bird. Some cooks add a chopped, hard-boiled egg to the finished gravy.

The liver is usually left out when you're making stock for gravy. Unless you're particularly fond of a liver flavor in your gravy, separate the liver out of the giblets and save it for another use or discard it. Sometimes giblets will include an extra heart or gizzard—if you got extra, toss them in the stock. This recipe works equally well with turkey giblets.

For the stock:	For the gravy:
1 neck	2 tablespoons butter
1 heart	2 tablespoons all-purpose flour
1 gizzard	Salt and pepper
1 small onion	
1 bay leaf	
1/2 teaspoon salt	
5 peppercorns (optional)	
2–3 cups water	

1. Place the neck, heart, gizzard, bay leaf, onion, salt, and peppercorns in a medium saucepan and cover with 2–3 cups of water.

2. Simmer gently for about an hour, cool and strain out the solids. Pick the meat off the neck and return it to the stock, and finely chop the remaining innards and put them back in the stock.

3. To make the gravy, heat the butter in another small saucepan, stir in the flour, and cook, stirring, for several minutes over medium heat. Don't let the flour or butter brown.

4. Slowly stir in the stock and meat bits, blending carefully to keep lumps from forming. Season to taste with salt and pepper. Serve over sliced roasted chicken and mashed potatoes.

Dirty Rice

A spicy dish from frugal Cajun cooks, Dirty Rice probably evolved as a way to use up every part of a chicken, but what was once a side dish is hearty enough to serve as a main course. The chopped-up giblets and plethora of seasonings give it the characteristic "dirty" appearance. Vary the amount of cayenne to your taste, and serve with Louisiana hot sauce on the side for those who like their dirty rice a little more spicy.

Serves 6–8

6 chicken necks	2 stalks celery, chopped
1 bay leaf	1 green bell pepper, cored, seeded, and diced
6 chicken gizzards	1 1/2 teaspoons salt
6–8 chicken hearts	1/2 teaspoon cayenne
1/2 pound chicken livers (about 3/4 cup)	1/2 teaspoon freshly ground black pepper
3 tablespoons olive oil	1/2 teaspoon cumin
1 large onion, chopped	1/2 teaspoon thyme
2 cloves garlic, minced	4 cups freshly cooked white rice

1. In a small saucepan, cook the chicken necks with the bay leaf in water to cover until the meat is falling off the bones. Pick the meat off the bones, discard the bones, and set the meat and cooking liquid aside.

2. Rinse and trim as needed the hearts, gizzards, and livers. Mince all the giblets with a large knife (you can chop the hearts and gizzards in the food processor but not the livers, which will turn to mush).

3. Heat the olive oil in a large Dutch oven or stewpot. Stir in the livers, gizzards, and hearts, and cook 6–8 minutes, till meat is browned. Add the onion, garlic, celery, and bell pepper, and cook until the vegetables start to soften, 4–5 minutes. Stir in the salt, cayenne, black pepper, cumin, and thyme.

4. Add the cooked meat from the necks and 1/2 cup of the broth from cooking the neck. Stir in the hot cooked rice and toss well to combine. Moisten with a little more of the broth if necessary and serve.

Country Pate

This is a quick and easy rustic pate that can go from frying pan to food processor to hors d'ouevre in about fifteen minutes. It's terrific served on bruschetta, which is an Italian method of scraping the surface of toasted bread with raw garlic, then painting it with olive oil. Make a plateful of bruschetta, using a good bakery bread such as sourdough, and serve it with a knife and a bowl of this pate. It's so addictive, your guests may not even want dinner. You need a food processor to make this pate.

Serves 4–6

2 tablespoons butter	Pinch of nutmeg
1 onion, diced	1 teaspoon salt
2 cloves garlic, minced	1/2 teaspoon freshly ground black pepper
1/2 teaspoon dried thyme	1/3 cup red wine
1 pound chicken livers (about 1 1/2 cups), cleaned and trimmed	

1. Heat the butter in a skillet over medium heat and cook the onions and garlic until softened and translucent. Watch the heat and do not allow them to brown.

2. Add the livers and cook through, about 5 minutes, stirring occasionally. Stir in thyme, nutmeg, salt, pepper, and wine, and cook another 2–3 minutes, until wine has evaporated somewhat.

3. Pour the hot liver mixture into the bowl of a food processor and whizz for 2–3 minutes until the mixture achieves a pastelike consistency. Scrape into a serving dish and serve with bruschetta or slices of French bread or crackers.

    If storing, smooth it into a dish and top with a layer of melted butter to seal before covering. Keeps in refrigerator for up to a week, and freezes well for up to three months.

Don't Fowl Up

If you don't have a thermometer to test your oil temperature, heat the oil until it's just beginning to smoke and then lower the temperature slightly so it doesn't get any hotter. If the oil is really smoking, it's too hot, so cool it slightly before adding any food. If you want to test the oil, stick a fork in a cube of bread and hold it in the hot oil. It should immediately start to sizzle and brown. If it doesn't sizzle right away, your oil isn't hot enough.

Ginger-Fried Chicken Livers

This is an unusual Asian recipe to stretch your chicken liver horizons. Chinese cooks have long used every part of whatever bird or beast they're cooking, and that resourcefulness certainly extends to the innards. In this dish, livers are soaked in a garlicky fresh ginger sauce before being shallow-fried. Spicy and crispy, they're also quite good cold.

Serves 4

For the marinade:

1/2 teaspoon salt

3 cloves garlic, minced

1 teaspoon finely minced ginger

1/2 teaspoon honey

1 teaspoon sesame oil

1/2 pound (about 3/4 cup) chicken livers, rinsed and trimmed

3 tablespoons all-purpose flour

Oil for frying

For sauce:

2 teaspoons finely minced ginger

1 tablespoon soy sauce

1 teaspoon sherry or rice wine

1 teaspoon cider vinegar

1/2 teaspoon sugar

1 teaspoon sesame oil

Chopped scallions for garnish

1. Mix together marinade ingredients in a medium bowl and stir in the chicken livers, tossing well to coat. Leave to marinate 30 minutes.

2. Heat 2 inches of oil to 350° in a wok or heavy-sided saucepan.

3. Toss the chicken livers in the flour and cook in two batches. They will be brown and crispy in 2–3 minutes. Remove to a paper towel-lined platter.

4. Heat one tablespoon of the cooking oil in a clean skillet over medium heat. Stir the 2 teaspoons of ginger in the oil for 30 seconds, then add the remaining sauce ingredients and bring to the boil. Turn the heat down and simmer for 3–4 minutes.

5. Add the chicken livers and stir them in the sauce for another 3–4 minutes. Sprinkle with chopped green onions for garnish. Serve hot, or allow to cool and serve cold that same day.

Chicken Livers with Mushrooms and Bacon

This is an elegant ragout, perfect for a cold night. (*"Ragout"* is a French term for a thick, highly seasoned stew. The word comes from the verb *"ragouter,"* meaning "to stimulate the taste buds.") Serve tiny plates of it sprinkled with parsley as an appetizer, or serve larger portions over toast points with a glass of red wine for a main dish. It's hearty and heavy, so serve it with a tartly dressed green salad to cut the richness.

Serves 6 as an appetizer, 4 as a main dish

3 slices bacon, diced

1 small onion, chopped

1/2 pound fresh mushrooms, sliced

1 tablespoon all-purpose flour

1 cup dry white wine

1 cup heavy cream

2 tablespoons chopped fresh oregano or 1 teaspoon dried oregano

1 teaspoon salt

1/2 teaspoon freshly ground black pepper

1 tablespoon butter

1 pound (about 1 1/2 cups) chicken livers

Chopped fresh parsley for garnish

1. Cook the bacon in a skillet over medium heat until the fat runs. Add the onion and cook for 4–5 minutes, until translucent but not browned. Add the mushrooms and cook until tender, 5–7 minutes.

2. Stir in the flour and add white wine, blending well. Stir until the sauce comes to a boil, then add the cream and return to a boil. Remove from heat and add oregano, salt, and pepper. Cover to keep warm and set aside.

3. In a clean skillet, heat the butter over medium-high heat. The butter will foam up. As soon as the butter foams but before it turns brown, add the livers and cook quickly, tossing in the butter, until browned, about 4–5 minutes.

4. Stir hot livers into the cream sauce and serve immediately, garnished with parsley.

Secret-Ingredient Bolognese Sauce

There are endless recipes for Italian meat sauces, but many cooks swear that the secret ingredient for a classic Bolognese sauce is chicken livers. The one below is a particularly delicious version, hearty and meaty, with ground sirloin and chicken livers, flavored with bacon and the traditional Bolognese vegetables of onion, carrot, and celery and a minimum of tomato. Let it cook slowly and gently to allow the flavors to meld, then serve it sparingly over hot spaghetti. The chicken livers make the sauce very rich, and a little goes a long way.

Serves 4–6

4 strips of bacon, diced

1 small onion, chopped

1 carrot, peeled and finely diced

1 stick celery, finely chopped

1/2 pound ground sirloin

1/4 pound chicken livers (a little less than 1/2 cup), coarsely chopped

2 tablespoons tomato paste

2/3 cup white wine

1 1/2 cups beef stock (or chicken stock)

1/2 teaspoon dried oregano

1 teaspoon salt

1/2 teaspoon freshly ground black pepper

1. Fry the bacon in a heavy Dutch oven or stewpot over medium heat. As the fat begins to run, add the onion, carrot, and celery, and cook about 5 minutes, until they start to brown slightly.

2. Add the ground sirloin and cook 3–4 minutes, breaking it up. As the meat starts to brown, stir in the chicken livers and cook for a further 5 minutes, stirring occasionally until the livers are browned.

3. Blend the tomato paste into the meats and vegetables, stirring well. Add the wine, stock, oregano, salt, and pepper. Bring to a boil, stirring, then reduce the heat. Cover partially and cook at a low simmer for 30–40 minutes, stirring from time to time.

The Least You Need to Know

➤ The giblets of a chicken consist of the neck, heart, gizzard, and liver.

➤ A package of giblets wrapped in a small paper or plastic bag can usually be found in the inner cavity of a whole chicken.

➤ Chicken livers, though somewhat high in cholesterol, are low in saturated fat and full of vitamins and iron, and they're the secret ingredient for absolutely wonderful Bolognese Sauce.

Chapter 21

What Do I Do with It? Light and Tasty Ground Chicken

In This Chapter

➤ It's not pale hamburger

➤ Grinding your own

➤ This is chicken?! Great ground chicken recipes

If you expect it to act like ground chuck, you're in for a disappointment. But treat it right and ground chicken can be your new best friend.

It's Not Pale Hamburger

When ground poultry first hit the shelves, hamburger got worried. Consumers wanted lower fat ground chicken and ground turkey in place of hamburger in everything. But then the popularity of ground chicken waned as people started to notice, Hey, this doesn't taste like much.

The problem is that ground poultry is not merely a pale substitute for ground beef. That same lower fat content that drew us to ground chicken in the first place also means that chicken must be handled more gently and flavored differently from hamburger. Because it has so much less fat, it's far more likely to burn when browning it the way you might burn regular hamburger, and you may even need to add some oil to the pan to help it brown properly. The lower fat content also means that ground chicken may need a little extra "body" when used for, say, chicken burgers. You can accomplish this by stirring in breadcrumbs and other additions such as beaten egg.

So don't automatically toss in a pound of ground chicken where your recipe calls for a pound of hamburger. Treated with a little respect, ground chicken has its own delicate flavor that can be accented with judicious use of herbs and spices. Chicken burgers, chicken meatloaf, and chicken sausages are all terrific foods on their own unless you expect them to taste just like their beef versions. Try the recipes below created expressly for ground chicken to see that it's much, much more than "white hamburger."

Don't Fowl Up

In a dish that's already strongly flavored, such as a spaghetti or lasagne sauce or a pot of chili, ground chicken can indeed provide the texture of ground beef while cutting the fat content of the overall dish. But taste your sauce and add a touch of extra oregano or some more chili powder, or perhaps a little extra salt and pepper to make up for the more delicate chicken flavor.

Grinding Your Own

If you're eating ground chicken because you think it's much lower fat than ground beef, make sure you read the package label very carefully or ask your butcher. Ground chicken can, by law, contain ground-up chicken skin to give it some added fat, and depending on the mix of dark and white meat and how much skin is added, the fat content can be as high as 15 percent, which is similar to that of hamburger. Dark meat is a definite plus because of the extra flavor it adds, but a lot of skin in your ground chicken is to be avoided, both for the fat content and the lowered quality of the meat.

The best way to avoid the skin is to grind your own chicken. For the absolute lowest fat type of ground chicken, trim all the skin and fat off chicken breasts, cut them into large pieces, and pulse briefly in your food processor or run it through a meat grinder once on the coarsest plate (what butchers call the chili plate). Don't just turn your food processor on and let it run or the chicken will quickly become a smooth, tasteless, useless paste. You just want to break the meat down as coarsely as possible, and you can judge by the look. After a few pulses, it will very soon look like coarse-ground hamburger.

You can vary the mix of chicken as well. Try two to three boneless, skinless breasts and add five thighs which you have boned and trimmed of all fat and skin. This blend of half dark, half white meat makes for a terrific balance of chicken flavor and gives the chicken a little more body for making burgers, meatballs, and loaves. If you're making chicken sausages (see p. 147), you can add the spices and breadcrumbs (not the whole pieces of bread) directly to the food processor before you grind and the sausage practically makes itself. If you're adventurous, you may want to toss in a few chunks of veal or pork loin to vary the flavors and textures of your chicken meatloaf. Experiment to see what works best for you.

This Is Chicken?! Great Ground Chicken Recipes

The secret is to let chicken be itself, and not try to make it look, taste, or act like ground beef. You don't expect your chicken breast to stand in on your plate for a steak. Use the recipes below to get a feel for handling ground chicken, and note the use of herbs and citrus to accentuate chicken's lighter flavor. You'll soon develop the instinct for modifying your ground beef recipes to accommodate ground chicken.

Wing Tips

Ground chicken is much more tender than ground beef, even more tender than ground turkey, so expect your meatloaf to be delicate and almost mousse-like in texture.

Best Chicken Loaf

Chicken loaves are not meat loaves, and if you try to follow your usual meatloaf recipe, you'll end up with something utterly tasteless and dry. For a good chicken loaf, you must accommodate the lower fat content and try to heighten the chicken flavor. Soaking the breadcrumbs in buttermilk adds a great deal more flavor than soaking the bread in regular milk, and the wet bread makes the whole loaf moister when cooked. And a ketchup topping leaves chicken loaf uninspired—a liberal coating of mustard strikes just the right note. If you're lucky you'll have a couple slices left over for sandwiches.

Serves 6

2 tablespoon olive oil

1 large onion, finely chopped

2 cloves garlic, minced

2 medium carrots, peeled and grated

3 slices stale white bread, crusts removed

1/3 cup buttermilk

2 pounds ground chicken

1/4 cup chopped fresh parsley, preferably flat-leaf Italian

1 egg, beaten

1 teaspoon dried thyme

2 teaspoons salt

1/2 teaspoon white pepper

Dijon or spicy brown mustard

1. Preheat oven to 350° and lightly grease a loaf pan.

2. Heat the olive oil in a skillet over medium-low heat and cook the onion, garlic, and grated carrot until vegetables are tender but not browned, 12–15 minutes. While vegetables are cooking, soak the bread in the buttermilk in a small bowl until bread falls apart.

3. In a large bowl, combine chicken, cooked vegetables, soaked bread, and all remaining ingredients. Mix well with your hands and pack the mixture into the loaf pan.

continues

continued

4. Create a water bath by setting the loaf pan in a larger glass casserole and fill with hot water till water is 1 inch up the sides of the loaf pan. (A water bath is created when a baking dish is set into a larger dish and the larger dish is filled with hot water. The water comes up the sides of the inner pan and prevents the food being cooked in the inner pan from drying out. It's used when baking delicate foods such as custards, eggs, and pates.) Bake for 1 hour and 15 minutes.

5. Remove from oven and take loaf pan out of the water. Cool loaf in pan for 20 minutes and then run a knife around all four sides to loosen it before inverting on a serving platter. Spread mustard across the top of the loaf and serve, cutting into 3/4-inch slices.

Tarragon Chicken Burgers

The tarragon in these juicy burgers makes for a far more elegant burger than what usually graces a bun. A creamy sauce and toasted sourdough buns set them off to perfection, and a slice of Monterey Jack cheese is merely gilding the lily. For an extra touch of flavor, use sourdough bread crumbs instead of plain. Be sure not to overcook the burgers and serve them good and hot.

Serves 6

1 1/2 pounds ground chicken

1/2 cup white breadcrumbs

1 clove garlic, minced

1 teaspoon dried tarragon or 2 teaspoons fresh, chopped

1 teaspoon salt

1/2 teaspoon freshly ground black pepper

2 tablespoons olive oil

1/4 cup mayonnaise

1/4 cup Dijon mustard

1/4 teaspoon dried basil

6 sourdough buns

6 thin slices fresh tomato

6 leaves of romaine lettuce, rinsed and dried with paper towel

6 thin slices Monterey Jack cheese (optional)

1. In a medium bowl, combine chicken, breadcrumbs, garlic, salt, and pepper, mixing gently with your hands or a wooden spoon. Form into 6 patties, each about 3 1/2 inches across.

2. Heat olive oil in a skillet over medium heat and fry the burgers, turning once, about 10–12 minutes. They should be lightly browned on the outside and white through, with no trace of pink.

3. While the burgers are frying, blend the mayonnaise, Dijon, and basil in a small bowl. Toast the sourdough buns.

4. To assemble burgers, lay the hot burger on the bottom of the bun, top with cheese if using, then lettuce and tomato. Slather 1 1/2 tablespoons of Dijon sauce on bun top and close. Serve immediately.

Zesty Chicken Sausage Patties

Don't consider this a substitute for your usual pork breakfast sausage but as a sausage in its own right. The light flavors of apple and orange paired with the traditional flavoring of sage make for an unusual and refreshing blend that makes an excellent accompaniment to your breakfast egg or perfect for a light supper with some fried potatoes and a green salad.

Serves 6

1 pound chicken breasts, boned	1 teaspoon orange zest
1 pound chicken thighs or drumsticks, boned	1 teaspoon dried sage
1 large Granny Smith apple	1 teaspoon freshly ground black pepper
1 medium onion	2 tablespoons orange juice
1 tablespoon salt	

1. Cut the chicken pieces into large chunks. Peel, core, and dice the apple and onion. Place all ingredients in a food processor and pulse just until coarsely chopped and combined. Do not overprocess into a paste.

2. Divide the mixture into 12 patties. Wrap in waxed paper and refrigerate at least 4 hours, preferably overnight.

3. When ready to serve, broil for 5 minutes on each side, until white throughout with a browned crust. Don't overcook or the sausages will be dry. Serve immediately while still hot and juicy.

Don't Fowl Up

Because this is a sausage, some of the fat and skin should remain on the chicken to bind the sausage together and keep it from drying out while it cooks. Make sure the pieces are completely boned, but don't remove the fat and skin from more than half of it.

Chicken Sloppy Joes

Instead of the traditional Sloppy Joes of ground beef with a heavy, barbecue-like red sauce, Chicken Sloppy Joes have a lighter, tangier sauce with a hint of citrus and cinnamon, and some chopped green pepper and mushroom to vary the texture. Serve on soft hamburger rolls, ladling on enough of the mix that it spills off the bun, and eat with a knife and fork.

Serves 6

2 tablespoons olive oil	1/4 cup orange juice
2 pounds ground chicken	1 tablespoon Worcestershire sauce
1 medium onion, chopped	1/2 teaspoons salt
1 green pepper, cored, seeded, and chopped	1/2 teaspoon freshly ground black pepper
1 clove garlic, minced	1/2 teaspoon cinnamon
1/2 cup sliced fresh mushrooms	6 hamburger buns
1 8-ounce can tomato sauce	

1. Heat the olive oil in a skillet over medium heat, and add the ground chicken and onions. Cook, stirring occasionally, for 7–10 minutes, until chicken is white through and onions are tender and translucent.

2. Stir in green pepper, garlic, and mushrooms and cook another 5 minutes, till vegetables soften.

3. Add remaining ingredients, except for buns, and stir well. Bring to a boil and then reduce heat to low. Cook gently, stirring now and then, for about 30 minutes, until flavors have blended.

4. Taste and adjust seasonings—you may want a touch more Worcestershire or orange juice for tanginess. Spoon over bottom half of buns on each plate and top with upper half. Serve immediately.

White Chicken Chili

Ground chicken has a hard time standing up to the traditional red kidney beans and tomato sauce of beef chili, so this is a chili designed to let the chicken flavor come through. Green peppers and red onions provide a little more body, and white beans are used, either cannellini, navy, or Great Northern.

Chicken broth and white wine provide a light sauce that allows the oregano, bay leaf, and fresh cilantro to shine. Still, there's a kick of chili powder and extra cumin that you can turn up to your taste—after all, it may be chicken but it's still chili!

Serves 4–6

2 tablespoons olive oil

1 red onion, chopped

3 cloves garlic, minced

1 pound ground chicken

1 green pepper, cored, seeded, and diced

2 cups chicken broth

1/2 cup dry white wine

1 16-ounce can white beans, drained and rinsed

1–3 pickled jalapeno peppers, seeded and minced

2 teaspoons dried oregano

2 teaspoons chili powder

2 teaspoons salt

1 teaspoon cumin

1 bay leaf

Chopped fresh cilantro for garnish

1. Heat the olive oil in a deep, heavy-sided saucepan. Add onion and cook for 7–10 minutes, until it begins to turn golden and translucent.

2. Stir in ground chicken, garlic cloves, and green pepper and cook 4–5 minutes till chicken is white through and slightly browned.

3. Add remaining ingredients and stir well. Bring to a boil and reduce heat. Cover pot with lid slightly askew and simmer for 30 minutes, until vegetables are tender and sauce has cooked down and thickened.

4. Taste and adjust seasonings, adding more salt or jalapeno if desired. Serve in bowls with a generous sprinkle of chopped cilantro as garnish.

The Least You Need to Know

➤ If you try to treat ground chicken as a pale replacement for ground beef, you'll be disappointed.

➤ Think of ground chicken as a food in its own right, a light, low-fat ground meat that needs delicate handling to bring out its best flavor.

➤ Some commercially produced ground chicken has so much skin ground with the meat that the fat content approaches that of ground beef.

➤ To make sure your ground chicken is low fat, grind boneless, skinless breasts in the food processor.

➤ When using ground chicken in place of hamburger in traditional recipes such as chili, be generous with seasonings such as salt and chili powder to make up for the less robust flavor of the chicken meat.

Part 4
Chicken by the Course

So now you know what to do with every possible part of a chicken that might come your way. But what to do when you're not trying to deal with a package of thighs but instead trying to prepare a tasty tray of appetizers? "Chicken by the Course" will show you how to bring chicken into pretty much every part of the meal except dessert.

Chapter 22

Appetizers, Snacks, and Sandwiches

> **In This Chapter**
>
> ➤ Appetizers
>
> ➤ Snacks
>
> ➤ Sandwiches

Chicken appetizers and snacks run the gamut from fast and easy to elaborate preparations that can turn into a meal.

Appetizers and Snacks

Rumaki

A terrific little nibble reminiscent of 1970s dinner parties, Rumaki is a great item to hand round with drinks. It's a small mouthful but it's meaty, crisp, and savory, an appetizer in the truest sense.

Makes about 2 dozen pieces

1/2 pound chicken livers	1 teaspoon grated fresh ginger
1/4 cup soy sauce	1 6-ounce can whole water chestnuts
2 cloves garlic, minced	10–12 slices bacon, halved

1. Rinse and pat dry the chicken livers and trim them into pieces about the size of a walnut.
2. In a small bowl, mix the soy sauce, garlic, and ginger. Put the livers into the soy sauce mixture and toss well to coat. Marinate for at least 15 minutes, and up to an hour.
3. Preheat oven to 400°. Wrap a strip of bacon around a piece of liver and a water chestnut and secure with a toothpick. Discard the marinade.
4. Arrange in a single layer on a baking sheet and bake for 8–10 minutes, until the bacon is crisp and browned. Serve hot.

Chicken Nachos

Nachos are a constant favorite. They range from the simplest version of tortilla chips with melted cheese to elaborate creations with meat, beans, guacamole, and sour cream. Chicken Nachos offer a whole new take, with thin strips of chicken breast marinated and cooked like fajitas, then poured over chips and cheese.

Serves 4

2 boneless, skinless chicken breasts	1 9-ounce bag tortilla chips
2 tablespoons lime juice	1 tablespoon vegetable oil
1 teaspoon cumin	1/2 cup diced tomatoes
1 teaspoon chili powder	1 cup salsa
1/2 teaspoon salt	1/2 cup sour cream
1 1/2 cups grated Cheddar or Monterey Jack cheese	

1. Rinse and pat dry the chicken breasts. Slice thinly in 1/4-inch slices. Put chicken slices in a medium bowl and toss with lime juice, cumin, chili pepper, and salt. Marinate for 10–15 minutes.

2. Preheat the oven to 350°. Spread the tortilla chips in a 9 x 13-inch glass pan. Top with cheese and put in the oven while the chicken cooks, just long enough to melt the cheese, about 5 minutes.

3. Heat the oil in a skillet over medium-high heat. When the oil just starts to smoke, put in the chicken and toss over the heat for 4–5 minutes, until chicken is cooked through and browned on all sides. Remove chips from oven. Spread the hot chicken over the cheese and tortilla chips.

4. Sprinkle with diced tomato and spoon the salsa over all. Top with spoonfuls of sour cream and serve immediately.

Don't Fowl Up

To slice chicken in 1/4-inch strips, place the breasts in the freezer for about fifteen minutes, until the meat is deeply chilled and firm. This will allow you to cut more thinly.

Devilled Chicken Spread

Potted chicken is a British spread made mostly of cooked chicken ground up and seasoned with butter, a bit of onion, a touch of cloves or allspice, and salt. It's not bad, but it's a bit bland. A little mustard and spice, however, jazzes up the old-fashioned potted meat and transforms it into a tasty and unusual filling for sandwiches and a terrific spread for crackers. You need a food processor to make this spread.

Makes about 2 cups

2 cups cooked chicken, coarsely chopped

2 tablespoons mayonnaise

1 tablespoon Dijon mustard

2 tablespoons softened butter

1/2 teaspoon salt

1/4 teaspoon cayenne

1/4 teaspoon freshly ground black pepper

1. Place all ingredients in a food processor and process until smooth. Serve spread on crackers or lightly buttered white bread or toast. Keeps for about two days tightly covered in refrigerator, can be frozen for up to three months.

Golden Chicken Nuggets with Sweet and Sour Sauce

Homemade chicken nuggets tend to be far more tender and juicy than the restaurant and store-bought kind, which are often made of ground up chicken meat formed into a nugget shape. The bit of cornmeal in the coating ensures an extra-crispy crust. The butter coating makes these especially succulent, but if you want a slightly lower-fat version, dip the chicken in two beaten egg whites instead of butter.

Makes about 4 dozen nuggets

For sauce:

1 cup apricot preserves

1/4 cup white wine vinegar

1 teaspoon hot pepper sauce

For nuggets:

2 pounds boneless, skinless chicken breasts

2 cups fine, dry breadcrumbs

1/2 cup cornmeal

1/2 teaspoon whole dried oregano

8 tablespoons (1 stick) butter, melted

Oil for frying

1. Make dipping sauce by stirring ingredients in a small saucepan till warm. Set aside.

2. Rinse chicken breasts and pat dry. Cut chicken into 1-inch pieces.

continues

continued

3. Combine breadcrumbs, cornmeal, and oregano in a medium bowl. Put the melted butter in a small bowl nearby. Heat 1 inch of oil in a heavy skillet over medium heat.

4. Dip a chicken piece in the butter, then roll it in the breadcrumb mixture and slip into hot oil. Fry in batches till golden brown and crispy, about 5 minutes, turning once. Drain cooked nuggets on a paper towel-lined platter and keep warm in a low oven while cooking remaining pieces. Serve hot with warm dipping sauce.

Sesame Chicken Strips

A little more grown-up than nuggets, these elegant strips are an excellent snack for parties, especially if you use snazzy black sesame seeds instead of white. You might even try a racy combination of the two. You can eat them plain or with any type of sauce such as Honey-Mustard or the Sweet and Sour Sauce above, but try them with the simple, thin, Asian-inspired sauce below to really accentuate the sesame flavor. Serve on a platter with toothpicks to skewer the chicken pieces and dip them in the sauce.

Makes 2 dozen

For dipping sauce:	For chicken breasts:
1/2 cup light soy sauce	4 boneless, skinless chicken breasts
1 tablespoon finely chopped scallions	2 egg whites, beaten
1 teaspoon sesame oil	1 tablespoon soy sauce
1 teaspoon grated fresh ginger	2 teaspoons dark sesame oil
	1/4 cup sesame seeds

1. Combine sauce ingredients in a small bowl and set aside.

2. Rinse and dry the chicken breasts, and slice each one longways into 6 pieces. In a medium bowl, blend the egg whites with the soy sauce and sesame oil and stir in the chicken pieces. Marinate for at least an hour, but no more than 2 hours.

3. Preheat broiler. Stir the sesame seeds into the chicken and egg whites, tossing to cover the chicken pieces with seeds. Lift each chicken piece out, being careful not to knock off the seeds, and lay it on the broiler pan.

4. Broil for 4–5 minutes, watching to make sure seeds aren't burning, then turn pieces and broil another 2–3 minutes. Discard the marinade. Chicken should be browned on the outside and white through to the middle.

Don't Fowl Up

To ease cleaning, you may want to cover the broiler pan with aluminum foil before putting the chicken on it.

Sandwiches

The Modified Kentucky Hot Brown

The legendary Brown Hotel in Louisville, Kentucky, was famous for its elegant sandwich featuring a cheesy cream sauce over sliced turkey on toast points. The Brown Hotel was closed for many years, but when it reopened, the Hot Brown was again on the menu, redeveloped from memories of the original. Many versions of the recipe exist, some with sauteed mushrooms, with onions, with varying types of cheese, but here's one with chicken.

Serves 4

4 tablespoons (1/2 stick) butter	2 tablespoons sweet sherry (optional)
4 tablespoons all-purpose flour	4 slices white or whole-wheat toast
2 cups milk	8 thin slices chicken breast
1/2 teaspoon salt	8 slices bacon, fried crisp
1/3 cup grated Cheddar cheese	1 medium tomato, cut in 8 wedges (optional)
1/3 cup grated Parmesan cheese	

1. Melt butter in a saucepan over medium heat and stir in flour. Cook 2–3 minutes, then slowly blend in the milk, whisking to prevent lumps from forming. Add salt and cook until thickened. Slowly stir in cheeses and turn off heat. Stir until cheeses melt and sauce is thick and smooth. Stir in sherry.

2. Preheat broiler. Cut each slice of toast in half diagonally and lay two triangles on each of four ovenproof dishes or plates.

3. Layer two slices of chicken in each dish, then ladle a quarter of the sauce over each.

4. Place under the broiler for 2–3 minutes until sauce begins to bubble and brown. Garnish each dish with two slices of bacon, crossed, and two wedges of tomato, and serve immediately.

Ranch Chicken Club Deluxe

Club sandwiches are triple-deckers that usually start with a basic BLT base with chicken or turkey. The addition of sliced avocado makes this an especially hearty meal, and when dressed with a good-quality ranch dressing, you've got something really special. Buy the thicker kind of dressing found in the refrigerated case at the supermarket. Use any leftover cooked chicken. Slices of roast chicken breast are perfect (p. 55) or see p. 80 to poach whole breasts.

To make 4 sandwiches

12 slices white or whole wheat bread	8 slices tomato
2/3 cup ranch dressing	8 slices bacon, cooked crisp
8 slices cooked chicken breast	4 leaves romaine lettuce, washed and dried
1 ripe avocado	

1. Toast the bread. Spread ranch dressing on one side of each piece, reserving some for assembling the sandwiches. Peel and slice the avocado into 16 wedges.
2. Place two slices of chicken on each of four pieces of toast. Put four slices of avocado on each, and top with another four slices of toast, dressing side down. Spread remaining dressing on the other side.
3. Layer two slices of tomato and a leaf of lettuce on each sandwich and top with the remaining bread, dressing side down. Secure with toothpicks to keep them from toppling.

Pulled Chicken Barbecue

This is an unusual and much lower fat alternative to pulled pork barbecue. It doesn't mimic the flavor of pulled pork so much as the texture, but the hearty, tangy, homemade barbecue sauce offers added depth of flavor and makes this a special treat in its own right. Serve on soft hamburger rolls with cole slaw on the side.

Makes about 6 cups, to serve 6–8

3 tablespoons butter	1/2 teaspoon dried oregano
1 cup cider vinegar	3 tablespoons Worcestershire sauce
3/4 cup ketchup	1 teaspoon sugar
1/2 cup water	1/2 teaspoon cayenne
1 teaspoon dry mustard	1 tablespoon hot sauce
1 small onion, minced	4 boneless, skinless chicken breasts
2 cloves garlic, minced	

1. Blend all ingredients except chicken breasts in a medium saucepan. Put the chicken breasts into the cold sauce and turn the heat on.
2. Bring to a boil, reduce to a gentle simmer, and cover. Cook for about an hour, till meat is tender.
3. With two forks, pull the breasts into shreds in the sauce, till it resembles shredded pork barbecue. Simmer with the lid off till sauce thickens slightly. Serve hot on buns. Store in the refrigerator up to a week.

Chicken Meatball Subs

The secret to chicken meatballs that aren't dry and tough is lots of breadcrumbs, well-soaked in milk or buttermilk to keep the meat moist while cooking. These spicy meatballs are then simmered in a quick tomato sauce and spooned into submarine buns. Top with a thick layer of Parmesan cheese for a luxurious, hearty sandwich.

To make 6 subs

For meatballs:

1 cup breadcrumbs

1 cup milk or buttermilk

1 1/2 pounds ground chicken

1 egg, beaten

2 cloves garlic, minced

1 teaspoon dried oregano

1 1/2 teaspoons salt

2–3 tablespoons olive oil

For sauce:

2 tablespoons olive oil

1 medium onion, minced

1 clove garlic, minced

1 28-ounce can crushed tomatoes

2 tablespoons tomato paste

1 teaspoon salt

1/2 teaspoon freshly ground black pepper

1/2 teaspoon oregano

1/2 teaspoon red pepper flakes (optional)

6 submarine rolls, split

1. Put the breadcrumbs in a large bowl and pour in the milk or buttermilk. Stir and leave to soak till the crumbs have absorbed all the liquid, about 10 minutes.

2. Add the remaining meatball ingredients and combine with your hands. Roll into 25–30 meatballs, about 1 inch in diameter.

3. Heat a skillet over medium heat and add the olive oil. Fry the meatballs, a batch at a time, till browned and cooked through.

4. While the meatballs are cooking, heat the 2 tablespoons of olive oil for the sauce in a large saucepan and saute the onions and garlic till tender. Stir in remaining ingredients and simmer gently while tending to the meatballs.

5. When the meatballs are all cooked, add them to the sauce all at once and simmer 10–15 minutes, till meatballs and sauce are hot through and sauce has thickened slightly. Divide meatballs and sauce among the sub rolls and serve immediately.

Chicken Tortilla Roll-Ups

Wrapped sandwiches are a relatively new food fad that, like so many others, has its roots in long-established cuisines. The rolled sandwiches with ingredients folded inside flat breads and flour tortillas echo Mexican burritos, Middle Eastern pitas, even Ethiopian and Afghani flat breads used instead of utensils to scoop up food. This version with grilled chicken and vegetables makes a filling, healthy meal. If you don't want to grill, you can broil the chicken and vegetables instead.

To make 4 wrapped sandwiches

2 boneless, skinless chicken breasts	Olive oil
1 small zucchini	2 tablespoons balsamic vinegar
1 red bell pepper	4 10-inch flour tortillas
1 large yellow onion	

1. Wash and slice the vegetables. Cut the zucchini into long, thin diagonals slices, cut the pepper into strips, and the onion into rounds 1/2-inch thick.

2. Brush the vegetables and chicken breasts with olive oil and season with salt and pepper. Grill over a medium fire until the chicken is browned and cooked through and the vegetables are soft and browned, about 10 minutes. Remove to a platter and slice the breasts into 1/4-inch slices.

3. In a small jar, place 1/4 cup olive oil and the balsamic vinegar and shake till well blended.

4. Divide the chicken and vegetables onto the four tortillas. Drizzle thickly with the balsamic vinaigrette and roll up. Cut each roll in half diagonally and serve.

The Least You Need to Know

➤ You can bring chicken into nearly every part of a meal except dessert.

➤ Chicken snacks and appetizers include classics such as rumaki, the party fare of chicken livers broiled with bacon and water chestnuts, and old favorites updated with chicken, such as hearty nachos with strips of chicken breast.

➤ Chicken sandwiches can be much more than sliced cooked chicken with toppings—you can make a delicious and much lower fat version of pulled pork barbecue by simmering chicken breasts till tender in a tangy sauce and shredding them with two forks.

160

Chapter 23

Soups and Salads

In This Chapter

➤ Soups that start with the whole chicken

➤ Classic soup recipes

➤ Chicken salads with pizzazz

Soups

Nothing says home and comfort more than homemade chicken soup, the stock long simmered to extract every hint of flavor from the bones, and the ingredients selected and added with care. If you're in the habit of opening a can when you want chicken soup, you may be surprised to find how wholesome and satisfying real homemade chicken soup can be.

In 1835, H.W. Brand left the employ of King George IV to start a shop in London selling his Essence of Chicken, a concoction he had created in the kitchens of Buckingham Palace as a health tonic for the king. So say the purveyors of Brand's, a health supplement whose popularity seems largely confined to Asia. Over 100 million bottles are sold every year of this chicken essence that promises to act as a general panacea, to increase energy levels, and to promote mental alertness and memory skills. When tested on memory skills, the company says "those who consumed Brand's made less mistakes." Presumably grammar is not part of the test.

Chicken Soup with Matzoh Balls

The classic Jewish soup, with hearty matzoh balls floating in rich stock, promising relief from whatever ails you, be it a cold or flu, or weariness in body or spirit.

The quality of the matzoh balls are the subject of endless debate. Some are heavy and doughy, sinking to the bottom of the soup and the stomach like lead, and the best float in the soup like little yellow clouds. There are all sorts of tips for getting it right, but you won't know what kind of matzoh ball maker you are until you try. Some people, it seems, are just blessed with a lighter hand. (And some use schmaltz, rendered chicken fat, instead of butter.)

Serves 6–8

For the chicken soup:

1 4–5-pound stewing hen

2 stalks celery, roughly chopped

1 medium carrot, roughly chopped

2 bay leaves

1 1/2 teaspoons salt

1/2 teaspoon whole peppercorns

1 large sprig parsley

3 1/2 quarts cold water

For the matzoh balls:

1 cup matzoh meal

2 eggs, beaten

1/2 cup water

3 tablespoons butter or margarine, melted

1 teaspoon salt

1. Rinse the chicken inside and out under cold running water and joint it into pieces (p. 24).

2. Place the pieces in a 6–8-quart stockpot. Add the carrot, celery, parsley, bay, salt and pepper and cover with the water. Slowly bring just to a boil over medium heat, then immediately reduce the heat to low and let simmer gently for 2 1/2–3 hours.

3. Strain the soup into a clean container and skim off the fat. Chop up the breast meat and return it to the soup, and add some of the dark meat if desired. Discard the remaining chicken and vegetables.

4. While the chicken soup is cooking, combine all of the ingredients for the matzoh balls in a medium bowl and stir well. Let the mixture sit in the refrigerator until the soup is ready, then use your hands or two teaspoons to form the dough into balls, about 1 1/2 inches in diameter, and drop them into the boiling soup.

5. Let the matzoh balls simmer in the soup for 20 minutes before serving.

Greek Chicken and Rice Soup

Avgolemono, egg and lemon, is the Greek name for this heavenly soup of rich chicken stock with rice. Just before serving, a mixture of beaten egg and lemon juice is stirred into the soup, enriching the stock and making the soup thicker, with a fine tangy flavor of lemon. Use fresh lemon juice for the best results, and don't be shy about the amount. Avgolemono should have a distinctive lemon flavor.

Serves 6

1 3-pound stewing hen or 3 pounds chicken pieces

1 medium onion, coarsely chopped

1 stalk celery, coarsely chopped

1 medium carrot, coarsely chopped

1 teaspoon salt

1/2 teaspoon whole black peppercorns

2 1/2 quarts cold water

1 cup long grain rice

1/4 cup lemon juice

2 eggs

Chopped fresh parsley, for garnish

1. Rinse the chicken well under cold running water. If you are using a whole chicken, joint it into 8 pieces.

2. Place it in a 6–8 quart stock pot. Put in the onion, carrot, celery, salt, and pepper and cover with the water. Slowly bring just to a boil over medium heat. Immediately reduce the heat to low and let simmer for 2 1/2–3 hours.

3. Strain the soup into a clean container and skim off the fat. Return some of the chopped breast meat to the soup, and some of the dark meat if desired. Discard the remaining chicken and vegetables.

4. Add the rice to the broth, cover and cook for 12–18 minutes or until the rice is cooked.

5. In a bowl, beat the eggs with a whisk and beat in the lemon juice. When the chicken soup is ready, slowly whisk one cup of soup into the egg mixture before gradually beating this soup-egg mixture back into the soup.

6. Simmer over low heat until the soup thickens, about 5 minutes. Serve garnished with a little chopped parsley.

Best-Ever Chicken Noodle Soup

This is a very simple soup if you have rich chicken stock ready to go. Finely chopped vegetables are cooked in butter, then a little flour is added to ensure the soup will be thick and velvety. The stock goes in to cook the wide egg noodles, and then the finishing touch is a splash of light cream to enrich and unify. It's not a heavy, hearty soup, but an elegant and comforting one for an afternoon lunch. If you're only accustomed to salty chicken noodle from a can, give this a try.

Serves 6

2 tablespoons butter	2 quarts Elaborate Chicken Stock (page 52)
1 small onion, finely chopped	1/4 pound egg noodles
1 medium carrot, diced	1/4 cup light cream
1 stalk celery, finely chopped	1/2 teaspoon white pepper
2 tablespoons flour	Fresh chopped parsley, for garnish

1. Heat the oil in a heavy pot or Dutch oven (4-quart or larger). Add the onions and cook over medium heat for 3–4 minutes until transparent. Stir in the carrot and celery and cook for 5 minutes longer. Add the flour and stir to combine. Cook for another minute, stirring occasionally.

2. Slowly pour in the chicken stock, stirring vigorously. Bring the soup to a boil. Add the noodles to the soup. Cook for 10 minutes, or until the noodles are cooked.

3. Stir in the cream and black pepper and heat through. Taste and add salt if necessary, depending on your stock. Garnish with parsley and serve.

Tortilla Soup

The usual tortilla soup is a chicken stock laced with onions, peppers, chiles, chicken, and some chopped tomatoes, spooned over tortilla chips and topped with grated cheese. This version has a hearty tomato base that turns the soup into an entire meal. Spicy hot and completely satisfying, it's the perfect lunch for a chilly afternoon. Canned tomatoes usually contain salt, so you probably won't need to add any.

When chopping fresh jalapenos or any other fresh chile, remember that the main source of heat, the chemical capsaicin, lies in the interior membranes that contain the seeds. For a milder flavored dish, carefully remove all seeds and membranes.

Serves 6

2 tablespoons vegetable oil	2 28-ounce cans whole tomatoes
2 chicken breasts, cut into thin strips	1 teaspoon ground cumin
1 large onion, chopped	1 chipotle pepper, finely chopped (optional)
1 green pepper, seeded and chopped	2 tablespoon lime juice
3 cloves garlic, minced	Tortilla chips
1 quart Quick Chicken Stock (p. 51)	Grated Cheddar or Monterey Jack cheese
4 fresh jalapenos (or to taste), seeded and chopped	

1. In a large pot, heat the oil over medium heat. Stir in chicken strips and cook till they just start to brown, then add the onion, green pepper, and jalapenos and saute 4–5 minutes, till they start to become tender. Add garlic and saute another minute, then pour in chicken stock.

2. Puree the cans of tomato in a blender or food processor (or break up the tomatoes with a knife) and add them to the soup. Stir in cumin and chipotle, if using, and bring to a boil.

3. Reduce heat and simmer for 45 minutes, till vegetables are tender and soup has thickened slightly. Stir in lime juice and taste and adjust seasonings, adding salt if necessary.

4. To serve, put a handful of tortilla chips in the bottom of each bowl. Ladle soup over the chips and top with a generous handful of grated cheese. Serve immediately.

Don't Fowl Up

Always, always wash your hands immediately after cutting chiles for recipes like Tortilla Soup—juices and oils from the fresh chiles can cling to your fingertips. You may inadvertently transfer the heat to the tap on the sink, the knife blade, or the spoon you're using to stir the soup, and if you later rub your eyes, you'll feel the pain. If this happens, immediately rinse with clear water till the pain subsides.

Vegetable-Chicken Soup

It seems as if it should be easy to make a chicken soup with vegetables, but it's hard to get the blend just right so that the vegetables complement the rich stock and tender meat while retaining their flavor. The secret lies, however, in making not so much a chicken-vegetable soup as the reverse: vegetables simmer till just tender in a light chicken stock and cubed white-meat chicken is added at the very end.

Serves 6–8

3 tablespoons butter

1 medium onion, chopped

1 stalk celery, chopped

1 large carrot, cut in 1/4-inch rings

2 medium leeks, white parts only, cleaned and chopped

2 medium potatoes, peeled and diced

1 cup fresh green beans (or 1 cup frozen)

2 medium tomatoes, chopped, or 1 cup canned tomatoes, drained

1/2 teaspoon dried thyme

1/2 teaspoon dried basil

1 cup white wine

3 quarts Quick Chicken Stock (p. 51)

1 cup white-meat chicken, cubed

1. In a large pot, heat the butter over medium heat. When foam subsides, add the onions and saute till they start to become translucent but not browned, about 3–4 minutes.

2. Add celery, carrot, leeks, potatoes, and green beans (if using fresh; if using frozen, don't add them till you add the stock). Turn the heat to medium-low, cover, and let them sweat for about 10 minutes, stirring occasionally. (To sweat vegetables is to soften them without browning by heating them in a small amount of oil, then covering and cooking over a medium-low heat. The steam softens the vegetables more quickly than sauteing and the low heat keeps them from browning.)

3. After vegetables are softened, add tomatoes, thyme, basil, and the white wine. Turn up the heat and bring to a simmer. Add stock and simmer for 10–15 minutes, until vegetables are tender.

4. Just before serving, add the chicken and stir. Let soup heat through and serve immediately, garnished with fresh parsley if desired.

Salads

Chicken goes with salad like no other meat or poultry does. It can be the basis of the whole salad, or it can accentuate greens or other ingredients; it can provide the main flavor, complemented with a mild creamy dressing, or it can recede from center stage to allow curry or toasted sesame oil to star.

Ladies Lunch Chicken Salad

Whenever a recipe promises "traditional" or "old-fashioned" chicken salad, it usually ends up being whatever the writer's mother used to make, with all sorts of ingredients ranging from sweet pickle relish and olives, dressed with cream or yogurt and spiked with herbs or spices. If your mother always added chopped green pepper or some other particular ingredient, it's hard for chicken salad to taste right without it.

Here's a really basic chicken salad that takes well to those special added ingredients: The basic dish is nothing but tender white meat with celery, in the requisite creamy mayonnaise dressing with extra lemon juice. This kind of salad tastes best with poached chicken breasts and not roast chicken. For a real old-fashioned approach, stuff it into hollowed-out tomatoes served on a plate of Bibb lettuce. (If you're going to do that, ladies should probably wear hats and gloves while eating it.)

Serves 6

3 cups cooked white-meat chicken, cut into cubes	1/2 teaspoon freshly ground black pepper
1 cup thinly sliced celery	1/2 teaspoon salt
3/4 cup mayonnaise	Paprika for garnish, if desired
3 tablespoons lemon juice	

1. Toss the chicken and celery in a medium bowl. Blend the mayonnaise, lemon juice, salt, and pepper, and pour over the chicken.

2. Stir together gently to keep the chicken from breaking apart too much. Taste and adjust seasoning. Use on sandwiches, or serve mounded on lettuce or stuffed into hollowed-out tomatoes, garnished with a sprinkle of paprika.

167

Chicken Cranberry Salad

Fresh cranberries and pecans make this unusual salad into a whole new taste treat. You can use canned whole cranberry sauce, drained, if you like, but cooking the cranberries yourself means the salad is tart and tangy and as fresh-tasting as it can be. The creamy dressing unifies the whole, and the chopped chives add a savory note to keep it from being too sweet. Although it makes a wonderful sandwich, especially on multigrain bread, this is a salad that stands up well as an entree. Try serving it with wild rice and hot rolls.

Serves 4–6

1 cup whole fresh cranberries, uncooked

1 cup water

1/2 cup sugar

1/2 teaspoon freshly ground black pepper

2 tablespoons chopped fresh chives or 1 tablespoon finely chopped scallions (green part only)

1/3 cup pecans, coarsely chopped

3 cups cooked chicken, cubed

1/2 cup thinly sliced celery

1 cup mayonnaise

1 teaspoon salt

1. In a small saucepan, combine the cranberries with the sugar and water and cook over medium-low heat for about 10 minutes, till the cranberries are softened. You should hear them burst in the hot water. Set aside and allow to cool completely.

2. Toast the pecans by heating a skillet over medium heat and adding the nuts. Toss in the hot dry pan for about 30 seconds, no longer than one minute, and immediately pour them into a bowl to cool. (If you leave them in the hot skillet, the nuts will scorch.)

3. When ready to serve, combine chicken, pecans, and celery in a large bowl. Mix the mayonnaise, salt, pepper, and chives and pour over the chicken.

4. Before mixing, drain the cranberries and add to salad. Toss quickly and gently and serve right away.

Grilled Chicken Caesar

Caesar salad with chicken can be found on practically any restaurant menu these days. It's a delicious twist on original Caesar and turns it into a full meal. It's also an easy enough dish to reproduce at home, but the reason that restaurants do it so well is that they sear the chicken breasts over high heat, so they taste pleasantly of the grill and have appetizing char marks. You can make a tasty salad cooking your chicken breasts in a frying pan, but for best results, either cook on the outdoor grill or in a stove-top grill pan.

Good Caesar salad is all about the best ingredients: Use Parmigiano Reggiano if you can, not just pregrated Parmesan. You can use store-bought croutons, but the best are made from crusty bakery bread, olive oil, and garlic. Use the freshest, greenest romaine, extra virgin olive oil, and don't skip the anchovies for authentic flavor. You won't even know they're there once the dressing is mixed, but they add a salty undertaste that's indispensable for the true Caesar connoisseur.

Serves 4

For dressing:

1/2 cup extra virgin olive oil

3 tablespoons lemon juice

1 tablespoon Dijon mustard

1/2 teaspoon Tabasco

4 anchovy filets, finely chopped,
or 1 1/2 teaspoons anchovy paste (optional)

For croutons:

2 thick slices French or Italian bread

1/4 cup olive oil

2 cloves garlic, finely minced

For salad:

2 heads romaine lettuce

1/2 cup freshly grated Parmesan cheese

4 chicken breasts

Salt and pepper

1. Place all dressing ingredients in a jar with a tight-fitting lid, cover, and shake till well combined.

2. Cut the bread into 1/2-inch cubes. Heat the olive oil over medium-low heat in a nonstick skillet. Toss in the garlic and just as it starts to sizzle, add the bread and toss well to blend. Cook 3–4 minutes, till bread is crispy, then pour into a bowl and leave to cool.

3. Clean and dry the romaine and tear into bite-size pieces in a large bowl.

4. Season the chicken breasts with salt and pepper. Either grill for 5–7 minutes on an outdoor grill, sear quickly in a stove-top grill pan, or fry in a couple tablespoons of oil in a frying pan over medium-high heat, until chicken is cooked through. Remove to a plate and allow to cool slightly.

5. Just before serving, assemble the salad by tossing the lettuce with the dressing, the grated parmesan, and the croutons.

6. Divide salad among four serving plates. Slice each chicken breast into thin slices on the diagonal and fan the slices over each salad. Sprinkle additional Parmesan for garnish if desired. Serve immediately.

Curried Chicken Salad

If you've never tasted curried chicken salad, it may look like an unusual combination. But the edge of mildly spicy sweetness in the dressing is a perfect foil for the chicken, especially if you include some dark meat, and the nuts and raisins add texture. It's regular chicken salad taken one step further for grown-ups.

Try stuffing it into lightly toasted pita pockets. Even better, make open-faced sandwiches on thick-sliced whole wheat bread, preferably one made with several grains. The hearty salad stands up well to a fully flavored bread, or even to a sweet bread such as toasted cinnamon-raisin. For a low-fat salad, you can replace the mayonnaise with nonfat plain yogurt. It will be a good bit tangier, so leave out the vinegar and add 1/4 teaspoon of sugar to smooth out the flavors.

Golden raisins are also called sultanas. They're the dried fruit of white grapes, and they have a mellower flavor than regular dark raisins, almost honeyed and perfume-like. You can also use regular raisins in this recipe, but golden raisins will add a different level of flavor.

Toasting the nuts before adding them to the salad will add depths of flavor. Heat a skillet over medium heat (don't use a nonstick, which shouldn't be heated without something in it). When the pan is hot, put in the nuts and swirl them around until they start to brown, usually less than a minute. Dump them out immediately into a bowl to cool before adding to the salad. If you let them cool in the pan, they'll burn.

Serves 6

3 cups cooked chicken, cubed	1 cup mayonnaise
1 cup thinly sliced celery	1 tablespoon lemon juice or white wine vinegar
1/2 cup golden raisins	1 1/2 teaspoons curry powder
1/2 cup slivered almonds	1/2 teaspoon salt

1. Toss the chicken, celery, raisins, and almonds in a large bowl.

2. Blend the mayonnaise, lemon juice or vinegar, curry powder, and salt and pour over the salad.

3. Toss gently and serve. This salad tastes better if it's not icy cold. If it's been refrigerated, let it sit on the counter for 15–20 minutes (but no longer) before serving.

Cold Sesame Chicken Salad

This is a fabulous dish for a summer evening, satisfying without being heavy, cool to the tongue but full of zingy hot flavors. Cantonese egg noodles are available dry in many grocery stores in the Asian foods section, or you can substitute any long, thin noodle, preferably one made with eggs.

Don't be put off by the amount of peanut butter. It adds a suaveness to the sauce and perfectly complements the salty soy sauce and nutty sesame oil. You can make this in the morning and leave it chilling in the refrigerator until supper. Take it out about fifteen minutes before serving.

Serves 4

1 pound Cantonese noodles or vermicelli egg noodles

1 tablespoon sesame oil

1 cup shredded cooked chicken (preferably all white meat)(roasted, p. 55, or poached, p. 80)

1 medium cucumber, peeled, seeded, and cut into matchsticks

1/4 cup chopped scallions

For dressing:

1/4 cup cider vinegar

3 tablespoons soy sauce

3 tablespoons peanut butter

1 teaspoon Tabasco sauce

1 clove garlic, finely minced

1 teaspoon sugar

1. Cook noodles according to package directions. Drain and rinse under cool water to stop them cooking.

2. In a large bowl, toss noodles with the sesame oil to stop them from sticking. Add chicken, cucumber, and scallions.

3. Whisk together dressing ingredients until smooth and pour over noodles. Toss well to combine, cover and store in refrigerator for at least an hour to let the flavors blend and to cool salad before serving.

The Least You Need to Know

➤ The basis of many soups is a good chicken stock, whether or not you add chicken meat.

➤ When you add chicken to soup along with other ingredients, be it noodles, matzoh balls, or tortilla strips, chicken soups are among the most hearty and comforting of all homemade food.

➤ Chicken is perfect for salads, whether playing the starring role, as in traditional chicken salad with mayonnaise and celery, or appearing as a special guest, as when broiled and sliced onto an upscale Chicken Caesar Salad.

Chapter 24

Pastas, Pies, and Pastries

In This Chapter

➤ Quick and delicious pasta dishes with chicken

➤ How to wrap chicken in a crust, from pies to pastry

➤ The versatile bird—fabulous chicken pizza

Chicken goes wonderfully well with flour-based foods, from pastas to crusts, such as rich empanada dough or a quick topping made from packaged biscuit mix. Pasta recipes always work well with a vegetable mixed in with the chicken, while anything with a crust, such as Chicken Pot Pie, cries out for gravy.

Pasta

If you've got some kind of pasta in the cabinet and some kind of chicken in the fridge, you've almost certainly got a dinner ready in minutes. It helps to have a vegetable for color and texture, but you don't need an elaborate sauce—once you've browned the chicken, a splash of wine and the pan scrapings can be all you need. Below are some simple recipes for quick chicken and pasta meals, and some slightly more complicated, such as that potluck classic Chicken Tetrazzini. Al dente is an Italian phrase that literally means "to the tooth." It tends to be an unfamiliar term to Americans, who tend to like their pasta cooked super-soft, but it refers to pasta that still has a bit of texture and bite, that is just short of being "done." Al dente pasta stands up better to chunky sauces such as the one in Carnival Chicken Pasta.

Chicken Primavera

Primavera is Italian for spring, and any dish Primavera-style usually includes a selection of early season vegetables such as asparagus and sugar snap peas. However, any mix of vegetables in a light buttery sauce will work well, so feel free to vary the suggested vegetables below with whatever you have in the refrigerator. Be sure to cut the vegetables into slender pieces so they cook through. Bow-tie pasta makes a festive-looking meal, but other pastas such as fettucine, spaghetti, or even wide egg noodles taste terrific.

Serves 4–6

1 pound pasta	1 medium zucchini, cut in matchsticks
3 boneless, skinless chicken breasts	1/2 cup peas, fresh or frozen
2 tablespoons olive oil	1/2 cup chicken stock (p. 51)
2 tablespoons butter	1/4 cup light cream
1 medium onion, sliced into thin rings	Salt and freshly ground black pepper
1/2 cup sliced fresh mushrooms	Grated Parmesan cheese
1 carrot, peeled and cut into very thin matchsticks	

1. Cook pasta in salted boiling water according to package instructions. Drain all the water, then return the pasta to the pot to keep warm.

2. Cut the breasts into 1/2-inch strips. Heat the olive oil in a large nonstick skillet over medium-high heat and saute the breasts until browned and cooked through. Remove the chicken breasts to a bowl large enough to hold all the ingredients and toss the pasta in, and set aside.

3. Add the butter to the oil in the pan and cook the onions and carrot slices for 7–8 minutes until carrots are softened and onions are browned. Add the mushrooms and zucchini and cook 3–4 minutes till softened. Add peas, asparagus and chicken, and pour chicken broth over all. Bring to a boil and simmer 2–3 minutes.

4. Stir in cream. Heat through and season to taste with salt and pepper. Toss with pasta, sprinkle with Parmesan cheese, and serve immediately.

Carnival Chicken Pasta

Zesty with tomatoes, olives, rosemary and wine, packed with nutritious vegetables, and served over fusilli, this pasta dish bursts with flavor and color. If you use multicolored fusilli, it's like a carnival on your plate. You won't need to serve anything on the side but a green salad. Use either a small chicken, jointed into eight pieces, or boneless, skinless breasts for speed.

If you add a tablespoon of olive oil to the pasta water while cooking, your finished noodles will be less likely to stick together—or if they do, more easily separated—if the pasta has to wait while you finish preparing a dish.

Serves 6

1 pound fusilli

1 small chicken (2 1/2–3 pounds), jointed, or 4 chicken breasts

3 tablespoons olive oil

1 medium onion, diced

3 cloves garlic, minced

1 small green bell pepper, cored, seeded, and sliced

1 small red bell pepper, cored, seeded, and sliced

1/2 cup sliced fresh mushrooms

1 carrot, sliced into thin matchsticks

1/2 cup white wine

1 cup chicken stock

1 medium tomato, diced, or 1/2 cup whole canned tomatoes

1 teaspoon dried rosemary

1/2 cup black olives, pitted and sliced

Freshly ground black pepper

Grated Parmesan cheese

1. Heat the olive oil in a large, nonstick skillet over medium-high heat. Add the jointed chicken or the whole breasts and saute until well browned. Remove to a platter and set aside.

2. Add the onion to the oil left in the pan and cook till it starts to soften and brown. Add the garlic, peppers, mushrooms, and carrots, and cook, stirring frequently, for 3–4 minutes.

3. While the vegetables are cooking, bring a large pot of water to a boil and cook pasta according to package directions.

4. Stir in the wine, stock, tomatoes, and rosemary. Return the chicken to the pan and bring the sauce to a boil. Reduce the heat and simmer 8–10 minutes, until chicken is cooked through and vegetables are tender. Drain the pasta and return it to the pan to keep warm.

5. Stir the olives into the sauce and heat through. Season with salt and pepper to taste. Pour sauce over pasta and toss. Garnish with Parmesan cheese and serve immediately.

Chicken Alfredo

The classic creamy and cheesy pasta presentation takes on new depth when chicken is added. Even though this is a slightly lighter recipe than traditional Alfredo, it still tastes very rich, so serve smaller portions and accent it with a green vegetable such as steamed asparagus. It's amazingly fast and a good dish for dinner in a hurry.

Serves 6

1 pound fettucine	1/2 cup grated Parmesan
3 skinless, boneless chicken breasts	1/2 teaspoon salt
4 tablespoons butter	Freshly ground black pepper
1/3 cup half and half	Fresh parsley for garnish, chopped

1. Cook the fettucine in boiling salted water. Drain and keep covered with the pan's lid so the pasta stays warm.

2. Cut the chicken into strips 1/2-inch thick. Heat the butter in a large, nonstick skillet over medium-high heat, making sure not to burn it. As soon as the foam subsides, add the chicken breasts and cook till brown.

3. Reduce heat slightly and add the cream to the pan. Heat it through but don't bring it to a boil. Quickly stir in the Parmesan. Season with salt and pepper and pour over the pasta.

4. Toss well, sprinkle fresh parsley on the top for color, and serve immediately.

Chicken Tetrazzini

In its original form, Chicken Tetrazzini was grand gourmet fare, created by no less a chef than Auguste Escoffier for an opera star, Luisa Tetrazzini. Even if you are using leftover components (and it is ideal for that), a good cream sauce spiked with a healthy dollop of sherry will reveal Tetrazzini's appeal. Leftover holiday turkey is often employed, but the more subtle flavor of chicken makes a more elegant dish.

Serves 4–6

8 ounces spaghetti or egg noodles, uncooked	2 tablespoons sherry
5 tablespoons butter	1 teaspoon salt
1 stalk celery, finely diced	1/2 teaspoon freshly ground black pepper
8 ounces fresh mushrooms, sliced	3 cups cooked chicken, cubed
1/4 cup flour	1/2 cup Parmesan cheese
2 1/2 cups chicken broth	1/2 cup slivered almonds
1/2 cup milk	

1. Preheat oven to 350°. Bring a pot of salted water to a boil and cook the pasta according to package directions. Drain and keep covered in the pot so the pasta stays warm.

2. Melt the butter over medium heat in a large skillet and saute the celery for 2–3 minutes. Add the mushrooms and saute another 5 minutes, till tender.

3. Sprinkle on the flour and stir to combine. Cook 2–3 minutes, then slowly stir in the chicken broth, adding a little at a time. Stir in the milk and cook till mixture is thick and smooth, stirring frequently.

4. Remove from heat and stir in sherry, salt, and pepper. Add cooked pasta and chicken and combine.

5. Pour into a glass 9 x 13-inch baking dish. Sprinkle Parmesan and almonds evenly on top and bake for 30–35 minutes, until bubbly and browned.

Lemon Cream Chicken

The lemon and grapes keep the flavor light, but the cream and pasta make sure this unusual dish is hearty and satisfying. Serve on a platter over mixed green and white tagliatelle for a colorful and exciting main dish.

Serves 6

1 1/2 cups seedless green grapes

1 pound tagliatelle

4 boneless, skinless chicken breasts

2 tablespoons olive oil

1 cup chicken stock

1/2 cup light cream

Juice and zest of 1 lemon

1 tablespoon chopped fresh parsley

Salt and freshly ground black pepper

1. Halve the grapes and set aside. Cook the pasta in salted boiling water according to package directions. Drain pasta and keep covered in pan so it stays warm.

2. Cut the chicken breasts into strips 1/2-inch thick. Heat the olive oil in a large, nonstick skillet over medium-high heat and fry the chicken strips until lightly browned.

3. Add the chicken stock, cream, lemon zest and juice, parsley, and salt and pepper to taste. Bring liquid to a boil, reduce heat, and simmer gently for 10 minutes, until sauce reduces slightly. (To reduce a sauce is to cook it down till some of the liquid evaporates, leaving the sauce thickened. It is a thickening method that requires no starch such as flour or cornstarch.)

4. Stir in sliced grapes and heat briefly. Pour the sauce over the warm pasta, toss well, and serve immediately.

Pies and Pastries

Let the British keep their pork pies, Cornish pasties, and steak and kidney pies. Since colonial days, Americans have loved chicken pies, from the biscuit-topped kind to the early American type baked in a pie crust. And then there's chicken pizza, a typically American way to get chicken—and cheese—on a crust.

Classic Biscuit-Crust Pot Pie

Real, old-fashioned chicken pot pie starts with a whole chicken and ends with a biscuit crust, the top golden brown, the underside soaking up gravy from the delicately seasoned pie below. This kind of pot pie takes a little bit of extra effort, but when you dig your serving spoon into that fluffy biscuit crust and turn up the tender chicken meat, you'll know it was all worth it.

Serves 6

1 3 1/2–4-pound chicken	For biscuit topping:
2 stalks of celery, chopped	2 1/2 cups all-purpose flour
2 medium carrots, diced	1 teaspoon salt
2 medium potatoes, diced	1 teaspoon baking soda
2 tablespoons butter, softened	1 teaspoon baking powder
2 tablespoons flour	4 tablespoons (1/2 stick) butter
Salt and freshly ground black pepper	1 1/4 cups buttermilk

1. Poach the chicken according to the instructions on p. 81, reserving the stock. Allow to cool and strip all the meat off the bones, removing and discarding the skin and bones. Set the meat aside.

2. Place 4 cups of the cooled stock in a medium saucepan and add the celery, carrots, and potatoes. Bring to a boil, reduce heat, and simmer 10 minutes, until just tender. Remove from heat but do not drain.

3. On a small saucer or plate, use a fork to make a paste of the softened butter and flour and stir this paste into the vegetables and stock. Add the chicken meat and several grindings of black pepper. Pour this mixture into a tall-sided 3-quart casserole.

4. Preheat the oven to 425°. In a medium bowl, blend all the dry ingredients for the biscuit topping. Cut the butter in using two knives until the mixture resembles fine crumbs. (To cut butter or shortening into flour is to work the fat into the dry ingredients until the fat binds to the flour particles and the dry ingredients take on the texture of cornmeal or fine crumbs. You can accomplish this with a fork, mashing the butter and flour through the tines, or with two knives, slashing back and forth through the mixture, or fastest of all, in a food processor, which will cut butter into flour in seconds.) Make a well in the center and stir in the buttermilk to make a soft dough.

5. Drop large spoonfuls of the biscuit dough evenly across the top of the pot pie, leaving about 1 1/2 inches between biscuits. Bake uncovered for 25 minutes, or until pot pie is bubbling and biscuits are puffy and golden.

Quick Chicken Pot Pie

It's incredibly quick and easy, relying on a can of soup, packaged biscuit mix, frozen peas, and precooked chicken. But for all the ready-made ingredients, this pie is more than the sum of its parts. Beware, though—the price you'll pay for the convenience of processed ingredients is a dish higher in fat and sodium than if you started from scratch. But for a delicious and comforting dinner in a hurry, this is hard to beat.

Serves 6–8

1 rotisserie (or any precooked) chicken	1 cup biscuit mix
1 cup frozen green peas	1 cup milk
1 can cream of celery soup	1 stick butter or margarine, melted
1 cup chicken stock	

1. Preheat oven to 400°. Strip the chicken meat from the bone, removing skin if desired, and put the meat in a 9 x 13-inch glass casserole (don't use a smaller pan or the crust won't work well).

2. Sprinkle the peas over the chicken. In a small bowl, whisk the soup mix with the chicken stock till smooth, and pour over chicken and peas.

3. In the same bowl, blend the biscuit mix with the milk and melted butter, beating till smooth. Pour gently and evenly over the chicken. (Don't worry if the crust seems to be sinking beneath the other ingredients—it will rise.)

4. Bake for 30 minutes, until pie is bubbling and crust is a delicate golden color. Allow to cool 5–10 minutes before serving.

Moravian Chicken Pie

The Moravians were a religious sect that emigrated to North Carolina from Germany in the eighteenth century. Moravian communities still thrive throughout the state (and elsewhere) and they help keep their congregations close-knit through traditions of music and wonderful food.

Moravian Chicken Pie is a signature dish, a homemade pie crust filled with cooked chicken, then topped with another pie crust, as if it were a fruit pie, and baked. The wedges of pie are served with a lightly thickened chicken gravy. Using a food processor makes the pastry wondrously fast, or you can also use packaged pie dough. These uncooked pies freeze particularly well, and you can put them in the oven frozen. Just add about 1/2 hour to the cooking time.

To make 1 10-inch pie, serving 6

continues

179

continued

Pastry:

2 cups all-purpose flour

3/4 cup solid vegetable shortening

6–8 tablespoons cold water

1 teaspoon salt

1 tablespoon flour

Filling:

3 cups cooked chicken, chopped

1 hard-boiled egg, mashed with a fork

Salt and pepper

1 tablespoon butter

2 1/2 cups chicken broth

1. Preheat oven to 375°. In a food processor, blend the shortening, flour, and salt till it resembles cornmeal. With the machine running, add 6 tablespoons of water. If the dough does not swiftly form a ball, add a tablespoon more. The pastry should rapidly form a ball. (If mixing by hand, cut the shortening into the flour and salt with a fork till it resembles fine crumbs, then swiftly mix in the water and gather the dough together into a ball.)

2. Grease a 10-inch pie plate. Divide dough in half and roll out one half into a 10-inch circle. Press that half of the dough into the pie plate.

3. Place chicken in the pie shell and scatter with the mashed egg. Sprinkle with salt and pepper to taste.

4. In a small saucepan, heat the butter over medium heat. As soon as it melts, stir in the flour. Cook for 1 minute, then slowly pour in the chicken stock, whisking to combine. Cook 2–3 minutes, till slightly thickened. Pour 1 cup of this gravy over the chicken and reserve the rest for serving with the finished pie.

5. Roll out the second half of the pastry and place over pie. Cut off the excess and press the edges together with a fork all the way around. Cut a few slits in the top with a sharp knife to let steam escape. (At this stage, pie can be wrapped in foil and frozen if desired.)

6. Bake for 50–60 minutes, till top is browned. Serve in wedges and pass the rest of the gravy to spoon over each slice.

Chicken Empanadas

Empanadas are a sort of turnover made both in Spain and Mexico. The pastry is a very rich shortcrust, full of butter or shortening, resulting in a tender, flaky dough to wrap around a savory chicken filling.

Save the egg whites when making the pastry and brush a little on the finished empanadas before putting them in the oven. If you want to be really authentic, give each one a very light sprinkling of sugar as they do in Mexico, to make the finished crust sparkle.

Let the eggshell do the work for you when separating eggs. Break the egg gently against the rim of a glass bowl, but don't let the insides fall into the bowl. Turn the eggshell halves upward, like two cups. The yolk will be caught in one side, along with much of the white. Tip the yolk into the other half of the shell, then back again, letting the white fall into the bowl while the yolk stays in the shell. Similarly, if you've dropped a bit of broken shell into the bowl when breaking whole eggs, use the sharp edge of the shell to fish the broken piece out. The broken bit will cling to the shell, whereas if you use your fingers or a spoon, it will slip away from you.

Serves 4–6

For filling:

1 tablespoon olive oil
1 small onion, diced
2 cloves garlic, minced
2 fresh jalapenos, minced
1 cup canned crushed tomatoes
3 cups cooked chicken, finely chopped
Salt

For pastry:

3 cups all-purpose flour
1 teaspoon salt
2/3 cup butter or solid shortening
1/2 cup ice water
1 tablespoon white vinegar
2 egg yolks

1. To make filling, heat olive oil in a skillet over medium heat. Add onions and saute until translucent and lightly browned. Stir in garlic and fresh jalapenos and cook 2–3 minutes.

2. Add the tomatoes, bring to a simmer, and cook 4–5 minutes, till tomatoes reduce slightly and mixture thickens slightly. Stir in the chicken and heat briefly. Taste and add a small amount of salt if necessary. Remove from heat and allow to cool.

3. To make pastry, put the flour and salt in a food processor and pulse briefly. Add the butter or shortening, cut into chunks or dropped in by the spoonful, and process until the mixture resembles fine crumbs.

4. In a small bowl, whisk the water, vinegar, and egg yolks together with a fork. Add this mixture to the food processor slowly, with the machine running, and stop as soon as the pastry forms a ball. You may not need all the liquid. Wrap the ball of pastry in plastic wrap and place in the freezer for 15 minutes.

5. Preheat oven to 400°. Lightly grease a baking sheet. Divide the pastry in half and divide each half into five, so you have ten equal pieces. On a floured surface, roll a piece into a circle about 5 inches across.

6. Put a few tablespoons of filling in the center of the circle. Brush the edges with a little water, and fold the pastry over. Use a fork to crimp where the two edges meet. Place on baking sheet and repeat with remaining dough and filling.

7. If desired, brush each finished pastry with the egg whites left from making the pastry. Use a fork or a small knife to poke a few holes into each pastry so the steam can escape. Bake for 20–25 minutes, until empanadas are golden brown.

Deep-Dish Barbecue Chicken Pizza

Sure, you can use a ready-made pizza crust, but with an extra five minutes of effort you can make an incredibly easy homemade crust that beats out the store-bought kind by a mile. Thinly sliced chicken breasts are quickly fried and tossed with bottled barbecue sauce, and piled on the pizza crust with sliced onions and cheese. You might call it fancy designer pizza—but you'll probably just call it delicious.

Makes one 15 1/2 x 10 1/2-inch pizza

For pizza crust:	For pizza:
1 package active dry yeast	2 boneless, skinless chicken breasts
1 cup warm water	2 tablespoons olive oil
2 1/2 cups all-purpose flour	3/4 cup bottled barbecue sauce
2 tablespoons olive oil	1 cup grated cheddar cheese
1 teaspoon sugar	1 cup grated mozzarella cheese
1 teaspoon salt	Pickled jalapenos, finely minced (optional)
	1 medium sweet onion, such as Vidalia or Walla-Walla, sliced

1. To make crust, dissolve the yeast in the warm water in a medium bowl. Stir in remaining ingredients to form a soft crust and let sit for 10 minutes. Pat down into a 15 1/2 x 10 1/2-inch jelly roll pan or cookie sheet.

2. Preheat the oven to 425°. Cut the chicken breasts into 1/2-inch strips. Heat the olive oil in a skillet over medium-high heat and quickly saute the chicken and onions, until chicken pieces are cooked through and onions have softened slightly.

3. Remove from heat and pour in barbecue sauce. Spread this mixture over the pizza crust. Sprinkle evenly with both cheeses, and top with minced jalapenos to taste.

4. Bake for 15–20 minutes, until edges of crust are browned and cheese is bubbling.

The Least You Need to Know

➤ If you have boneless, skinless chicken breasts and a package of noodles, you can have dinner on the table in a hurry, with easy chicken pasta dishes that are long on flavor and short on work.

➤ Chicken pies are American classics and they range from elaborate crusts made by dropping homemade buttermilk biscuit dough on top to ultra-simple but yummy versions made with biscuit mix and canned soup.

Chapter 25

Stews and Casseroles

It's serious meal time now, with a succession of stews and casseroles that are perfect for family suppers on a weeknight but also good enough to feed special guests. The standard rubber chicken breast in a sauce is a joke at corporate and political dinners, but people wouldn't mind going to these functions if they were served any of the home-cooked meals below. The casseroles and stews in this chapter store well in the refrigerator for up to four days, when tightly covered with a lid or plastic wrap. Stored in the freezer, they'll still taste good up to three months, but any longer than that and you're in danger of having that "freezer" taste when you thaw and reheat them.

Stews

Chicken soups are always delicious, but sometimes you want something more solid and hearty, and that's where stews come in. Some chicken stews, such as Southern Chicken and Dumplings, are an entire meal in a bowl, while others, such as Paprikash, require simple egg noodles or mashed potatoes as a bed.

Southern Chicken and Dumplings

It takes a little extra effort to make Southern Chicken and Dumplings, but the finished dish ranks high on the list of all-time favorite comfort food. The succulent stewed chicken and the velvety dumplings bobbing in a rich broth are hearty, delicious, and soothing. It's a mildly flavored dish, but be careful how you season—the doughy dumplings absorb salt like sponges.

If you don't have time to make homemade dumplings, follow the recipe up to the end of step 2, then open a can of refrigerator buttermilk biscuits. Flatten each biscuit with the palm of your hand, cut in half and then half again, as if you were cutting a cake, and drop the pieces into the simmering stock, following the cooking instructions in step **5**.

Serves 6

1 4–5-pound stewing hen, jointed
(see p. 24), skin removed

1 medium white onion, cut in half

2 ribs of celery, roughly chopped

1 carrot, peeled and cut into 2-inch chunks

1 bay leaf

2 teaspoons salt

1/2 teaspoon freshly ground black pepper

2 quarts water

For dumplings:

1 cup flour

2 teaspoons baking powder

2 tablespoons butter, softened

1/2 teaspoon salt

1/2 cup milk

1. Place the hen with the onion, celery, and carrot into a large heavy-sided saucepan with the water. Add bay leaf, salt, and pepper, place over a medium heat, and bring to a boil.

2. When it boils, immediately lower the heat, skim off and discard the scum that rises, and allow the chicken to simmer gently for about 2 hours, until the meat falls off the bones.

3. Turn off the heat and allow to cool for several hours, until cool enough to remove and discard the bones, bay leaf, celery, onion, and carrot.

4. To make dumplings: About half an hour before you're ready to eat, sift into a medium bowl the flour, baking soda, and salt. Using a fork, blend the softened butter into the flour, until large crumbs form. Make a well in the center of the flour mixture and pour the milk into it, stirring briefly with a fork just until dough clings together.

5. Bring the chicken stock to a boil. Using two spoons, pick up about a tablespoon of dough with one spoon, and use the second spoon to push it off the first spoon and into the boiling stock. Repeat until all of dough is used.

6. Stir the dumplings, cover the pot, lower the heat, and simmer for about 10 minutes. Remove the lid and simmer for another 10 minutes. You will have a stew with meat and dumplings floating in a thickened stock. Taste and adjust salt and pepper. Serve hot, in bowls. Store covered in the refrigerator for up to four days, and up to three months in the freezer.

Paprikash

Paprikash is essentially the chicken version of Hungarian goulash, which is a beef stew flavored with paprika and thickened with sour cream and flour. Chicken takes even better to this treatment, and this rich, creamy stew is delicious served over wide buttered egg noodles. The sour cream sauce is so rich, you'll probably want to serve small portions.

To make real Paprikash, you must have the right paprika. If you have an old spice tin collecting dust in the cabinet, throw it away and buy new paprika. Fresh sweet paprika is ground from dried Hungarian paprika peppers. It has a remarkable flavor, smoky and pungent, with a deep, dark red color. It doesn't compare in any way to the dry, faintly orange dust that passes for paprika in the average supermarket, though more and more of them are carrying an improved variety. Try to buy a paprika imported from Hungary for authentic flavor and best results.

Serves 4–6

4 boneless, skinless chicken breasts	1 medium red bell pepper, diced
1/4 cup Hungarian sweet paprika	1 cup chicken stock
1 teaspoon salt	1 cup sour cream
3 tablespoons butter	2 tablespoons flour
2 large onions, coarsely chopped	Salt and pepper

1. Slice the chicken breasts into narrow strips and sprinkle with the salt and 1 tablespoon of the paprika.

2. Heat the butter in a large, heavy skillet over medium-high heat and cook the breast strips and the onions, stirring frequently, until golden and brown, about 7–10 minutes. Add the red pepper and the remaining paprika and cook for 3–4 minutes.

3. Pour in the chicken stock. Bring to a boil and reduce heat. Cover the pan loosely and simmer gently for 10–15 minutes, until chicken is cooked through and vegetables are tender.

4. In a small bowl, whisk the flour into the sour cream until smooth and blend this mixture into the chicken. Bring to a boil and immediately reduce heat.

5. Simmer until sauce thickens, 3–5 minutes. Taste sauce and add salt and pepper as needed. Serve immediately.

Chicken Stew with Apples and Cabbage

There are overtones of Autumn in this stew of chicken, cabbage, and apples, fragrant with caraway. It's wonderful with a hot mound of mashed potatoes on the side. Use the best apple cider you can find, preferably the freshly milled kind found at farmers' markets. Thinner apple juice will do in a pinch, but it doesn't have as much body. A food processor will make short work of slicing the cabbage. If you don't like caraway seeds, add one teaspoon of dried thyme instead.

Serves 6

4 strips bacon, diced	1 teaspoon salt
1 2 1/3–3-pound chicken, jointed (p. 24)	1/2 teaspoon freshly ground black pepper
1 medium onion, chopped	1/2 small head green cabbage, thinly sliced
4 cups apple cider	Juice of 1/2 lemon
1 teaspoon caraway seeds	

1. Remove chicken skin if desired. Heat the bacon over medium heat in a large stewpot or Dutch oven. When the fat starts to run, add the chicken pieces and cook till browned, about 10 minutes. As the chicken starts to turn golden, add the onions and cook till softened and starting to brown, about 5 minutes.

2. Pour in the apple cider, caraway, salt, and pepper. Bring to a boil, then reduce heat and simmer gently for 30 minutes.

3. Stir in the shredded cabbage, cover, and cook an additional 15 minutes, till cabbage is tender. Squeeze in the lemon juice and serve.

Chicken and Rice

Here's one version of a classic South Carolina pilau, or "perlow" as local dialect has it. Chicken pieces are browned in bacon and butter before being slow-cooked with rice until the dish cooks down into a thick, mild stew, the chicken pieces buried in the stock-enriched rice.

For a true pilau, don't overcook. The rice is briefly sauteed in the fat before liquid is added, and each rice grain should remain whole and separate, glistening with fat, in the finished pilau.

Serves 6

2 tablespoons butter	6 cups water
2 tablespoons olive oil	1 1/2 teaspoons salt
1 3 1/2–4-pound chicken, jointed	1 teaspoon freshly ground black pepper
2 cups rice, uncooked	1/4 teaspoon ground nutmeg

1. Place the butter and olive oil in a large heavy stewpot or Dutch oven over medium heat. Add the chicken pieces and brown them lightly on both sides, 7–10 minutes.

2. When the chicken pieces are golden, add the rice and stir over the heat for a couple of minutes, making sure it's well coated with the fat in the pan. Add the water, salt, pepper, and nutmeg, and stir well.

3. Cover and cook over medium-low heat for 30–35 minutes, until all the water had been absorbed and the chicken is cooked through.

Chicken and Artichoke Stew

Tangy and delicious, this aromatic stew hints of Mediterranean sunshine. It calls for a whole chicken, but it's perfect for a meaty package of thighs or drumsticks. Don't use breasts alone, as they can get a little dry during the long simmering. Frozen artichokes are fast and easy, but you can also use artichokes bottled in brine if you like (drain them first). Serve over rice, with crusty bread and a salad garnished with feta cheese.

Serves 6

1/4 cup olive oil	1 cup dry white wine
1 (3–4-pound chicken, jointed into 8 pieces	2 cups chicken stock
3 cloves garlic, minced	1 10-ounce package frozen artichoke hearts
2 medium onions, chopped	1 teaspoon dried dill
1 6-ounce can tomato paste	1/4 cup lemon juice
1/2 cup chopped parsley	Salt and freshly ground black pepper

1. Heat the olive oil in a stewpot or Dutch oven over medium heat. Add the chicken pieces and cook 8–10 minutes, turning to brown evenly.

2. Add the garlic and onion to the browned chicken and cook till onions soften and become translucent.

3. Stir in the tomato paste and parsley. Turn the heat up to high and add the white wine. Cook for 2–3 minutes, until wine reduces, then add chicken stock. Bring to a boil. Reduce heat and cover loosely. Simmer very gently for about an hour.

4. Add the artichokes, dill, and lemon juice and cook an additional 15–30 minutes. Taste and add salt and pepper as needed. Garnish with additional parsley, if desired.

Casseroles

The classic French meaning of casserole refers to a dish, usually a deep oval porcelain or stoneware pan, in which meat is cooked, with other ingredients and not much liquid, in the oven, to emerge soft and tender in its own sauce. The standard American meaning tends to be something mixed with rice or noodles and a can of condensed soup and baked. The recipes below are somewhere in between the two. True, canned condensed soup is mentioned (it does have its occasional uses), but the dishes here involve savory, real food, casseroles that emerge steaming from the oven to be served with little more than a salad and bread. From the proper version of Chicken Divan (no soup, please!) to an unusual Chicken Lasagne in which chicken and vegetables are rolled inside cooked noodles and baked in a sauce, there's a hearty dinner awaiting every cold winter afternoon when you want an excuse to turn on the oven and warm up the kitchen.

Chicken Divan

Named after Divan Parisien, a long-defunct restaurant in New York City, Chicken Divan is supposed to be broccoli and juicy sliced chicken breast broiled under a rich cream sauce spiked with dry sherry and topped with Parmesan cheese. It has devolved into a way to get rid of leftover chicken (or turkey), and frequently features packaged frozen broccoli and canned cream of mushroom soup. You can still use leftover cooked chicken, but this version is more akin to what the original might have been like, with a rich white sauce enriched with an egg yolk, a splash of sherry, and cream.

Serves 4–6

1/2 cup (1 stick) butter	1/2 teaspoon freshly ground black pepper
1/2 cup flour	1/2 cup cream
2 cups milk	1/2 cup Parmesan cheese
1 egg yolk	1 bunch broccoli
3 tablespoons sherry	1 pound sliced cooked chicken, mostly breast meat
1 teaspoon salt	

1. Melt butter in a saucepan over medium heat and stir in flour. Cook, stirring, for 1 minute, then slowly blend in milk, whisking to make sure there are no lumps. Cook for 2–3 minutes until sauce starts to thicken.

2. Beat the egg yolk up in a cup and blend a few spoonsful of the cream sauce into the cup. Then stir this mixture back into the saucepan. (This procedure ensures the delicate yolk won't be shocked by the hot liquid and curdle on you.)

3. Add sherry, salt, pepper, and cream, and cook, stirring, for another 2–3 minutes, until sauce is thick. Remove from heat and cover.

4. Bring a saucepan of water to a boil. Wash the broccoli and trim off the end of the stems. Peel the thick skin off the long stems with a vegetable peeler or paring knife, and cut the broccoli into long florets. Immerse the florets in the boiling water and cook for 5 minutes, until just tender. Drain.

5. Preheat the broiler. Butter a shallow 2-quart casserole and arrange the broccoli in a single layer in the bottom. Cover with the sliced chicken and pour the cream sauce over all. Sprinkle the remaining 1/4 cup of Parmesan cheese over the cream sauce.

6. Place the casserole under the broiler for 3–5 minutes, watching closely, until sauce bubbles and browns. Serve immediately.

Chicken and Asparagus Casserole

Canned soup and canned asparagus make preparation speedy for this meal in a dish. With rolls and green salad on the side, you have an entire meal. Canned asparagus is a little mushy to some tastes. If you prefer, substitute either fresh cooked asparagus or frozen green beans.

Serves 6

4 cups cooked rice	1 teaspoon white pepper
2 cups cooked chicken, chopped	1 10-ounce can asparagus, drained
1 can cream of mushroom soup	1/2 cup bread crumbs
1/2 cup milk	2 tablespoons butter, melted
1 small onion, finely chopped	

1. Preheat oven to 375°. In a large bowl, mix the rice, chicken, soup, milk, onion, and pepper. Smooth half of this mixture in a 9 x 13-inch glass casserole.

2. Lay the asparagus spears in one layer on top of the rice mixture. Spread the remaining rice mixture over the asparagus. Sprinkle with crumbs and drizzle evenly with the melted butter.

3. Bake for 40–45 minutes until crumbs are browned and casserole is bubbly.

Chicken Tamale Pie

Real Mexican tamales are made of a lime-treated cornmeal called masa harina, which is mixed with water and lard and packed around a meat, cheese or chili filling before being wrapped with corn husks and steamed. They're delicious, but represent a hard day's work for the cook. This tamale pie cheats by using regular cornmeal cooked as if for polenta, layering it in the bottom of a casserole and covering it with a spicy chicken filling. The top layer of cornmeal is covered with some spicy tomato sauce, the pie is baked, and presto! all the flavor of tamales with about a quarter of the effort.

The chipotle peppers in adobo sauce are available in the Mexican section of most supermarkets. They are smoked jalapenos in a red sauce, extra hot and spicy.

Serves 6–8

For cornmeal layer:

1 cup yellow cornmeal

1 teaspoon salt

2 tablespoons olive oil

4 cups water

1/2 teaspoon cayenne

For tomato sauce:

2 tablespoons olive oil

2 cloves garlic, minced

1 medium yellow onion, chopped

1 16-ounce can whole tomatoes

2–3 pickled jalapenos or
1 chipotle in adobo

1 teaspoon lemon juice

For filling:

1 tablespoon olive oil

1 medium onion, chopped

3 cloves garlic, minced

1 8-ounce can tomatoes with green chiles

1 cup tomato sauce (see above)

1 teaspoon ground cumin

3 boneless, skinless chicken breasts, cut in 1/2-inch strips

1. Using a whisk, combine all ingredients for the cornmeal layer in a medium saucepan. Cook, stirring frequently, over medium heat till mixture starts to bubble and thicken, about 10 minutes. Remove from heat and set aside.

2. To make tomato sauce, heat olive oil in small pan and saute the onions and garlic till translucent and lightly browned. Add the onions and garlic to a food processor or blender with the tomatoes, jalapeno or chipotle, and lemon juice, and pulse till smooth. Set aside.

3. To make filling, heat the olive oil in a skillet over medium-high heat and saute the chicken breast strips with the onion and garlic till lightly browned. Stir in the tomatoes with green chiles and 1 cup of the tomato sauce you just made, and the cumin.

4. Preheat oven to 375°. Using a rubber spatula, spread half the cornmeal mixture in the bottom of a 9 x 9-inch glass baking dish. Dip the spatula in cold water if the cornmeal sticks.

5. Spread the chicken mixture evenly over this layer and top with the remaining cornmeal mixture. Spoon the rest of the tomato sauce over the top and bake for 35–40 minutes, until heated through.

Chicken Noodle Casserole with Green Peppers

The green peppers and onions add a fresh piquancy to this quick and creamy casserole which makes a perfect weeknight supper without a lot of advance preparation. You can even prepare it the night before and leave it, unbaked and covered in the refrigerator until you come home. The potato chip topping will take you straight back to dinnertime, 1974, but you can substitute 1/2 cup breadcrumbs drizzled with two tablespoons melted butter if you prefer not to go back in time.

Serves 4

8 ounces wide egg noodles

3 cups cooked chicken, diced

1 green bell pepper, seeded and diced into 1/2-inch squares

1 medium onion, finely diced

1 can condensed cream of chicken or mushroom soup

3/4 cup milk

2 tablespoons chopped parsley

1 tablespoon lemon juice

1 teaspoon paprika

1/2 cup crumbled potato chips

1. Cook the egg noodles according to package directions. Drain and return to cooking pan.

2. Stir in remaining ingredients except for potato chips and pour into a lightly greased 3-quart baking dish.

3. Sprinkle the top evenly with potato chips. Bake for 40–50 minutes, until casserole is bubbly and top is browned.

191

Chicken Lasagne Roll-Ups

Cooked lasagne noodles are rolled around a filling of chicken and vegetables, covered in a store-bought marinara sauce, and baked to bubbling goodness in this unusual and attractive dish. Serve with a crispy green salad and garlic bread for an elegant and delicious supper.

Serves 8

For roll-ups:

8 uncooked wide lasagne noodles	1 teaspoon dried oregano
2 tablespoons olive oil	1 teaspoon salt
3 boneless, skinless chicken breasts, diced	1 12-ounce carton cottage cheese
1 small onion, chopped	1 egg
2 cloves garlic, minced	1/4 cup Parmesan cheese
1 medium yellow squash, cut in thin matchsticks	1/4 cup chopped fresh parsley
1 red bell pepper, seeded and cut in thin strips	1 16-ounce jar marinara sauce (or spaghetti sauce)
1 green bell pepper, seeded and cut in thin strips	1 cup grated mozzarella cheese
1 cup whole canned tomatoes	
1/4 cup fresh basil, chopped (or 2 tablespoons dried)	

1. Prepare lasagne noodles according to package directions. Drain and rinse.

2. Heat olive oil in a large nonstick skillet. Add the diced chicken pieces and saute till they turn white, about 5 minutes. Stir in onion, garlic, squash, and peppers. Saute 4–5 minutes, till vegetables start to soften, then stir in tomatoes, basil, oregano, and 1/2 teaspoon of the salt, breaking up tomatoes with a spoon. Bring to a boil, then reduce heat and simmer 3–4 minutes. Set aside.

3. In a large bowl, stir together cottage cheese, egg, Parmesan, parsley, and 1/2 teaspoon of salt. Set aside.

4. Preheat oven to 350°. Lightly grease a 9 x 9-inch glass baking pan and prepare the roll-ups. At one end of each lasagne noodle, place about 1/2 cup of the chicken and vegetables. Spoon 1/8 of the cottage cheese mixture over the chicken and vegetables, and roll up the noodle. Place each roll seam-side down, in the pan. Repeat with remaining mixture and noodles, and then pack any extra chicken, vegetables, or cheese around the sides.

5. Pour the marinara sauce over all, top with grated mozzarella, and bake 30 minutes, until sauce is bubbly and cheese starts to brown. Let sit 10 minutes before serving.

The Least You Need to Know

➤ Hearty chicken stews can often serve as a whole meal in one pot, such Chicken with Cabbage and Apples or a steaming bowl of Southern Chicken and Dumplings.

➤ Paprikash, a Hungarian chicken stew thickened with sour cream, is an elegant topping for noodles or mashed potatoes, to be served with a vegetable or green salad.

➤ Chicken casseroles featuring cooked chicken are not only a good way to use up (and disguise) leftovers but many are terrific dishes in their own right, such as Chicken Tamale Pie, offering the flavors of fresh tamales with a fraction of the work.

Part 5
Chicken Around the World

The world was cooking chicken before America was ever discovered, and other cultures and cuisines offer a wealth of delicious chicken recipes to keep your taste buds happy. From the rich sauces of France to the buttery Chicken Kiev of Russia, from spicy South American chicken with chocolate to the fabulous and plentiful flavors of Southeast Asia, there's something here for everyone's taste.

Chapter 26

Chicken and the Frozen North

In This Chapter

➤ Icy little birds

➤ Sweden: Swedish Meatballs, Roasted Chicken with Warm Spices

➤ Norway: Chicken and Rice in White Sauce

➤ Denmark: Smørrebrød

➤ Canada: Maple-Cranberry Baked Chicken

➤ Russia: Chicken Kiev

Icy Little Birds

Chicken doesn't play a huge part in the cuisine of the Northern part of the world, probably because chickens like to be warm. It can be costly and difficult to mass-produce poultry (or even produce it on a small level) in a place where the weather is working so hard against you.

Of course chicken is available in colder parts of the world, but the rarity of chicken in the diet from earlier days means that there aren't a lot of classic chicken recipes in Scandinavian cuisine, although chicken can be incorporated into familiar dishes such as Swedish Meatballs.

Canada, like the United States, doesn't have as clearly defined cuisine as some countries, but the recipe here pays homage to the maple syrup that our neighbors to the north supply us with so liberally, not to mention the cranberry bogs that thrive in cooler regions.

Geographically, Russia might as easily belong in the western Europe chapter, but it takes a very cold nation to produce the fat and warming dish that is Chicken Kiev.

The Recipes

Sweden: Swedish Chicken Meatballs

Perhaps the most widely known of all Swedish dishes, classic Swedish meatballs are made of a blend of ground beef and ground pork. Adding ground chicken instead of beef makes the meatballs lighter in color and more delicate in flavor. The chicken is perfectly complemented by the hint of nutmeg. While the fresh dill in the sauce doesn't appear in every traditional recipe, it adds freshness and vibrant flavor to the cream sauce.

Serve with mashed potatoes and a green vegetable, or let the meatballs grace a buffet table, kept warm in a chafing dish.

Serves 6

4 tablespoons (1/2 stick) butter	1 teaspoon salt
1 small onion, finely chopped	1/2 teaspoon nutmeg
3/4 pounds ground chicken	1/4 teaspoon allspice
3/4 pounds ground pork	2 tablespoons all-purpose flour
1/2 cup dry white breadcrumbs	1/2 teaspoon salt
1/2 cup buttermilk	1 cup chicken stock
1 egg, beaten	1/2 cup light cream
1 teaspoon sugar	2 tablespoons chopped fresh dill

1. Heat 2 tablespoons of the butter in a skillet over medium heat and saute the onion until translucent but not browned.

2. Place in a large bowl and add the ground chicken and pork, breadcrumbs, buttermilk, egg, sugar, salt, nutmeg, and allspice. Mix well with your hands and shape the meat into 1-inch balls.

3. Heat the remaining 2 tablespoons of butter in the same skillet over medium-high heat and cook the meatballs till browned. Turn them frequently to brown evenly. Remove to a bowl and keep warm in oven set at 180°.

4. Add the flour and salt to the fat remaining in the skillet over medium heat. Stir and cook for 1–2 minutes, then slowly blend in the chicken stock, stirring till there are no lumps. Bring to a simmer and cook 1–2 minutes, then pour in the cream. Bring to a simmer and cook another 2 minutes, till sauce is thick and smooth.

5. Stir in the fresh dill, pour the sauce over the meatballs in the bowl, and serve immediately.

Sweden: Roasted Chicken with Warm Spices

Inspired by Marcus Samuelsson, the chef of Aquavit, a Swedish restaurant in New York City, this roasted chicken is coated with warm spices, something he says his grandmother used to do in Sweden. Fresh herbs weren't often available during the long winters, but spices are always available. The resulting chicken smells rich and sweet in the oven and results in tender, lightly spicy meat, perfect with a mound of mashed potatoes.

For extra orange flavor, save the orange you use for zesting, cut in half, and place the halves inside the chicken.

1 4–5-pound chicken, giblets removed	1/2 teaspoon ground cardamom
4 tablespoons butter, softened	1/2 teaspoon cinnamon
1 teaspoon grated orange zest	1/4 teaspoon cloves
1 teaspoon salt	

1. Preheat the oven to 400°. Rinse and pat dry the chicken.

2. Mix the softened butter with the orange zest, salt, and spices. Use your hands to spread this mixture all over the chicken, sliding some in under the skin. Lay it breast side down on a rack in the roasting pan, and place in the oven.

3. Roast for 15–20 minutes, then lower heat to 350°. Baste the chicken with the pan juices and roast 40 minutes, basting every 10 minutes.

4. Turn the chicken breast-side up and baste with pan juices. Continue roasting for 20 minutes, or until the leg joints move easily, chicken is golden brown, and juices run clear.

Norway: Chicken and Rice in White Sauce

Among Scandinavian-Americans, Scandinavian "white cooking" is almost something of a joke, except for the fact that they cling to it faithfully. It's a cuisine where everything is either white, or enrobed in a white sauce, and herbs and spices are kept at a distinct minimum. Chicken and Rice in White Sauce is perhaps the epitome of white cooking.

There's something inestimably soothing about the gently poached chicken served over white rice cooked with the poaching stock, then covered in a creamy white sauce enriched with an egg yolk. Offer spinach and a Scandinavian beet salad on the side to brighten up the plates.

If you want to violate the pure whiteness of this dish, sprinkle it with paprika and chopped fresh parsley before serving.

Serves 6

continues

continued

1 3 1/2–4-pound broiler-fryer, giblets removed	2 tablespoons all-purpose flour
2 small onions, quartered	2 cups chicken stock
2 sticks celery, chopped	1 cup light cream
1 teaspoon salt	1 egg yolk
10 black peppercorns	1/2 teaspoon salt
1 1/2 cups rice, uncooked	1/2 teaspoon freshly ground black pepper
2 tablespoons butter	

1. Put the chicken in a pot with the onions, celery, salt, and peppercorns and add water just to cover. Simmer gently, without boiling, for 50–60 minutes, until chicken is tender. Remove from pot and set aside, reserving the stock.

2. Put the rice in a pot and add 3 cups of the stock from poaching the chicken. Cover, bring to a boil, reduce heat, and cook for 15–20 minutes, until all the liquid has been absorbed.

3. While the rice is cooking, melt the butter in a skillet over medium heat. Add the flour and cook 2–3 minutes. Slowly blend in 2 cups of the stock from poaching the chicken, stirring till there are no lumps. Add the cream and bring to a boil, cooking 2–3 minutes till sauce is thick and smooth. Whisk the egg yolk into the hot sauce and season with salt and pepper.

4. Spread the cooked rice on a warmed serving platter and set the chicken on top of it. Pour any juices that have accumulated under the chicken on top of the rice. Pour the hot white sauce over the chicken and rice and serve immediately.

Denmark: Smørrebrød

Smørrebrød are open-faced sandwiches and they're one of Denmark's main contributions to world cuisine. Smørrebrød are little works of art, the sandwiches as carefully and creatively composed as a painting. They're meant to delight the eye as well as the palate, so the ingredients must be arranged on the face of the bread carefully, and ingredients are also meant to be selected so that their flavors complement each other well.

Rye bread is common, and when white bread is used, it's usually toasted. Use a sturdy white bread, not an overly soft and moist packaged bread. Seasoned butters are used occasionally, but you can use plain butter or mayonnaise as well. Below is simply one idea for a chicken sandwich—don't hesitate to mix and match other ingredients. The smørrebrød menu is limited only by your imagination.

To make 4 smørrebrød

4 slices white sandwich bread	1 cucumber, peeled and sliced as thin as possible
2 tablespoons butter, softened	2 hard-boiled eggs, each cut into 8 thin slices
1 teaspoon chopped chives	1 tablespoon very finely minced onion
1 teaspoon lemon juice	1 tablespoon finely chopped fresh parsley
4 thin slices cooked chicken breast	Paprika

1. Trim the crusts off the bread and toast. Allow the toast to cool.

2. Blend the softened butter with the chives and lemon juice. Spread on the cooled toast. Lay the chicken slices on the toast, then lay the cucumber slices over the chicken in a shingle pattern, each piece overlapping.

3. Place four pieces of egg on each sandwich, like a four-leaf clover. Sprinkle minced onion and parsley over each sandwich, and finish with a dash of paprika for color.

Canada: Maple-Cranberry Baked Chicken

This is less a Canadian dish than a dish in honor of Canadians, who tend to eat in a similar manner to the rest of us North Americans. That far north, there's plenty of sap flowing from the maple trees and there are plenty of cranberry bogs. Mind you, there's a whole school of thought (inspired, it must be admitted, by a pair of Canadian comedians) that holds that Canadians eat nothing but bacon and beer. But Canadian food is a lot more sophisticated than that, and some of the best of it draws on the natural resources of the country. Ideally, this Maple-Cranberry Baked Chicken should be served with Canadian wild rice.

Serves 4

1 3 1/2–4-pound broiler-fryer, jointed, with the skin on

Salt and pepper

1/2 cup canned cranberry sauce

1/2 cup maple syrup

1/4 cup cider vinegar

3 tablespoons water

1. Preheat the oven to 375°. Rinse and pat dry the chicken pieces, season them with salt and pepper, and place them, skin side-up, in a greased 9 x 13-inch glass baking dish. Bake 25–30 minutes.

2. While the chicken is roasting, mix the remaining ingredients in a small saucepan over medium heat and stir till smooth. Pour over the chicken and stir to coat each piece in the mixture.

3. Bake an additional 10–15 minutes, till the chicken is well browned and the skin is crispy.

Russia: Chicken Kiev

Russians eat more fat in their diet than any other people in the world, upwards of 45 percent of the daily intake, and so it's not surprising that this classic Russian method for preparing chicken is all about butter. And how! If you're going to make a dish so rich in butterfat, thank goodness it tastes this good.

The secret to good Chicken Kiev is to pound the breasts very thin, and then to roll them tightly around the chilled lumps of seasoned butter, so you don't lose all the butter inside during cooking.

Serves 6

For filling:

3/4 cup (1 1/2 sticks) butter, softened

3 cloves garlic, minced

2 tablespoons chopped scallion

1 tablespoon chopped fresh parsley

1/2 teaspoon freshly ground black pepper

For chicken:

6 boneless, skinless chicken breasts

1 1/2 cups dry breadcrumbs

1/4 cup chopped fresh parsley

1/2 teaspoon salt

1/2 teaspoon freshly ground black pepper

1/2 cup (1 stick) butter, melted

1/2 cup olive oil

1. Blend the softened butter with the garlic, green onion, parsley, and black pepper. Divide the butter mixture into six little patties, wrap in waxed paper, and place in the freezer for at least 30 minutes.

2. Working on one breast at a time, place each between two sheets of waxed paper and pound out to an even 1/4-inch thickness using a meat mallet or a rolling pin.

3. Place one of the butter patties in the middle of each flattened breast, and roll up tightly by flipping the narrowest end of the breast up over the patty, then closing in the two sides, like an envelope, and rolling the remaining side down and over the whole package. Secure firmly with a wooden toothpick.

4. Preheat the oven to 350°. Mix the breadcrumbs with the parsley, salt, and pepper on a large plate. Have the melted butter ready in a bowl, and heat the olive oil in a large skillet over medium-high heat.

5. Roll each chicken package liberally in the melted butter, then in the bread crumbs, pressing the crumbs on with your hands.

6. Gently slide each breaded roll into the hot oil and fry till golden brown, turning once, 6–8 minutes altogether. Lay the browned rolls on a jelly roll pan and drizzle with any melted butter remaining in the bowl. Bake for 15–20 minutes. Serve immediately.

The Least You Need to Know

➤ The Scandinavian countries don't have a lot of traditional chicken dishes in their cuisines because historically they didn't raise a lot of chicken in such cold climes.

➤ Adapting a classic recipe, Swedish meatballs, by using ground chicken in place of beef, is a new take on an old favorite.

➤ If you make this fabulous Russian Chicken Kiev, with each chicken breast wrapped around a mound of butter, you won't be surprised to learn that Russians as a group eat more fat in their diet than the people of any other country, with up to 45 percent of calories coming from fat. It's a dish to save for an infrequent treat.

Chapter 27

Chicken and the Sizzling South

¡Pollo Ay Caramba! and Others

Chicken in the southern part of the world doesn't only mean the Latin countries, though chicken, and indeed all poultry, is treated very well there and served in many imaginative ways. Chicken was well established in South America in pre-Columbian times, and the varied cuisine reflects many centuries of getting to know chicken and all its intricacies. Even so, it still has a celebratory aspect. Empanadas with cheese or other fillings might be served regularly, but add a chicken filling, and they're probably being served at a wedding feast.

Africa falls geographically into this category of countries south of the equator (as do Australia and a lot of other places not discussed) and there's a fine Chicken and Ground-nut Stew here representative of the Gold Coast on the west side of the continent. Morocco, in northwest Africa, is famous for its slow-cooked tagines, which are meat and vegetable stews moistly cooked in a special clay pot. (You can approximate the flavor here without one.) These are slightly different chicken flavors than the ones most Americans encounter regularly, and well worth the detour off the beaten food track.

The Recipes

Mexico: Chicken Tacos

Tacos may seem too simple to warrant a recipe. After all, you just buy the crisp shells and fill them with meat, cheese, lettuce, and salsa. But those are American tacos, and while they're tasty, they don't even approach the hearty, delicious, and satisfying qualities of real Mexican tacos.

For those, you must have soft corn tortillas, steamed, and stacked two-deep to hold beef or chorizo, peppers or lamb and potatoes, and best of all, sauteed strips of chicken and onions, topped with a sprinkle of cheese and some guacamole. The soft tortillas enfold a perfectly seasoned mix of sliced chicken and sauteed onions, topped only with a dollop of fresh guacamole, though you can add a spoonful of salsa if you like. They're warm and soft and filling, real Mexican comfort food. They make the hard shells seem like a dry memory—but for speed and ease, you can use them here if you wish.

Serves 4–6

3 boneless, skinless chicken breasts

2 tablespoons vegetable oil

2 large onions, thinly sliced

1 clove garlic, minced

1 teaspoon cumin

1 teaspoon dried oregano

1 teaspoon chili powder

1/2 teaspoon salt

16 soft corn tortillas

For guacamole:

2 large ripe avocados

Juice of 1 lemon or lime

1 clove garlic, minced

1/2 teaspoon chili powder (optional)

1. Cut the chicken breasts into narrow strips, about 1/4-inch wide. Set aside.

2. Heat the oil over medium heat in a large nonstick skillet and saute the onions till softened but not browned, 4–5 minutes. Increase heat to medium-high, add the chicken and garlic and saute till onions are lightly browned and chicken is cooked through, 7–8 minutes. Stir in the cumin, oregano, and chili powder and cook 2–3 minutes. Set aside.

3. Lightly dampen a clean kitchen towel and wrap the tortillas in it. Lay them in the microwave and cook on high for 2 minutes till tortillas are soft and steaming. (Alternately, follow package instructions for steaming or frying.)

4. While tortillas are heating, place the avocado flesh in a bowl with the lemon or lime juice, garlic, and chili powder, if using. Mash and whip with a fork until mixed.

5. Place all the ingredients on the table and have each diner assemble his or her own tacos by laying two warmed tortillas together on a plate and placing a generous spoonful of filling down the middle. Top with a dollop of guacamole and fold the tortillas in half over the filling. Eat immediately.

Don't Fowl Up

Don't overcook the tortillas in the microwave or they'll dry out and crack when folding.

Peru: Braised Chicken in Chocolate Sauce

Native tribes of South America were the first people to eat the cocoa bean, and early versions of hot chocolate were bitter and unsweetened. Chocolate lovers will appreciate the fact that South American cooks get more chocolate into their lives by using it as a savory as well as a sweet ingredient. The dark, bitter flavor of unsweetened chocolate adds depth and bite to a sauce or stew, and the richness brings out new flavors in meat. When chicken is slowly braised in a spicy chocolate sauce, the meat becomes as moist, silky, and velvety as the sauce. Make sure you use a high-quality unsweetened chocolate. Rice is a good accompaniment.

Serves 6

1 large (4–5-pound) broiler-fryer, jointed

1/4 cup olive oil

4 cloves garlic, minced

2 large onions, chopped

2 stalks celery, finely chopped

1 carrot, finely chopped

3 tablespoons all-purpose flour

1/2 teaspoon cayenne

1/4 teaspoon ground cloves

1 cup red wine

6 cups chicken stock

2 ounces unsweetened chocolate, chopped

1 teaspoon salt

Freshly ground black pepper

1. Rinse and pat dry the chicken pieces, removing skin if desired. Heat the olive oil in a large skillet over medium-high heat and saute the chicken parts till well browned. Remove to a platter and set aside.

2. Place the garlic, onions, celery, and carrots in the skillet and saute 8–10 minutes, till softened and lightly browned. Stir in the flour, cayenne, and cloves and pour in the wine. Bring to a simmer and cook, stirring, till most of the wine is evaporated.

3. Stir in the stock and bring to a simmer. Add the chocolate and stir till smooth. Return the chicken to the pan and add salt and pepper. Cook, covered, for an hour, stirring occasionally, till the sauce is thickened and chicken is tender. Serve right away, with hot white rice if desired.

Brazil: Chicken Salpicòn
with Ginger

Ginger is not native to South America. It was first brought there by Spanish and Portuguese sailors but it was taken up by Brazilian cooks as if they'd always had it, and it figures prominently in their cuisine.

Salpicòn is a fresh mixed dish usually of meat with thinly sliced raw vegetables and a tart sauce. The cabbage in this version makes it taste like a meaty slaw, and is perfect served cool for a summer supper. Prepare it several hours in advance of serving so the flavors have time to mingle.

Serves 6

For the dressing:

2/3 cup extra virgin olive oil

1/4 cup lemon juice

2 tablespoons Dijon mustard

1 tablespoon grated fresh ginger

1 teaspoon paprika

1 teaspoon salt

Freshly ground black pepper

For the salad:

6 cups finely shredded cabbage

2 red bell peppers, cored, seeded, and diced

1 red onion, thinly sliced

1/4 cup finely chopped fresh parsley

3 cups cooked chicken, chopped (use leftover roast chicken or poached)

1. Place the dressing ingredients in a small jar, cover, and shake until well blended.
2. Put the salad ingredients in a large bowl and toss with the dressing. Cover and refrigerate for several hours before serving.

Africa's Gold Coast: Chicken
in Peanut Sauce

There are many variations on this chicken stew with its sauce of ground peanuts in many African countries. The sauce is rich and smooth, spicy with chiles and creamy with the ground peanuts. African cooks use roasted peanuts ground to a paste, like American peanut butter but without the added sugar. If you can find unsweetened peanut butter at a health food store or gourmet market, use that. If not, smooth peanut butter will let you approximate the flavor.

Modify the chili to your taste, but don't leave it out altogether—that spicy hint of heat keeps the stew from tasting too heavy. Serve the stew over white rice.

Serves 6

1 3 1/2–4-pound broiler-fryer, jointed

1/4 cup peanut oil or olive oil

2 large onions, thinly sliced

2 cloves garlic, minced

1 teaspoon red chili flakes

1 teaspoon cumin

1 teaspoon salt

3 cups chicken stock

1 1/2 cups smooth peanut butter

1. Rinse and dry the chicken pieces, removing skin if desired. Heat the oil in a large skillet over medium-high heat and saute the chicken pieces till golden, about 10 minutes. Remove to a platter and set aside.

2. Add the onions to the oil remaining in the pan and cook till softened and lightly browned. Add the garlic, cumin, and salt, and stir in the stock. Bring to a simmer, and return the chicken to the pan. Simmer, covered, for 15 minutes.

3. Put the peanut butter in a bowl and spoon in about a cup of the hot chicken stock from the skillet. Stir into the peanut butter to thin it, then stir the thinned peanut butter into the sauce.

4. Stir to combine well and then simmer, covered, for another 15–20 minutes, till the chicken is tender and the sauce is thick and smooth.

Morocco: Chicken with Preserved Lemons

Preserved lemons are one of the most distinctive flavors of Moroccan cuisine, adding a memorably tart and salty flavor to tagines and salads. If you can't find preserved lemons in a gourmet market, you can make your own, but remember to start them at least a week before making the dish. (You can also just leave them out altogether, which will make quite a different but still tasty dish.)

Make your own preserved lemons by cutting two lemons lengthwise into quarters (traditional Moroccan methods leave the quarters attached at the stem end). Rub the inside of each lemon generously with salt and push the quarters into a small jar. Add 1/3 cup of salt to the jar and 1/2 cup of fresh lemon juice. Cover and shake well and leave in a cool place for a week. Shake the jar occasionally. After seven days, store in the refrigerator. Keeps in the fridge for up to two months.

Chicken with preserved lemons and olives is a classic Moroccan dish, succulent and flavorful. It's a terrific introduction to Moroccan cuisine. As with many Moroccan dishes, it's terrific served with couscous and a fresh salad (try chopped tomatoes with parsley, vinegar, olive oil, cumin, and salt).

Serves 6

1 3 1/2–4-pound broiler-fryer, jointed	1/2 teaspoon freshly ground black pepper
3 tablespoons olive oil	1 15-ounce can whole tomatoes, with juice
1 large onion, chopped	1/4 cup chopped fresh cilantro
4 cloves garlic, minced	1/4 cup chopped fresh parsley
1 teaspoon cumin	1/2 cup green olives, pitted
1 teaspoon ground ginger	1 preserved lemon, rinsed and chopped
1 teaspoon salt	

1. Rinse and pat dry the chicken pieces and remove skin if desired. Heat the olive oil in a large skillet and brown the chicken. Remove to a platter and set aside.

continues

continued

2. Add the onions and garlic to the oil remaining in the pan and saute 6–7 minutes, till softened and lightly browned. Stir in cumin, ginger, salt, and pepper and cook 2 minutes. Stir in the tomatoes, breaking apart large pieces.

3. Return the chicken to the pan and add cilantro, parsley, olives, and chopped lemon. Cover and simmer gently for 30–35 minutes, till chicken is tender and sauce has thickened slightly.

Morocco: Chicken Tagine

Tagines are classic Moroccan stews, taking their name from the clay pot in which they're cooked. Tagines consist of a flat, rimmed base covered with a cone-shaped clay top with a hole in the top for the steam to escape. You don't need a tagine, however, to make a tagine, which are traditionally served with couscous. The stews of meat and vegetables are cooked long and slow until the meat is meltingly tender and falling off the bone and the flavors of the vegetables have completely blended. It's considered good luck in Morocco to have seven kinds of vegetables in a dish.

You need a heavy stovetop pot to try to approximate the cooking method of a tagine pot. A Dutch oven is ideal.

Serves 6

1 4–5-pound stewing hen, jointed	1/2 teaspoon freshly ground black pepper
1/4 cup olive oil	1 large carrot, diced
1 large onion, diced	1 medium zucchini, diced
2 cloves garlic, minced	1 small turnip, diced
2 teaspoons ground cumin	1 green bell pepper, cored, seeded, and diced
1 teaspoon curry powder	2 cups chicken stock
1/2 teaspoon cinnamon	1 ripe tomato, diced
1 teaspoon salt	1/4 cup raisins
2 medium potatoes, peeled and cut into thin slices	

1. Rinse and pat dry the chicken pieces, removing skin if desired. Heat the olive oil in a large skillet over medium-high heat and brown the chicken 6–8 minutes, till lightly browned. Remove to a platter and set aside.

2. Add the onions and garlic to the oil remaining in pan and saute till softened and lightly browned. Stir in the cumin, curry powder, cinnamon, salt, and pepper. Add the potato, carrot, zucchini, turnip, and pepper. Saute 10 minutes, till vegetables start to soften.

3. Return the chicken to the pan and stir in chicken stock, tomatoes, and raisins.

4. Cover and cook over low heat for 1 1/2 hours, till vegetables are tender and chicken is falling off the bone. Check and stir occasionally and add another 1/4–1/2 cup chicken stock if necessary, but don't make the tagine soupy. It should be a very moist stew, without too much liquid.

The Least You Need to Know

➤ South American cooks treat chicken with flair, pairing it with zesty seasonings ranging from ginger to chili to chocolate.

➤ In Africa, chicken pieces are often stewed with a spicy ground peanut sauce. American cooks can reproduce the taste with peanut butter.

➤ Tagines are hearty and filling Moroccan stews of chicken (and sometimes other meats) slow-cooked with vegetables, spiced with warm flavors such as cinnamon and curry, and accented with raisins and tomatoes.

Chapter 28

The Chicken Rises in the East

In This Chapter

➤ The start of it all

➤ China: Peking Chicken, Chicken and Broccoli

➤ India: Chicken Korma

➤ Malaysia: Nasi Goreng

➤ Indonesia: Gado Gado

➤ Japan: Chicken Katsu

➤ Thailand: Thai Basil Chicken

➤ Vietnam: Pho Ga, Vietnamese Pate Sandwiches

The Start of It All

Domesticated chicken is believed to have originated in Asia at least four thousand years ago in the Indus River valley. By the 5th century B.C., it appeared in Greece, but the cradle of chicken civilization is Asia and it's from Asia that some of the world's finest chicken recipes come.

Roost Rap

Peanut oil is used for cooking many Asian dishes because it can withstand the high temperatures of stir-frying and it has a very neutral flavor. You can substitute any vegetable cooking oil, but don't use olive oil. The flavor isn't suitable for Asian food and it smokes at high temperatures.

Feathered Facts

Instead of cutting up chicken along the joints, Chinese chefs use heavy, powerful cleavers to crack the whole bird in half down the backbone. The halves are hacked into bite-size chunks. The whole leg and thigh, for instance, is usually divided into five to six pieces. If you hack tentatively, the bone may splinter, so give it a good sharp crack. Served this way, a whole chicken can be divided more evenly, instead of someone getting a breast and another only a drumstick.

Nowhere else is the bird so deeply ingrained in the cuisine. In India, chicken curry is ubiquitous; in China, it appears with countless vegetables, in a stunning array of preparations; and in Southeast Asia, in the recipes of Thailand and Vietnam and elsewhere, chicken is part of endless noodle dishes and stir-fries. The French colonial influence on Vietnamese cuisine results in the marvelous pate below, using ground chicken along with pork where the French might have used liver instead.

In many ways, it might be said that Asian cuisine is the most fearless about using chicken. The Chinese famously eat nearly every part from the cockscomb to the feet, and they are not hampered by our traditional Western ways of carving and jointing. Armed with a sharp cleaver, Chinese chefs make the chicken fit the recipe, not vice versa. Hence the chicken breast might be thinly sliced and delicately steamed, or the entire bird might be hacked into bite size pieces, bones and all. It's wonderfully innovative food, and the two recipes below don't even begin to do justice to it, but it's a start, along with the Malaysian, Indonesian, Japanese, Thai, and Vietnamese recipes here. If your taste buds yearn for these types of flavorings, the cuisine of more than half the world's population awaits to fulfill your desires.

The reason Chinese food cooked at home rarely tastes as rich as the restaurant version is that most American cooks don't know about oil-blanching the meat. Strips of meat for a dish are dropped into a wok full of hot oil and rapidly fried for one to two minutes before being removed and drained, later to be stir-fried into the dish. This step lightly caramelizes the surface of the meat and makes it tender and velvety. You can also drop the meat into boiling water for one to two minutes as a precooking step, a lower-fat method that improves the texture of the finished stir-fry although the meat will be somewhat chewier than when it's oil-blanched.

The Recipes

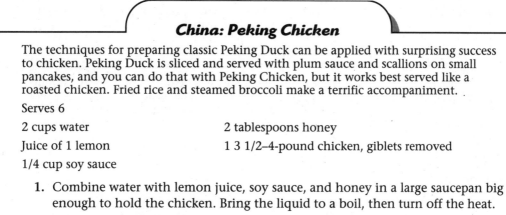

China: Peking Chicken

The techniques for preparing classic Peking Duck can be applied with surprising success to chicken. Peking Duck is sliced and served with plum sauce and scallions on small pancakes, and you can do that with Peking Chicken, but it works best served like a roasted chicken. Fried rice and steamed broccoli make a terrific accompaniment.

Serves 6

2 cups water	2 tablespoons honey
Juice of 1 lemon	1 3 1/2–4-pound chicken, giblets removed
1/4 cup soy sauce	

1. Combine water with lemon juice, soy sauce, and honey in a large saucepan big enough to hold the chicken. Bring the liquid to a boil, then turn off the heat.

2. Hold the chicken by one leg over the pot and ladle this mixture over the entire chicken for several minutes, until the bird is completely coated.

3. Lay it on a roasting rack in a shallow roasting pan and leave it uncovered in the refrigerator overnight. The skin should be very dry and slightly browned from the sauce. Store 1/2 cup of the basting sauce in a sealed glass jar in the refrigerator.

4. When ready to cook, preheat oven to 475°. Pour 1/2 cup of water in the roasting pan under the chicken to prevent the fat from splattering in the high heat. Roast for 20 minutes.

5. Lower heat to 350° and baste chicken with remaining sauce. Roast for another 75 minutes, without basting again, until skin is dark and crisp and legs move easily.

6. Carve and serve. If you'd like to serve the basting sauce on the side, boil it in a small saucepan for 3 minutes and serve in a clean dish.

China: Chicken and Broccoli

It's a simple Chinese dish, available in any Chinese restaurant, but too often it results in overcooked, over-sauced chicken served up with mushy broccoli. Tasty (and healthy) chicken and broccoli should be made quickly, with not too much sauce, itself just a light blend of sherry and soy sauce. The secret step to making the meat tender is oil-blanching, a lightning-fast fry in very hot oil, after which nearly all the oil is poured off.

The broccoli should be briefly blanched and added just before serving, so that it remains bright green with a bit of crunch. Tender white breast meat tastes best and cooks more quickly than dark meat. To turn this into a really healthful meal, serve it on brown rice instead of white or fried.

Serves 4

3 boneless, skinless chicken breasts	2 tablespoons light soy sauce
1 egg white	1 teaspoon sugar
1 tablespoon soy sauce	1 cup peanut oil
2 teaspoons cornstarch	2 cloves garlic, minced
1 head fresh broccoli	2 tablespoons chopped scallions
1 tablespoon rice wine or sherry	

1. Cut the chicken breasts into 1/4-inch strips and mix in a bowl with the egg white, soy sauce, and cornstarch. Leave to marinate for 15–20 minutes.

2. Trim the broccoli into florets. Peel the stems and slice them into rings or matchsticks. Bring a pot of water to boil, drop in the broccoli, and cook for no more than 5 minutes. Pour into a colander and immediately run cold water over the broccoli to stop the cooking. Set aside.

3. When ready to serve, combine the rice wine, light soy sauce, and sherry in a small cup. Put the peanut oil into a wok over high heat and when it starts to smoke, quickly drop in the marinated chicken pieces, stirring rapidly to separate them. Cook for 2 minutes, and immediately remove to a paper towel-lined plate or bowl.

4. Carefully pour the oil into a cup or bowl. Using a paper towel, carefully wipe the hot wok clean, and return 1 tablespoon of the oil to the wok. Heat over high heat and drop in the chopped garlic. Stir-fry for about 30 seconds, then return the chicken to the wok.

5. Add the broccoli and stir-fry about 1 minute to heat, then pour over the sherry mixture. Fry for another 1–2 minutes to heat through, then immediately pour into a bowl and serve with white or brown rice.

India: Chicken Korma

India has a wealth of curries in its cuisine, but they're not all the yellowish sauces many Americans expect. Korma is a mild white curry cooked in yogurt. The tangy taste of the yogurt blends all the curry flavors wonderfully, and the yogurt serves as an added tenderizer for the chicken. The dash of lemon juice added at the end perks up the sauce just before serving. Serve Chicken Korma over boiled white rice, and offer some chutney or spicy lime pickle on the side. A simple Indian salad of chopped cucumbers, onion, and tomato blended with yogurt, salt, and a touch of cumin rounds out the meal perfectly.

Serves 4

1 3-pound broiler-fryer, jointed and skin removed,
  or 3 pounds chicken thighs, skin removed

1/4 cup (1/2 stick) butter

4 large onions, finely chopped

6 cloves garlic, minced

1 teaspoon grated fresh ginger

2 tablespoons mild curry powder

1 teaspoon cinnamon

1 1/2 cups plain yogurt

1 1/2 cups chicken stock

1/4 cup ground almonds (optional)

3 tablespoons lemon juice

Chopped fresh cilantro

1. Rinse and pat dry the chicken pieces. If desired, bone the chicken thighs. Melt the butter in a large skillet over medium heat and add the chopped onions. Cook until softened and lightly browned. Remove to a bowl and set aside.

2. Saute the chicken pieces until well browned in the butter left in the pan. Return the onions to the pan with the minced garlic, ginger, curry, and cinnamon. Cook for 2–3 minutes until you can smell the spices strongly.

3. Stir in the yogurt and chicken stock. Bring to a boil, reduce heat, cover, and simmer very gently for 1–1 1/2 hours, until sauce is thick and chicken is tender and falling off the bone.

4. About 10 minutes before end of cooking, stir in the almonds if using. Just before serving, stir in the lemon juice, and garnish with chopped fresh cilantro.

Malaysia: Nasi Goreng

Nasi Goreng is an elaborate fried rice popular not only in Malaysia but also in Indonesia and Singapore. It is most definitely an entire meal in itself, and the ingredients can vary slightly depending on what you have on hand, although a few pieces of shrimp are customary. The addition of cooked chicken or even cubed breast pieces fried just for the Nasi Goreng make it a very elegant and substantial dish. Always use cold cooked rice for Nasi Goreng (indeed, for any fried rice dish). Warm rice becomes sticky if you try to stir-fry it.

Nasi Goreng is usually tightly pressed into a bowl and then the molded round pile of rice is turned upside down on the serving platter or individual plate. The traditional garnish is a few strips of quick-cooked omelette.

Serves 4

2 eggs, beaten

2 tablespoons peanut oil

2 chicken breasts, cubed, or 1 cup cold cooked chicken, diced

1 medium onion, finely chopped

3 cloves garlic, minced

2 fresh chiles, seeded and minced (try serrano or Scotch bonnet)

6 cups cold cooked rice

2 tablespoons soy sauce

1/2 cup frozen cooked shrimp

4 scallions, white and green parts thinly sliced

1. Heat one tablespoon of the oil in a nonstick skillet over medium heat and pour in the beaten egg. Let it set into a large thin omelette, then fold in half and then in half again. Slide it onto a plate and set aside.

2. Heat the remaining tablespoons of oil in the same skillet and toss in the chicken if using raw breast pieces (if using cooked chicken, add it later with the rice). Saute for 4–5 minutes, till cooked through and slightly browned, then add the onions and garlic and cook about 5 minutes, till onions become translucent.

3. Add the chiles and cook another 1–2 minutes, then stir in the rice, breaking up any lumps. Stir in the soy sauce and cook 4–5 minutes, till rice is heated through. Stir in the frozen shrimp and scallions and cook another minute to thaw and heat.

4. Mound into a large bowl, press down, and unmold onto a serving platter. Cut the omelette into narrow strips and crisscross these over the surface of the Nasi Goreng. Serve immediately with extra soy sauce if desired.

Indonesia: Gado Gado

Gado Gado is a cold Indonesian salad of blanched cooked vegetables, topped with an assortment of cooked meats or eggs, sometimes with pineapple and watercress, and drenched in a rich and spicy peanut sauce. It's delicious accompanied by the crispy shrimp crackers available in Asian markets. The crackers look like pieces of colored Styrofoam, and slightly shrimp flavored rather than being made of shrimp, but they add the perfect light crunch to accompany the salad.

It's a casual meal, with the vegetables and meats served in individual bowls for diners to build their own salads, so you can use leftover cooked vegetables or cook fresh ones just for this dish. Feel free to use any kind of vegetables and quantities that you have on hand. The unifying ingredient is the wonderful Gado Gado sauce, which is also great on cooked noodles, either hot or cold. Make the sauce as spicy or mild as you like. You'll need a blender to make the sauce creamy.

Gado Gado sauce is enough to serve 4–6

For Gado Gado sauce:

6 dried red chile peppers or 2 teaspoons red chili flakes

1 medium onion, chopped

2 cloves garlic, chopped

2 tablespoons peanut oil

1 13 1/2-ounce can unsweetened coconut milk

1/3 cup crunchy peanut butter

1 teaspoon brown sugar

3 tablespoons hot water

1 tablespoon lemon juice

1 teaspoon soy sauce

For the salad:

3 cups cold cooked chicken, sliced or cubed

3-4 cups very thinly sliced cabbage

3-4 cold boiled potatoes, sliced

2 cups cold cooked green beans, drained

1 cup fresh bean sprouts

3 hard boiled eggs, sliced or mashed

6 scallions, thinly sliced

1. To make sauce, soak dried chiles in 1 cup of just-boiled water for 10 minutes. Drain, reserving some of the liquid, and put the chiles in a blender along with the onion, garlic, and 1 tablespoon of the oil. Pulse to a thick puree. You may need to add a little of the soaking liquid to help grind the mixture up.

2. Heat the other tablespoon of oil in a nonstick skillet over medium-high heat and pour in the chili puree. Fry, stirring constantly, for 2–3 minutes, until the mixture is hot and smells pungent.

3. Lower the heat and slowly blend in the coconut milk, stirring constantly. Add all remaining sauce ingredients and cook for 4–5 minutes, until sauce is thick and smooth and hot. Allow to cool.

4. To serve the Gado Gado, place the salad ingredients in individual bowls on the table. Diners should make a pile of whichever ingredients they like, then pour the cooled Gado Gado sauce over the salads.

Don't Fowl Up

Make sure you use unsweetened coconut milk, available in cans in Asian markets and gourmet shops, for the Gado Gado sauce, and not the sweetened kind that is used in piña coladas.

Japan: Chicken Katsu

This is a chicken version of the famous Japanese dish tonkatsu, which is a breaded and deep-fried piece of lean pork, cut into thin slices and served with a tangy dipping sauce. The chicken cutlets are a little less heavy than the classic pork. You can buy bottled tonkatsu sauce, but the recipe below makes an almost perfect approximation of it. Serve the chicken katsu with rice and a shredded cabbage salad.

Serves 4

For sauce:

1/4 cup ketchup

1 tablespoon sugar

1 teaspoon soy sauce

1/2 teaspoon paprika

1/8 teaspoon nutmeg

For fillets:

4 boneless, skinless chicken breasts

Salt and freshly ground black pepper

1/4 cup all-purpose flour

4 egg yolks

3/4 cup dry white breadcrumbs

Oil for frying

1. Combine sauce ingredients in a small bowl and set aside.

2. Pound each chicken breast between two sheets of wax paper until they are a uniform 1/2-inch thick. Season each piece with salt and pepper and then dredge them in the flour.

3. Beat the egg yolks together in a bowl and have the breadcrumbs ready on a plate. Heat about 1 inch of oil in a large skillet over medium heat. Dip each breast in the egg yolk and then into the crumbs, pressing the crumbs in so they stick.

4. Fry each breaded fillet in the hot oil until golden brown, turning once, approximately 5 minutes altogether. To serve, slice the cooked chicken katsu patties on the diagonal into 1-inch strips. Serve with the dipping sauce on the side.

Don't Fowl Up

It's always good to have your ingredients chopped, measured, and laid out when cooking, but it's particularly important when making Asian food. The cooking methods tend to be so fast that if you stop to mix the soy sauce and rice wine or to blanch the broccoli or to wait for the rice to finish cooking, you run the risk of ruining the rest of the dish. Make sure all your ingredients are prepared and lying in readiness nearby before you start to cook.

Thailand: Thai Basil Chicken

If you can find fresh purple Asian basil at your Asian market or gourmet store, this is the dish in which to use it. The purple leaves have an intense flavor that permeates the whole dish. You can of course substitute regular basil, but make sure you only use fresh.

For this noodle dish, as with the Vietnamese dishes, you'll also need fish sauce. The Vietnamese version is nuoc mam, while Thai fish sauce is nam pla. There are slight differences that can be distinguished by experienced palates, but for our purposes, either is fine.

Pick up rice stick noodles at your Asian market as well, though you may be surprised to find how many average supermarkets have begun to stock them in their Asian food sections.

Serves 6

4 boneless, skinless chicken breasts	3–4 cloves garlic, minced
1/3 cup fish sauce	1 green bell pepper, cored, seeded, and sliced
1/3 cup soy sauce	1 red bell pepper, cored, seeded, and sliced
2 tablespoons rice wine or dry white wine	1 cup fresh bean sprouts
1/2 pound thin rice sticks	2 teaspoons dried red chili flakes
4 tablespoons peanut oil	1 tablespoon sugar
1 medium onion, thinly sliced	1 cup basil leaves, shredded

1. Thinly slice the chicken breasts 1/4-inch thick on the diagonal. In a glass bowl, combine the chicken slices with 2 tablespoons of the fish sauce, 2 tablespoons of the soy sauce, and the rice wine or dry white wine. Leave to marinate for 10–20 minutes.

2. Cook the rice sticks according to package directions. Set aside.

continues

continued

3. Heat a wok or a cast-iron skillet over high heat. When the pan is very hot, add 2 tablespoons of the oil and stir-fry the chicken for 4–5 minutes, till it turns lightly brown. Remove the chicken to a bowl and set aside. Wipe out the pan with a paper towel.

4. Heat the pan again and add the remaining 2 tablespoons of oil. When the oil starts to smoke, add the onions and stir-fry briefly. Toss in the garlic, then the green and red bell pepper, and stir-fry for 1–2 minutes, till the vegetables just begin to wilt.

5. Add the chili flakes and fry another 30 seconds. Add the remaining fish sauce and the sugar. Mix in the cooked chicken and the cooked rice sticks. Fry briefly to heat through, then toss with the shredded basil leaves and serve immediately.

Vietnam: Pho Ga

Pho (pronounced far) is the national dish of Vietnam, a noodle soup that inspires poems and songs among its devotees. Most major American cities feature a Vietnamese noodle shop where you can sample Pho Bo, the more traditional version of the soup with a ginger-laced beef broth and thin slices of just-cooked beef floating over the thin rice noodles. The beef version takes all day to cook, with elaborate preparation of the broth in particular taking up a lot of time.

The chicken version, however, is much quicker to make. Pho Ga, as it's called, features a chicken simmered in a gingery broth full of the flavors of star anise and cloves. The meat is shredded and returned to the strained stock, and then the soup is assembled.

For authentic pho taste, you will need nuoc mam, or fish sauce, a Southeast Asian condiment like a very pungent soy sauce. It's available in any Asian market and in gourmet stores, where you'll also find the most crucial ingredient to pho, the thin rice noodles known to the Vietnamese as banh pho. Ask for rice stick noodles, and if you can't find them, you can make a reasonable facsimile of the soup with regular vermicelli. Star anise, a fragrant star-shaped whole spice, is also available at Asian markets.

Serves 6

For stock:	For the pho:
1 4–5-pound stewing hen	1 1/2 pounds rice stick noodles (banh pho)
2 large onions, quartered	6 scallions, white and green parts finely chopped
2 4-inch pieces fresh ginger	1/3 cup chopped fresh cilantro
1/4 cup fish sauce	1 pound fresh bean sprouts
1/4 cup sugar	1/4 cup thinly chopped hot red chile peppers
5 whole star anise	2 limes, quartered
5 whole cloves	Sprigs of fresh basil or purple Asian basil (optional)
1 tablespoon salt	

1. Bring a large stockpot of water to boil. Using a cleaver or poultry shears, quarter the chicken by chopping in half down the breastbone and back, and then halving each of those pieces. When the water has come to a boil, drop in the chicken pieces and leave for 3 minutes, then remove the pieces and throw that water away. (This is blanching, as discussed on p. 49, to make a cleaner, purer stock.)

2. Bring 6 quarts of fresh water to a boil, add the blanched chicken parts, and reduce heat immediately. Add the remaining stock ingredients and simmer very gently, so that the water doesn't bubble but merely trembles, for about an hour.

3. Lift out the chicken pieces and strain and discard the other solids out of the stock. When the chicken is cool enough to handle, strip the meat off the bones, and set aside. Let the strained stock simmer very gently for another hour, to reduce it and concentrate the flavors.

4. When ready to serve, cook the rice sticks according to package directions (this usually involves a long soak and a brief boiling). Separate the noodles among large warmed bowls and ladle hot broth over them.

5. Lay pieces of the reserved meat in each bowl, and sprinkle generously with chopped scallions and cilantro. Serve the bean sprouts, chiles, and basil on the table for diners to add individually, along with the lime wedges to be squeezed over the soup. Once the broth hits the noodles, serve right away.

Vietnam: Vietnamese Pate Sandwiches

The French influence on Vietnamese cuisine is strong after years of colonial influence, and it has resulted occasionally in funky dishes that fuse the French and Vietnamese sensibilities. This unusual sandwich is one such case, with an Asian-spiced pate spread on crusty French baguettes and topped with distinctly Asian pickled vegetables. If you have a food processor, you can make short work of the pate by grinding your own whole chicken breast pieces and chunks of lean pork with the spices and flavorings.

The pate is good served on just about anything, so you don't need to construct the sandwiches if you prefer to serve it simply on bread or crackers. Again, you'll need the ubiquitous Vietnamese flavors of fish sauce (nuoc mam) and star anise, available at Asian markets and gourmet stores.

Baguette are long crusty French loaves made without any fat, just flour, water, yeast, and salt. They are only good on the day they are made, eaten preferably sooner rather than later. Many, many American supermarket bakeries have begun to offer surprisingly authentic tasting baguettes, often in paper bags striped with the colors of the French flag. Try to find a real, chewy baguette for this sandwich before settling for a substitute, but if in doubt, buy crusty sourdough rolls and toast them instead of using the pale, fat, white loaves often termed "French bread."

continues

continued

Makes 6 sandwiches

| For the pickles: | 2 eggs |
| For the pickles: | 2 tablespoons fish sauce |

For the pickles:

1 large carrot, grated

1/2 cup grated jicama or daikon or red radish

1 small serrano chili, minced

1/2 cup just-boiled water

5 tablespoons white or cider vinegar

2 tablespoons sugar

For the pate:

1/2 pound ground chicken

1/2 pound lean ground pork

1 small onion, very finely chopped

1 clove garlic, minced

2 eggs

2 tablespoons fish sauce

1 teaspoon sugar

1/4 teaspoon ground star anise

1/8 teaspoon cinnamon

For the sandwiches:

1 fresh, crusty baguette

Mayonnaise

Thinly sliced ripe tomatoes

Thinly sliced peeled cucumbers

Fresh mint and basil leaves

1. To make the Vietnamese pickle, combine the grated vegetables, chili, water, vinegar, and sugar in a small glass bowl and refrigerate for at least 4 hours before using.

2. To make the pate, preheat the oven to 350°. Combine all ingredients in a food processor, if using whole meats, or in a bowl if using already ground meat. Pulse or mix well.

3. Pack the mixture into a loaf pan and cover with foil. Place in a roasting pan and pour hot water into the pan until it comes about 1 inch up the sides of the loaf pan. Bake for about 45 minutes, until the pate is firm. Remove from the roasting pan and cool in the loaf pan.

4. To assemble the sandwiches, cut the baguette into six pieces. Halve each piece and lightly toast in a 350° oven or in a toaster oven. Spread the baguette pieces with a thin layer of mayonnaise and put a few slices of the pate on each bottom half.

5. Top with the pickle, slices of tomato and cucumber, and a sprinkling of torn mint and basil leaves. Store extra pate and pickle in the refrigerator for up to a week.

The Least You Need to Know

➤ The domestic chicken is believed to have originated in India some 4,000 years ago.

➤ Since that time, cooks on the continent of Asia have come up with some of the most delicious, imaginative chicken recipes to be found anywhere in the world.

➤ From India comes a wealth of pungent curries, from China comes chicken stir-fried and braised into succulent tenderness, and from various Southeast Asian countries come incredible noodle dishes, such as the Vietnamese chicken and noodle soup, Pho Ga.

Chicken and the Not-So-Wild West

In This Chapter

➤ Old-World chicken

➤ France: Coq au Vin, Poulet a l'Estragon

➤ Italy: Chicken Cacciatore, Chicken Piccata, Chicken Marsala

➤ Spain: Paella

➤ Switzerland: Chicken Cordon Bleu

Old-World Chicken

Western Europe has treated the world to some of the most elaborate chicken dishes available, cooking it in rich sauces, stuffing it with savory fillings, surrounding it with the finest ingredients.

It's not surprising that to our taste buds, the chicken occasionally seems eclipsed by what it was cooked in. This is more because of mass production having robbed modern chickens of a dominant flavor, however. The chicken that Europeans used to know, and for which these dishes were developed, were plump and flavorful birds, accustomed to wandering the fields and gardens eating what they liked and drinking fresh water. Battery chicken was not available in France until 1955, some thirty years after America had turned to mass production. It's not surprising that the French held out for so long against industrializing chicken. This is the country that still loves a sixteenth-century king, Henri IV, who promised "a chicken in every pot."

Feathered Facts

The best chickens in France happen to have the French national colors on their bodies. Bresse chickens from the Burgundy region have a red comb, white feathers, and distinctive blue feet, like a walking French tricolor flag. Like the finest wines, Bresse poultry has an "appellation d'origine controllee," meaning that each bird is certified to meet government criteria for being sold as Bresse poultry.

France's Bresse chickens live a luxury life by chicken standards, running free in yards and fed the finest grains as well as whatever insects and grass they can grub in the great outdoors. As a result, their meat is dense and firm and deeply flavored (not watery like so many mass-produced chickens in the US), and lightly marbled with fat, meaning the cooked bird will be as moist and tender as it can possibly be.

Poor Henry probably wouldn't recognize the taste of our birds today, but all is not lost. If you're going to take the time to assemble the ingredients for a fine paella, or use a whole bottle of good red wine for a Coq au Vin, or prepare an Italian chicken piccata where the taste of really good chicken is highlighted by the simple flavor of lemon and capers, take the time as well to find the best chicken you can afford. Even if regular mass-produced chicken is good for weeknight supper, the extra effort required for some of these dishes will be amply rewarded if you can find a farm-raised or free-range bird.

Don't Fowl Up

If you're buying a high-quality free-range, farm-raised bird, don't be surprised if it takes longer to cook than a mass-produced chicken. The flesh will be denser and less watery and may require extra time in the oven to reach perfection.

The Recipes

France: Coq au Vin

This classic French dish is ideal for older, bigger, or tougher birds. The long, slow stewing in red wine results in a tender, succulent bird, floating in a silky gravy that has absorbed the very essence of the wine. It's a proper fricassee, starting with a saute and moving on to a slow stew.

Coq au Vin is a good dish to cook on a rainy weekend afternoon, because it requires several steps that need you near the stove. It's terrific served right away, with mashed potatoes and green peas, but it takes on new depth and richness of flavor if you refrigerate overnight and reheat the next day.

Use a dry wine such as a Cabernet Sauvignon, and remember that the better quality of wine you use, the better the final dish. Don't use "cooking wine" or anything other than a bottle that you would drink yourself. You may need a leisurely glass of wine to keep you company while you cook, so buy more than one bottle.

Serves 4–6

6 slices of bacon, diced	1 tablespoon tomato paste
1 3 1/2–4 1/2-pound stewing hen, jointed	1 bottle (750 ml) dry red wine
1/4 cup flour	1/2 teaspoon dried thyme
1/2 teaspoon salt	2 bay leaves
1/4 teaspoon freshly ground black pepper	2 tablespoons butter
1 large yellow onion, sliced	1 pound button mushrooms, sliced
2–3 cloves garlic, minced	

1. In a large stew pot or Dutch oven over medium-low heat, cook the bacon till it's lightly browned and the grease runs. Toss the chicken pieces with the flour, salt, and pepper. Turn the heat up to high and add the coated chicken and saute till evenly browned, 7–10 minutes, turning once. Remove to a platter and set aside.

2. Lower heat to medium and saute the onions till softened and lightly browned. Add the garlic and cook a further 2–3 minutes. Stir in the tomato paste and return the chicken to the pot. Pour in the red wine, and add the thyme and bay leaves. Stir to blend. Bring to a simmer, cover loosely, lower heat, and cook until chicken is tender, 50–60 minutes.

3. Meanwhile, in a skillet over medium-high heat, melt the butter and saute the mushrooms until lightly browned, 6–7 minutes. The mushrooms will give off water, but keep the temperature up so it evaporates and they eventually brown. Add the mushrooms to the stew pot and cook an additional 10–15 minutes. Serve hot.

Don't Fowl Up

If you're using a particularly large stewing hen for your Coq au Vin, you may need to cook it longer than fifty to sixty minutes. Pierce a drumstick or thigh with a fork, and if the meat doesn't slide off easily, cook it longer, adding a little more wine, water, or chicken stock if necessary.

France: Poulet a l'Estragon

Estragon is not a famous French chef. It's the French word for tarragon, chicken's herbal soulmate. Nobody knows this better than the French, and no recipe reflects the loving relationship between chicken and the potent, gray-green, anise-flavored herb better than the one below. It's a fabulously simple dish, relying on top-quality ingredients. Cream and white wine bridge the two flavors, and even though a whole cup of heavy cream seems like a lot (and it is a lot, there's no denying it), you won't be sorry when you taste the finished dish. However, if you're going to use a whole cup of whipping cream, at least do the dish the justice of using only fresh tarragon. A rich but simple dish like this goes well with a slightly more elaborate side dish such as scalloped potatoes and green beans, perhaps the slender French haricots verts.

Serves 4–6

1 3 1/2–4-pound broiler-fryer, jointed	1 medium onion, finely chopped
1 teaspoon salt	2 tablespoons all-purpose flour
1/4 teaspoon freshly ground black pepper	3 tablespoons fresh tarragon
2 tablespoons olive oil	1 cup dry white wine
3 tablespoons butter	1 cup whipping cream

1. Rinse and pat dry the chicken pieces and sprinkle with the salt and pepper. Heat the olive oil in a large nonstick skillet over medium-high heat.

2. Add the butter and heat until it starts to foam. Immediately add the chicken pieces and cook for 6–8 minutes, turning occasionally, until golden brown. Add the chopped onions and cook until softened and translucent. Sprinkle with flour and stir to combine.

3. Add in 2 tablespoons of the fresh tarragon. Pour in white wine. Stir to combine with the onions and flour, bring to a boil, reduce heat, cover, and simmer gently for 20 minutes.

4. Remove the chicken to a serving platter and keep warm in a low oven. Add the whipping cream to the liquid left in the pan and bring to a boil. Cook for 5 minutes over a high heat, stirring frequently, until it thickens.

5. Stir in the remaining tarragon and pour this sauce over the chicken. Serve immediately.

Don't Fowl Up

Be sure to use fresh tarragon for the Poulet a l'Estragon. Dried tarragon has a pungent and delicious scent when you sniff it, but it doesn't have the delicious and elusive flavor of fresh. Most supermarkets nowadays have small packages of fresh herbs available in the produce section, and one package will probably be enough for this dish.

Italy: Chicken Cacciatore

The literal meaning of the name is "in the style of the hunter" and that usually means long–stewed with bacon and wine. It's a hearty and rugged way to cook the supposedly tough joints of meat that a hunter might bring home, such as wild boar or rabbit, but in practice, it's any meat cooked in a vibrant sauce, usually enriched with tomatoes, wine, bacon, pungent herbs such as rosemary and oregano, and often mushrooms.

Although the ingredients are quite similar to the French Coq au Vin, that dish is more elegant, with a silky sauce and refined flavor, while this is heartier and chunkier. It's best served on top of spaghetti, with a steaming loaf of homemade garlic bread wrapped in tinfoil. To be really authentic, serve it over toasted squares of polenta.

Serves 4–6

5–6 slices bacon, diced	3 cloves garlic, minced
1 4–5-pound stewing hen, jointed	1 tablespoon dried rosemary
1 cup flour	1 teaspoon dried oregano
1 teaspoon salt	1 cup dry Marsala or red wine
1/2 teaspoon freshly ground black pepper	1 28-ounce can crushed tomatoes
2 tablespoons olive oil	1/2 pound white mushrooms, sliced
1 large onion, chopped	

1. In a large stewpot or Dutch oven, cook the bacon over medium-low heat till lightly browned and the grease runs. Rinse and pat dry the chicken pieces and toss with the flour, salt, and pepper. Turn up the heat under the bacon, add the chicken, and brown, 7–10 minutes, turning so it browns evenly. Remove to a platter.

2. Add the olive oil to the pot, lower heat, and saute the onions till softened and translucent. Add the garlic, rosemary, and oregano, and cook for 2–3 minutes. Return the chicken to the pot. Turn up the heat and stir in the Marsala, stirring to coat the chicken pieces in the wine. (Marsala is a fortified red wine, available in any wine store and in most supermarkets. It has a pungent flavor, more reminiscent of a liquor than a wine. If you can't find it, use a good red wine.) Let the wine bubble and reduce a little.

3. Blend in the crushed tomatoes and bring to a simmer. Turn heat to medium-low, partially cover, and cook for 40–50 minutes. Stir in the sliced mushrooms and cook for 15–20 minutes, till sauce is thickened and chicken is tender.

Italy: Chicken Piccata

Chicken breasts are beaten into thin fillets, coated in breadcrumbs, and fried before being finished with a sharp sauce of lemon, capers, and butter. Piccata in fact means "sharp" in Italian and the lemon juice and vinegary caper make this an extremely fresh-tasting dish. The little bit of cornmeal mixed into the breadcrumbs makes the chicken breasts extremely crisp and toothsome.

It's ideal for a summer evening, served with a lightly steamed vegetable such as green beans or asparagus and a creamy potato salad to offset the piquant flavor of the chicken. Piccata can be made with medallions of pork or veal as well, but that makes a slightly heavier dish. The lighter flavor and texture of chicken is perfect for the piccata treatment.

Serves 6

6 boneless, skinless chicken breasts	1/4 cup olive oil
1 egg	2 tablespoons butter
2 tablespoons water	1/4 cup thinly sliced scallions
3/4 cup dry, very fine breadcrumbs	1/4 cup white wine
1/4 cup cornmeal	3 tablespoons lemon juice
1/4 cup chopped fresh parsley	2 tablespoons capers
1/2 teaspoon salt	Fresh parsley for garnish
1/4 teaspoon freshly ground black pepper	

1. Beat each chicken breast out to a uniform 1/4-inch thickness between two sheets of waxed paper with a meat mallet or rolling pin.

2. Beat the egg in a small bowl with the water. Mix breadcrumbs on a plate with the cornmeal, parsley, salt, and pepper.

3. Heat 2 tablespoons of the olive oil in a nonstick skillet over medium heat. Dip three of the chicken breasts in the egg, then in the breadcrumb mixture. Saute in the olive oil, turning once, till golden-brown on both sides, about 10 minutes altogether. Remove to a platter and keep warm in a low oven (set at 180°). Repeat with the last 2 tablespoons of olive oil and the remaining three chicken breasts and keep warm on the platter.

4. Melt the 2 tablespoons butter in the same nonstick skillet over medium heat. Stir in the sliced scallions and saute 2 minutes, then add wine and lemon juice and bring to a boil. Cook for 1 minute, then stir in capers and drizzle over chicken breasts. Garnish with fresh parsley and serve immediately.

Italy: Chicken Marsala

Marsala is a fortified Italian wine, reminiscent of sherry, but with a depth of flavor and a spiciness that make it ideal for saucing meats. There is also a sweet Marsala that is used as a dessert wine and in sweet dishes such as zabaglione, so make sure you have a dry Marsala for this dish, or use a heavy red wine.

Serves 6

6 boneless, skinless chicken breasts	1/2 teaspoon salt
1 egg	1/4 teaspoon freshly ground black pepper
2 tablespoons water	1/4 cup olive oil
1/2 cup flour	3/4 cup dry Marsala

1. Beat each chicken breast to an even 1/4-inch thickness between two sheets of waxed paper with a meat mallet or rolling pin. Mix flour on a plate with the salt and pepper.

2. Heat 2 tablespoons of the olive oil in a nonstick skillet over medium heat. Dip three of the chicken breasts in the flour. Saute in the olive oil, turning once, till golden brown on both sides, about 10 minutes altogether. Remove to a platter and keep warm in a low oven (set at 180°). Repeat with the last 2 tablespoons of olive oil and the remaining three chicken breasts and keep warm on the platter in the oven.

3. Melt the butter in the same nonstick skillet and stir in the Marsala, scraping up any browned bits off the bottom. Simmer for 2–3 minutes, until the butter and the wine combine to a velvety sauce. Return the chicken pieces to the pan, heat through in the sauce, sprinkle with fresh parsley, and serve immediately.

Spain: Paella

Paella (pie-AYY-ya) is one of those festive foods that signifies a celebration or at least a really fun dinner. There's something utterly hospitable about the amount of food, with rice and different meats and seafood all bursting out of one pot. It suggests generosity and openness, and if you add to the mix a pitcher of sangria, the Spanish punch of wine and fresh fruit, you've got almost a ready-made party. This is an especially easy version of the complicated dish, one that will give you the spirit of a true paella without an entire day's work in the kitchen.

The word paella actually refers to the large shallow pan in which the dish is made, and few American kitchens boast a frying pan large enough. If you have a 12-inch skillet with a cover, you'll manage, but a smaller skillet may make it difficult. If you don't have a very large skillet, try using a shallow stew pot or Dutch oven instead.

Serves 6

3 pounds chicken legs, jointed into thighs and drumsticks

1 teaspoon dried oregano

1/2 teaspoon freshly ground black pepper

1/4 cup olive oil

1 large onion, sliced

3 cloves garlic, minced

1 large green bell pepper, seeded and diced

1 large red bell pepper, seeded and diced

1/2 pound chorizo, cut in chunks (use kielbasa if chorizo is unavailable)

1 1/2 cups long grain rice

1 cup white wine

Generous pinch saffron threads

3 cups chicken stock

1 15-ounce can whole tomatoes

3/4 pound medium shrimp, shelled and cleaned

12 littleneck clams, scrubbed clean (optional)

12 mussels, scrubbed clean and debearded (optional)

1. Rinse and pat dry the chicken pieces. Season the pieces with the oregano and black pepper. Heat the olive oil in a very large skillet over medium-high heat. Add the chicken pieces and cook till browned, turning once, about 8–10 minutes. Remove the chicken to a platter and set aside.

2. Reduce the heat to medium-low and add the onions and garlic. Saute until onions are softened and translucent. Add the bell peppers and chorizo (or kielbasa) and saute briefly, 1–2 minutes.

3. Stir in the rice, making sure the grains are coated with the oil in the pan. Raise the heat and add the wine. Bring to a boil and cook until the wine is mostly absorbed. Add the saffron threads and then stir in the chicken stock.

4. Return the chicken to the pan, and add the tomatoes. Bring to a boil, reduce heat, cover loosely, and simmer for about 15 minutes, until the liquid has been absorbed, the rice is cooked, and the chicken is tender.

5. Distribute the shrimp over the top of the paella and push them down into the rice instead of stirring in. If using shellfish, distribute them over the top and also poke down into the rice. Cover and cook 5 minutes, or until the shrimp have turned bright pink and the shellfish have opened. Serve immediately.

Don't Fowl Up

Don't use any shellfish in your Paella that don't close when you touch them, and discard any shellfish that don't open when you cook them. Shellfish should be alive when you buy and cook them, for safety reasons, and not closing is a sign that they're either dead or close to it. If they don't open when you cook them, they were probably already dead and therefore are unsafe to eat.

Switzerland: Chicken Cordon Bleu

Although it's generally considered a French dish, Chicken Cordon Bleu actually originated in Switzerland (they speak French there, too, you know, along with German and Italian). The classic version of the dish consists of thinly pounded chicken breasts wrapped tightly around a slice of Gruyere and boiled ham, breaded, and deep-fried. It's labor-intensive (as is the Russian Chicken Kiev, p. 202) but utterly, decadently delicious.

The recipe for Chicken Cordon Bleu has come to be used with any sort of ham and cheese, so feel free to create variations on the theme below. You might try Italian prosciutto and Provolone, for instance, or bacon and creamy English Stilton, or Canadian bacon and Cheddar. The Swiss won't mind—they're neutral.

Serves 6

6 boneless, skinless chicken breasts

6 thin slices Swiss or Gruyere cheese

6 thin slices flavorful boiled ham

1 1/2 cups dry breadcrumbs

1/4 cup chopped fresh parsley

1/2 teaspoon salt

1/2 teaspoon freshly ground black pepper

1/2 cup (1 stick) butter, melted

1/2 cup olive oil

1. Working on 1 breast at a time, place each between two sheets of waxed paper and pound out to an even 1/4-inch thickness using a meat mallet or a rolling pin.

2. Place one slice of ham topped with one slice of cheese in the middle of each flattened breast, and roll up tightly by flipping the narrowest end of the breast up, then closing in the two sides, like an envelope, and rolling the remaining side down and over the whole package. Secure firmly with a round wooden toothpick.

3. Preheat the oven to 350°. Mix the breadcrumbs with the parsley, salt, and pepper on a large plate. Have the melted butter ready in a bowl, and heat the olive oil in a large skillet over medium-high heat.

4. Roll each chicken package liberally in the melted butter, then in the bread crumbs, pressing the crumbs on with your hands. Gently slide each breaded roll into the hot oil and fry till golden brown, turning once, 12–15 minutes altogether. Serve immediately.

The Least You Need to Know

➤ The French in particular are a chicken-loving nation—these are the people to whom King Henri IV promised "a chicken in every pot."

➤ From western Europe's long heritage come some of the richer and more elaborate recipes for chicken, including Switzerland's classic Chicken Cordon Bleu, with breasts wrapped around ham and Gruyere cheese and fried till golden.

Part 6

Beyond Chicken: Playing the Game

Chickens are not the only bird—but if you know how to cook one, it's just a short step to Cornish game hens, turkeys, ducks, geese, and more. Go beyond chicken to learn the secrets of moist and flavorful poultry, and start to explore the exciting world of game birds, from squab, guinea fowl, and pheasant to partridge and quail.

Chapter 30

Not Actually from Cornwall: Cornish Game Hens

> **In This Chapter**
>
> ➤ What are they anyway?
>
> ➤ Care and handling of your Cornish game hen
>
> ➤ Recipes: Roasted and grilled

Cornish game hens, chicken's tiny cousin, are always festive food, but they require special treatment to keep from overcooking.

What Are They, Anyway?

Usually referred to as "game hens" or "Cornish game hens," Rock Cornish game hens are actually a hybrid between strains of the meaty American White Rock chicken and the flavorful English Cornish hen. Because they are so small, the meat tends to be quite tender.

The Cornish game hen is an extremely close cousin of chicken, so, unfortunately, mass production has led to there being hardly any distinction in taste between it and the average broiler-fryer. So the original intent of creating a domestic table bird with a slightly more gamey flavor has been overthrown for the convenience of mass production. Nonetheless, even if there's not much game about game hens, there's still the fun of a single-serving bird—and it's a considerable amount of fun. The little birds are practically all breast meat and the teeny drumsticks and thighs are great, less for the quantity of meat on them but because they're in miniature.

Feathered Facts

Although Rock Cornish game hens are not baby chickens, there is such a thing. The French refer to them as "poussins" and in America, when you can find them, they're called "squab broilers" and they're far more expensive pound for pound than either mature chicken or Cornish game hens. If you are able to buy a poussin, however, you'll likely find it far more flavorful than its bigger cousins.

Although the size of Cornish game hens used to range from 3/4 of a pound to about 1 1/2 pounds, they've been growing on the US market. They seem to be increasingly large, which is presumably a side effect of mass production, so that more can be charged for the slightly bigger birds. You'll see them up to two pounds, but always try to buy the smallest ones you can find, so that each bird can serve one person.

A 2-pound bird can serve two, but it's best cooked split down the middle. The additional time needed to cook the larger birds whole often results in a dry, overcooked hen.

Well-cooked Cornish game hens make one of the most delightful poultry presentations. The thrill of individual birds on each plate transports children with delight, and usually provides adults with quite a kick, too, making them perfect dinner party fare.

Care and Handling of Your Cornish Game Hen

Dryness is the chief problem you'll face when cooking game hens. The short amount of time they need in the oven to cook through is not necessarily enough time to evenly brown the exterior, particularly if you're cooking more than two at once. The more birds you crowd into the pan, the paler your finished birds will be, especially if you use a high-sided roasting dish. The first thing to remember is not to crowd them, and always to elevate them on a baking rack.

Don't think you can brown better by just turning up the oven, either. A high temperature, so effective for rapidly browning larger birds, will leave little hens rapidly dried out. A steady temperature of about 400° produces the best results. Glazing the birds with soy sauce, a thinned jam, or balsamic vinegar will also help provide a better finish.

Butterflying the birds or splitting them right in half is a good way to cook them quickly. To butterfly, use a pair of poultry shears to cut down the middle of the back, leaving the breast intact. Bypass the backbone, then cut it off the side it's still attached to. Open the bird out and push down to flatten.

To halve the game hens, use a poultry shears to cut right up the middle all the way through the back and breast, splitting them in half with one wing, one breast, and one leg on each half. Cut off the back bone. After splitting, flatten them out with the heel of your hand or pound them gently, split-side down, with the bottom of a skillet.

Splitting the birds also splits the cooking time, down to twenty-five to thirty minutes in the oven, and even less under the broiler, about twenty minutes.

If there's time, always brine (see p. 41). Real game birds don't need brining, but the name notwithstanding, Cornish game hens are domesticated and mass produced and are definitely improved by a soak in a salty bath. When you take into account their tendency to dry out in the oven, there's even more reason to brine. For two quarts of water, use about 1/4 cup table salt or 1/2 cup kosher salt. (You may need to double the quantity of brine, depending on how many birds you're soaking.) To help brown the skin faster, try adding to the brine a few teaspoons of sugar, which will penetrate the surface and caramelize in the oven.

As with chickens, game hens are done when their leg joints move freely and the juices run clear when the thigh is pierced with a sharp knife. If the bird is browned but there are no juices, you may have overcooked. The flesh in the thickest part of the thigh (which admittedly isn't very thick in a Cornish game hen) should be 170° to 175°. If you're stuffing the hens, the stuffing inside must be at 160° for safety.

Although trussing makes a tidy-looking package when the bird comes to the table, it's all about presentation and is not strictly necessary. If you want to truss, just tie the tips of the drumsticks together with a short length of clean kitchen twine. Snip off the loose ends.

Wing Tips

To prevent the growth of bacteria from undercooked stuffing and to keep from having to overcook the bird to cook the stuffing through, heat the stuffing up in the micro-wave till it's hot and steaming before spooning it into the raw bird.

Recipes: Roasted, Grilled, and Stuffed

The recipes below offer simple techniques for preparing game hens. They're best roasted or grilled without a lot of fuss, but now and then you may want to stuff them for an elegant dinner. If you use these techniques and cooking times tailored to the needs of game hens, you can prepare Cornish game hens using practically any recipe for whole chickens. So consider the flavorings below as starting points for preparing them, then branch out to use any kind of herbs, marinades, or stuffings.

Wing Tips

The flavor and moistness of all the dishes in this chapter will be dramatically improved if you soak the Cornish game hens in a brining solution before cooking.

Herby Cornish Game Hens

Here's a straightforward recipe for roasting made even more flavorful by the addition of dried herbs. You may use any combination of herbs or any single one, such as tarragon or sage. For a simpler bird, follow this technique and don't use any herbs at all, just salt and pepper and butter on the outside, although the dab of lemon juice just before serving still makes a nice touch. The simple light glaze of balsamic vinegar or soy sauce helps ensure that your hens have a beautifully browned skin.

Serves 4

4 Cornish hens, each about 1 1/2 pounds

4 tablespoons (1/2 stick) butter, softened

1 teaspoon salt

Freshly ground black pepper

1 1/2 teaspoons each of dried thyme, rosemary, and basil

4 sprigs fresh parsley

2 lemons

1 tablespoon balsamic vinegar or soy sauce

1 tablespoon water

1. Preheat oven to 400°. Rinse the hens inside and out under cool running water and pat dry with paper towels.

2. Rub each bird with the softened butter, salt, and pepper. (Add a little salt and pepper to the inside cavity as well.) Place them at least two inches apart on a roasting rack.

3. Combine the dried herbs in a small cup and rub them all over the outside of each hen. Place a sprig of parsley inside each bird. Turn them breast-side down on the rack and place the roasting pan in the oven. Roast for 25 minutes, basting every 10 minutes with the pan juices.

4. Mix the balsamic vinegar or soy sauce and water in a small cup. Remove birds from oven, turn them breast-side up and brush each with this glaze. Pour 1 cup of water in the bottom of the roasting pan.

5. Return the birds to the oven and roast for 10–15 minutes longer, until a thermometer reads 170° when inserted in the thickest part of the thigh. Remove the birds from the oven. Half each lemon and squeeze a half over each bird. Serve immediately.

Don't Fowl Up

Adding water to the bottom of the roasting pan partway through the cooking will prevent the pan juices from drying out and burning. These recipes suggest adding the water twenty to twenty-five minutes into the cooking time, but if the fat is running and starting to smoke sooner than that in your oven, add water sooner.

Grilled Game Hens with Lemon and Oregano

A gas or charcoal grill is the perfect place to cook Cornish game hens. Grilling turns the birds into succulent, juicy little morsels, and splitting them in half ensures that each one cooks quickly enough to retain its tenderness and moisture. The Greek-inspired flavorings here stand up well to the smoky flavor. Serve the grilled birds atop a mound of pilaf, accompanied by a cucumber salad with yogurt and garlic in it. If you don't want to grill, cook the birds under the broiler for about eight minutes on each side.

Serves 2–4

2 Cornish game hens, 1 1/2–2 pounds each

1/4 cup extra virgin olive oil

1/4 cup lemon juice

2 cloves garlic, minced

1 teaspoon dried oregano

1 teaspoon salt

1/4 teaspoon chili pepper flakes

1/4 teaspoon freshly ground black pepper

2 tablespoons parsley, chopped

1. Split each bird in two and remove the backbone. Wash the halves under cold running water and pat dry.

2. In a large bowl, combine the olive oil, lemon juice, garlic, oregano, salt, chili flakes and pepper and whisk well until combined. Add the hen halves to the marinade and coat well. Cover and refrigerate for 20–30 minutes.

3. Cook on an outdoor grill over medium heat or under a broiler for 10–12 minutes on each side, brushing occasionally with the marinade until cooked through. Sprinkle with a little chopped parsley and serve. If you want to serve the remaining marinade on the side, boil it for 3 minutes and serve in a clean container.

Roast Cornish Game Hens with Celery and Almond Stuffing

The dollhouse tea party nature of game hens means they're begging to be stuffed, so that every guest gets something like a little holiday turkey on their individual plates. You can use any stuffing recipe for game hens, but this simple one with crunchy hints of almond, perfumed with celery and onion, makes a light stuffing that complements the delicate flavor of the bird.

Serves 4

4 Cornish game hens, about 1 1/2 pounds each

2 tablespoons butter, softened

1 teaspoon salt

Freshly ground black pepper

2 tablespoons apricot jam

2 tablespoons chicken stock

For stuffing:

1 1/2 tablespoons butter

1 medium onion, finely chopped

2 stalks celery, finely chopped

1/4 cup chicken stock

1 1/2 cups breadcrumbs

1/4 cup slivered almonds, toasted

2 tablespoons fresh parsley, chopped

1/2 teaspoon dried thyme leaves

1/2 teaspoon salt

1/4 teaspoon grated nutmeg

1/4 teaspoon freshly ground black pepper

1. Rinse the game hens and pat dry. Rub the hens with the butter and sprinkle the salt and pepper inside and out. Set aside while you prepare the stuffing.

2. Heat the butter in a skillet over medium heat until foaming. Add the onion and celery and cook for 3–4 minutes until soft and transparent. Remove the cooked onion and celery to a large bowl and add the remaining stuffing ingredients. Stir well to combine.

3. Preheat oven to 400°. Stuff each bird loosely with the stuffing and place on a rack, breast-side down, at least two inches apart.

4. Roast the game hens for 20–25 minutes until well browned. Stir together the apricot and chicken stock in a small cup. Turn the game hens breast-side up and brush with the apricot glaze. Add 1 cup of water to the pan and return to the oven.

5. Roast for a further 20–25 minutes until the birds are deep golden brown and a meat thermometer inserted in the stuffing registers 160°. Remove the hens from the oven and brush with the remaining glaze. Let rest for 5 minutes before serving.

The Least You Need to Know

➤ Rock Cornish game hens are not baby chickens, but a hybrid of the meaty American White Rock chicken and the flavorful English Cornish hen, and bred to be little.

➤ Buy the smallest game hens you can find, preferably 3/4 to one pound, although you may see them as large as two pounds.

➤ If you can only find the larger birds, split them right up the middle before roasting and serve one half per person.

➤ The meat tends to be quite tender, but the hens are also prone to dry out while roasting, so monitor them closely and don't overcook.

Chapter 31

The Big Challenge: Turkey

In This Chapter

➤ Who's afraid of the big bad turkey?

➤ Talking turkey: Tips for better cooking

➤ You don't have to get up at dawn: Turkey recipes

Roasting a whole turkey has long been a rite of passage for cooks, but the mythology surrounding the Thanksgiving bird is far more intimidating than the actual procedure.

Who's Afraid of the Big Bad Turkey?

As befits its status as the centerpiece of the Thanksgiving meal, turkey is an all-American bird. Turkeys, like potatoes, were introduced to Europe by explorers, in the turkey's case by Spaniards. They were called "turkeycocks" by the English, appropriating a then-current name for Guinea fowl, which were considered native to Turkish lands.

Nowadays we call females "turkey hens" and males are "toms" or "gobblers," the latter stemming from the fact that only males have the large red wattle hanging from their throats.

Only the nobility dined on the first turkeys in Europe, but gradually the bird began to be bred and made its way throughout the continent. Even in England, where the Christmas goose was a firmly enmeshed tradition, turkey grew in popularity to become the holiday bird, and even today, many in the British Isles celebrate Christmas dinner with a turkey (and a ham on the side for good measure).

Feathered Facts

Cooked turkey contains the chemical tryptophan, which can make you drowsy. (Tryptophan is also found in hot milk, created, as in turkey, through a chemical reaction in heating.) Tryptophan also creates a sense of well-being, which may be, scientists tell us, why so many people like to happily doze on the sofa all afternoon after Thanksgiving dinner.

Feathered Facts

George Washington named November 26 as a day of national thanksgiving in 1789, for that year only. That year, the Protestant Episcopal Church declared the first Thursday in November a regular day of thanks, "unless another day be appointed by the civil authorities." Different states named their own Thanksgiving Day, but there wasn't a national holiday until 1863, when Abraham Lincoln named the last Thursday in November as a national day of Thanksgiving.

The first Thanksgiving took place in Plymouth in 1621, when the colonists gratefully celebrated the harvest. The colonists had survived a terribly hard winter, and Governor William Bradford declared a three-day feast of thanksgiving and prayer. The misty-eyed memory of Indians delivering popcorn and pumpkin pie that appears in school plays probably never happened, but according to firsthand accounts, some ninety Indians joined the celebration and contributed deer and wild turkeys.

The birds that Americans have eaten since then have grown increasingly large. Turkeys have been bred over the years to be bigger and bigger, and this has often been to the detriment of flavor. Wild turkeys, such as the pilgrims ate, were much smaller and stringier, the flesh tasting more like the wild game they were than the domesticated birds we know. "Wild" turkeys are still available on the market, but today these tend to be more of a free-range product, raised eating a better supply of different grains and able to roam outside, but raised with human help nonetheless. If you know your supplier and sources, you may be able to find a real wild turkey, and the gamier taste is well worth the cost. (Perhaps the best, if not the most practical, way to get a real one is to hunt it yourself.)

There is a lesson to be learned from wild turkeys without hunting for them, though. The largest whole birds are usually no bigger than twelve to fifteen pounds and domestic turkeys tend to taste better when smaller, too. The smaller birds are usually hens, and the big ones, from twelve to twenty-four pounds or so, are gobblers or toms, though there's no real difference in taste in the sexes.

No matter what size turkey you buy, you can expect about twice as much white meat as dark. Turkey has very similar nutritional information to chicken's, and it's slightly lower in fat.

Turkeys are usually selected on the basis of how many guests are coming, figuring about a pound per person. If you're expecting a big crowd for Thanksgiving, you might consider roasting two smaller turkeys instead of sacrificing flavor and moistness by preparing one really big one. And with the techniques we'll discuss below, roasting two doesn't have to be appreciably harder than roasting one. Two birds will actually cook faster than one big one, with less chance of drying out.

Don't buy a bird whose package says it's "self-basting." This means that the turkey has been injected with, usually, a mixture of water and oil, often some heart-unhealthy palm oil. True, your turkey will probably taste a little moister, but at what cost? You're paying extra for an injection whose content you can't be sure of, when you can brine the turkey at home and use proper cooking methods for moisture.

Talking Turkey: Tips for Better Cooking

There are cooks who'll say that turkeys are just big chickens and the same techniques that apply to one apply to the other. But turkey is a different bird, with much dryer, coarser meat, particularly when you get into the really big turkeys of eighteen to twenty pounds or more. The bigger the bird is, the more tasteless the flesh is likely to be. Certainly, cooking methods are going to overlap, but you can't expect to drop a turkey in the roasting pan like a big chicken and simply extend the cooking time.

Turkey must be fully thawed before cooking. Most turkeys, whether they're labeled fresh or frozen, are actually going to feel frozen when you buy them. The fresh ones have been held at a low temperature which feels frozen to the consumer but which meets industry standards for fresh (see p. 12). Ideally, turkey should be thawed in its wrapping over several days in the refrigerator. This will take four to five hours per pound.

If you need to speed the thawing somewhat, you can put it in a sinkful of cold water (see p. 18) but never use hot water, which encourages the growth of bacteria. The cold water method will take an hour per pound. Even if the outside of the turkey feels thawed, you must also reach into the cavity and make sure the inside is not frozen. Frozen patches of flesh may well not reach the temperatures necessary in the oven to kill possibly harmful bacteria.

For this reason, it's best not to roast turkey at a temperature lower than 300°. Even though you can roast chicken long and slow at a low temperature, turkey needs to roast for so much longer that harmful bacteria may have too much opportunity to thrive. The optimal low temperature, should you wish to roast turkey slowly, is 325°.

For safety, and indeed, best taste, turkey should reach 160° to 165° in the breast, and 170° in the thigh. Don't trust the pop-out timers that come in some turkeys. They often don't release at the right temperature, either too soon or too late. It's best to use a digital instant-read thermometer, particularly if you've stuffed the turkey. The stuffing must register 160° to eliminate bacteria.

Like chicken, domestic turkey benefits particularly from brining. It takes much longer to brine a turkey than a chicken, so for best results when roasting the whole bird, put the turkey in a very large stockpot or brand-new, sterile bucket, and cover it with water (at least a gallon and probably more). Add two cups salt and a few tablespoons of sugar and stir well. Leave the turkey soaking in this solution overnight and your finished product will be moister and tastier.

251

The traditional method of roasting the whole turkey altogether can be improved dramatically by letting the bird lie on its side during the roasting. This lets the thighs and legs cook through nicely while keeping the breast from overcooking. The breast is, like chicken's, the part most prone to be dry, and when turkey breast is dry, its taste and texture are like cotton. Letting it rest on its side in the roasting pan lets the fat of the back and thighs drip down through the breast.

Start the bird in a hot oven, 400° to 425°, for about thirty minutes and then reduce the heat to 325° to 350° for the remaining cooking time. The high-heat start helps create a beautifully browned skin and speeds up the cooking when combined with the side-ways roasting technique.

How long to roast is not an exact science, despite what some cookbooks argue. The final cooking time can be altered by so many factors: there are variations in oven temperature, in degree of coolness in the bird going into the oven, in stuffing temperature, etc. An unstuffed turkey should roast in a 350° oven for approximately fifteen minutes per pound, and a stuffed one should roast approximately eighteen minutes a pound. Thus a 10-pound bird will roast in about 2 1/2 hours if not stuffed, and in three hours if stuffed.

The best way to judge is with a digital instant-read thermometer. The breast should be about 165° to be at its moistest, but the legs are better at a higher temperature, 170° to 175°. The stuffing should be, for safety, 160°. When cooked breast-side up, however, the breast will always reach a higher temperature more quickly than the legs, so read how to avoid this with breast-side down cooking below.

Even with carefully calculated times and instant-read thermometers, though, turkeys need a lot of attention in the oven. They should be basted every twenty minutes with the pan juices, turned occasionally if using the breast-side down method below, and sometimes the breast must be tented with foil if it's starting to overbrown near the end of cooking. A roasting turkey is a work in progress, and it should not be considered complete until it has been carved and brought to the table.

Some cooks like to ensure moisture by in essence steaming the bird, either in a tightly sealed foil tent or in a roasting bag. While this will let the turkey cook faster from the steam's concentrated heat, and also create moist breast meat, you won't end up with the beautifully caramelized skin of a perfectly roasted turkey. If you do want to seal up the bird, fit the inside of your roasting pan with long sheets of foil, with their edges folded together to create a seal. Set the stuffed and seasoned bird down on top of the foil in the pan, and bring the edges of the foil up over the turkey, rolling them together to lock in the steam. Roast in the foil, without opening, at 350° for about two hours for a 15-pound turkey. Carefully open the foil and brush some butter or olive oil on the turkey, then roast for another twenty to thirty minutes without covering, until the breast is browned.

Quick-Time Turkey

There is another method, however, to ensure that the turkey breast emerges from the oven in optimal condition. Dismantle your turkey before cooking by removing the legs whole and roasting them in the oven at the same time as the breast, but in a different pan.

Julia Child exhibited this method on a morning talk show some years ago to the utter astonishment of the host, who couldn't imagine that any American would want to desecrate a turkey before it had arrived on its serving platter at the table. But her method makes perfect sense, not to mention that it allows you to cook a whole turkey in less than a third of the usual amount of time. It's similar to the French method for cooking duck, where you eat the breast in its ideal state while the legs are removed and popped back into the oven to roast to dark-brown perfection.

This method of separate cooking works best with an unstuffed turkey—if your turkey is to be cooked in parts, no reason why the stuffing shouldn't also be baked separately, too. The legs will probably be done first, after about fifty minutes. Using an instant-read thermometer, check the breast and remove it from the oven when the breast reaches 160° to 165°, usually after about an hour in a 350° oven. But trust your thermometer over your clock.

Once you get used to the unorthodox cooking of turkey, you'll rapidly get more accustomed to unorthodox recipes. Despite turkey's healthful, low-fat qualities, and its increasing availability ground or in parts, Americans still tend to think of it as a holiday bird. But the Italians have none of the American reverence for turkey, and they subject it to some of the most interesting treatments anywhere. They slice the breast into medallions and deep-fry it or saute it with herbs and olive oil, tomato sauce, and olives. They fricassee the thighs and marinate the breast. And the turkey tastes wonderful. Turkey's distinctive flavor is strong enough to stand up to potent herbs such as basil and rosemary, but turkey also abides peaceably with acidic flavors such as tomato and even pomegranate.

Italian turkey recipes are a good way to bring turkey out of the Thanksgiving closet and into everyday cooking. So is simply buying a breast and either roasting or poaching it. You'll have sandwich meat on hand that's much lower in sodium content than the deli type, and you can substitute cooked turkey for nearly any recipe that calls for cooked chicken.

Feathered Facts

In 1939, President Franklin Delano Roosevelt changed the date of Thanksgiving to one week earlier to lengthen shopping time before Christmas. This lasted until 1941, when Congress ruled that starting in 1942, Thanksgiving on the fourth Thursday of November would be a legal Federal holiday.

You Don't Have to Get Up at Dawn: Turkey Recipes

First, here's a simple method with a couple of stuffing variations to help you make the best Thanksgiving or Christmas turkey. Then, to bring low-fat and delicious turkey into other days of the year, some exciting and different ways to prepare turkey that are a far cry from the usual holiday bird.

Turkey is carved just like chicken (p. 29), with the parts disjointed in the same way, except that the pieces are much larger. Although you can make long slices along the breast, an easier method is to slice off the whole breast, angling the carving knife down along the breastbone, and then slicing the breast shortways into serving pieces. The drumsticks and thighs may also be carved into slices for serving.

Roast Turkey with Sage and Onion Cornbread Stuffing

You can stuff the bird or bake the stuffing on the side in a separate dish. Either way, following the technique below, you should end up with just-cooked breast meat that's juicy and tender, and moist thighs that aren't underdone. A 10- to 12-pound bird provides the best flavor and enough meat to serve ten people, with enough leftovers for turkey sandwiches and maybe even a turkey divan.

Serves 10–12

1 10–12-pound turkey

4 tablespoons (1/2 stick) butter, softened

Giblets from turkey, with neck, without liver

1 onion, quartered

1 carrot, cut into chunks

1 bay leaf

5 black peppercorns

1 tablespoon salt

For the stuffing:

4 tablespoons (1/2 stick) butter

2 large onions, chopped

2 stalks celery, chopped

2 tablespoons dried sage (don't use ground sage, which can taste bitter)

1 cup chicken stock

1/2 teaspoon salt

1/2 teaspoon freshly ground black pepper

4 cups fresh cornbread crumbs

1. Prepare the turkey for roasting by brining overnight, if desired (see p. 41). Rinse and pat dry. Rub the turkey all over with the softened butter and tablespoon of salt. Place the turkey on a roasting rack in a roasting pan and set aside while you prepare the stuffing.

2. Preheat the oven to 400°. Put the giblets in a saucepan with the onion, carrot, bay, and peppercorns. Add a quart of cold water and bring to a simmer. Let cook, uncovered, very gently while turkey roasts.

3. Make the stuffing by melting the butter in a large skillet over medium heat. Saute the onions and celery until softened and translucent but not browned. Stir in the chicken stock, sage, salt, and pepper, and heat through. Place the cornbread crumbs in a large bowl and pour the stock and vegetables over the crumbs. Using a large spoon, mix the stuffing thoroughly.

4. Stuff the hot stuffing into the turkey and tie the legs together with a piece of clean kitchen twine if desired (trimming off the excess string). Turn the turkey on its side on the roasting rack and place pan in the oven immediately.

5. Roast at 400° for 30 minutes. Reduce heat to 350° and continue to roast, basting every 20 minutes with a large spoon or bulb baster. If you have a 10-pound stuffed bird, it will need approximately 18 minutes per pound, or about 3 hours.

6. About halfway through cooking time, turn the bird onto its other side. About 20 minutes before the end of cooking time, turn it breast-side up so the breast can brown.

7. The legs should move easily when the turkey is done. Pierce the thigh with a knife or skewer. The juices should run clear. A digital instant-read thermometer should register about 165° in the breast and 170° in the thigh, and 160° in the stuffing.

8. Remove the bird and let it sit at least 10 minutes before carving. If it needs to sit longer than 10 minutes while you finish cooking (up to about 30 minutes), lay foil lightly over the bird, but keep in mind that the skin won't be as crisp if the turkey has to sit underneath foil.

9. To make giblet gravy, if desired, strain the giblet stock and chop some of the giblets and return them to the stock. Collect the pan juices from the roasting pan and skim off the excess fat. Melt 3 tablespoons of butter and add 3 tablespoons all-purpose flour. Whisk in the pan juices and the giblet stock. Bring to a simmer. Cook till smooth and lightly thickened, 6–7 minutes. Season to taste with salt and pepper.

Stuffing Variation

This is a meaty and moist stuffing, combining the traditional flavors of apples and sausage but with the surprise addition of apple cider to moisten the stuffing. Sage appears here too—it's hard to do without it in stuffing—but you can substitute a combination of additional thyme and oregano or rosemary. If you want even more texture, add a handful of chopped toasted pecans.

To stuff 1 (10–12 pound) turkey

2 tablespoons butter

4 slices bacon, diced

1 large onion, chopped

1 tablespoon rubbed sage

1 teaspoon thyme

2 Granny Smith apples, peeled, cored, and grated

1 cup apple cider

1 teaspoon salt

1/2 teaspoon white pepper

1/2 pound mild breakfast sausage

3 cups dry white breadcrumbs

1. Melt the butter in a large skillet over medium heat and fry the diced bacon. When the grease runs, add the onion and cook till softened and translucent but not brown. Add the sage and thyme, then stir in the grated apple and cook till softened 3–4 minutes. Stir in the apple cider, salt, and white pepper, and bring to a boil. Remove from heat.

2. In a large bowl, place the sausage and breadcrumbs. Pour on the onion and apple mixture and mix well. Stuff into turkey and immediately put turkey in the oven, following instructions on p. 255.

Don't Fowl Up

Don't stuff your turkey until right before it goes in the oven to prevent bacteria from growing. To speed up cooking time, you can stuff the turkey with very hot stuffing. If the stuffing has to sit on the counter before you're ready to put the turkey in, heat it in the microwave and then spoon it into the bird. Don't overheat sausage stuffing or you'll cook the sausage.

Italian Turkey Medallions with Wine and Mushrooms

Here's a fine example of how Italians, not laden down with the patriotic associations turkey has for Americans, treat "tacchino" like any other pale meat. Although Italians will occasionally roast the entire bird, it's more common to see the boneless breast cut on the diagonal into thin slices, or medallions, and fried or braised. It's rare to find whole, boneless turkey breast in the US, but you can easily find a whole turkey breast on the bone. Trim one side of it off the bone, then slice this "tenderloin" of turkey into medallions yourself. In this dish, the thin slices are fried in olive oil and butter for flavor, then quickly cooked with a wine-flavored mushroom sauce. Serve over squares of toasted polenta, with a light fruity wine, such as a zinfandel, and a garlicky salad of ripe summer tomatoes and basil, dressed in olive oil.

Serves 6

One side of a turkey breast (buy a 6–8-pound breast and cut half of it off the bone to use here)

2 tablespoons butter

2 tablespoons olive oil

2 cloves garlic, minced

1/2 pound mushrooms, sliced

1/2 cup red wine

1/4 teaspoon dried oregano

1/4 cup light cream

1/2 teaspoon salt

Freshly ground black pepper

Freshly grated Parmesan cheese for garnish

1. Trim (or ask your butcher to trim) one side of the turkey breast off the bone, sliding the knife carefully around the breastbone. You should have a whole piece of turkey breast weighing 3–4 pounds. Slice this on the diagonal into medallions about 1/4-inch thick.

2. Heat the butter in a skillet over medium heat with 1 tablespoon of the olive oil. As soon as the butter stops foaming, add the turkey medallions in batches and cook till lightly browned, about 6 minutes for each batch. Remove to a platter and set aside.

3. Heat the remaining tablespoon of oil in the skillet and add the garlic. Saute for 1 minute, then add the mushrooms and cook till softened. Stir in the red wine and oregano, and bring to a boil. Immediately add the cream and return to a boil.

4. Stir in the salt and pepper and let simmer for 1–2 minutes, till sauce starts to reduce and thicken. Return the turkey to the pan, heat through briefly, and pour onto a serving platter. Garnish with a generous dusting of Parmesan cheese, if desired, and serve immediately.

For an Italian twist on roast turkey, combine 1 tablespoon of minced garlic with 1 1/2 tablespoons of dried rosemary, 1 teaspoon of salt, and 2 tablespoons of olive oil. Rub this under the skin and all over the outside of a 6-pound turkey breast, and roast on a rack in a 375° oven for about an hour, basting every fifteen minutes. The finished bird will have a crisp skin, and the meat is perfumed with the rosemary and garlic. It's delicious sliced hot, and perhaps even better on sandwiches the next day.

The Least You Need to Know

➤ When selecting a turkey, plan on about a pound of turkey for each diner, as well as a little extra for leftovers.

➤ Even though huge turkeys look impressive when you carry them to the table, for better flavor and moister meat it's best to buy and roast smaller birds, from ten to twelve pounds.

➤ When roasting a whole turkey, consider it a work in progress until it's carved and served. If you quit paying attention and forget to baste, it can easily overcook and dry out.

➤ For a more foolproof method for moist turkey, roast the bird on its side, turning to its other side occasionally, and only putting it breast side up to brown during the last twenty to twenty-five minutes of roasting. This lets the fat of the opposite leg drip down through the breast while cooking and helps keep the breast meat moist.

Chapter 32

Just Ducky: All About Ducks

In This Chapter

➤ Getting your ducks in a row

➤ Knowing when to duck: Tips for better cooking

➤ Roast duck and more: Recipes

Americans simply don't eat duck as frequently as the rest of the world, but we probably should. While duck meat is a little more fatty than other poultry (except for goose), the flesh is not only extremely delicious but also full of B-complex vitamins and iron.

Getting Your Ducks in a Row

Most of the time, the frozen bird you'll find at the supermarket labeled "duck" is a Pekin, a white-feathered strain that weighs from four to six pounds. In restaurants, you'll often see duck listed on the menu specifically as Muscovy. This is a black-feathered breed whose breast is much larger and meatier than the Pekin. It is also more expensive, and although increasingly available from gourmet markets, you may have to order in advance.

The other duck to look out for in US markets is the Moulard, a large, meaty cross between the Pekin and the Muscovy. Moulards are bred for their fattened livers, foie gras, and the meat is a little leaner than that of the Pekin.

If you live in a metropolitan area that has a Chinatown, you can probably find fresh ducks hanging in the window (and even live ones, should you wish). The ducks in Asian markets are often featured with their heads and feet intact to show the health of the bird. You can also buy them roasted.

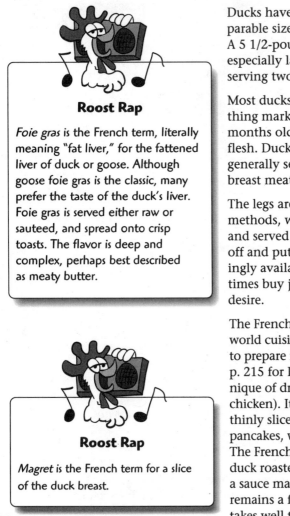

Roost Rap

Foie gras is the French term, literally meaning "fat liver," for the fattened liver of duck or goose. Although goose foie gras is the classic, many prefer the taste of the duck's liver. Foie gras is served either raw or sauteed, and spread onto crisp toasts. The flavor is deep and complex, perhaps best described as meaty butter.

Roost Rap

Magret is the French term for a slice of the duck breast.

Ducks have far less meat than a chicken of comparable size, so buy the biggest duck you can find. A 5 1/2-pound bird will make four servings that aren't especially large. You may want to plan on one duck serving two people, as most restaurants do.

Most ducks are no more than 3 months old, and anything marketed as duckling should be less than 2 months old. The younger the duck, the more tender the flesh. Duck meat should not be terribly chewy—it's generally served somewhat rarer than chicken, with the breast meat pink.

The legs are cooked longer in the traditional French methods, with the breast being removed from the oven and served while still slightly rare, and the legs carved off and put back into the oven. Duck parts are increasingly available in American stores, and you can sometimes buy just the legs or just the breasts, should you desire.

The French and the Chinese are the masters of duck in world cuisine, with each culture offering countless ways to prepare it. Peking Duck is one of the best known (see p. 215 for Peking Chicken, with the Peking Duck technique of drying the skin for greater crispness applied to chicken). It's served with great ceremony, the breast thinly sliced and layered with the crispy skin on little pancakes, with tangy plum sauce and sliced scallions. The French developed the classic Duck a l'Orange, the duck roasted with orange in the cavity, then coated with a sauce made of orange zest and the pan juices. It remains a favorite preparation because the rich dark meat takes well to the acid flavors of a wide variety of fruit.

Knowing When to Duck: Tips for Better Cooking

Duck is a fatty bird, but the fat is not marbled throughout the flesh. Rather, it's in a thick layer just under the skin, and with proper cooking, the fat can be made to drain away. It's this same fat separating the skin from the flesh that makes possible the crispy skin that's the hallmark of a well-roasted duck.

First, wash the duck inside and out and pat it dry with a paper towel. Then you want to remove all the obvious yellow fat, such as the clumps around the cavity opening. There will be two big flaps of fat, not skin, that can be cut or pulled off. Then using a fork or the tip of a sharp knife, prick the bird all over on the back, legs, and breast. This lets the fat drip out of the skin as the duck roasts. This is the most important step in cooking duck, and if you don't do this, you won't get a good result. Your duck will be fatty and the skin will be greasy and not crisp if the fat isn't allowed to drain out.

Duck should always be roasted on a rack, to elevate it from all the fat that's dripping down into the pan. This same fat means that duck doesn't need to be basted, nor does it need to lie on its breast to stay moist. The breast meat is dark meat in a duck, and it will stay moist on its own. Turning the roasting duck on its side will speed up the cooking of the legs, without overcooking the breast.

When you place the duck in the oven, put some water in the bottom of the roasting pan, about one cup. This small quantity of water will keep the fat from burning and smoking when it first hits the bottom of a hot dry roasting pan.

Duck is usually roasted in a 350° oven, no higher. The high fat content makes it unsuited to very high heat roasting, which will make the fat run out rapidly and start to smoke in the oven. Keep the oven at an even heat.

Duck is usually cooked for less time than chicken. Unlike chicken (and almost all other poultry), parts of the duck can be served slightly rare. For the average 5-pound duck, plan on about seventy-five to eighty minutes in the oven. The juices should run mostly clear, and the juices and meat can have a slightly rosy tinge.

Overcooked duck is tough and dry and flavorless. Even the largest duck, up to seven pounds, should not stay in the oven over two hours, and smaller ducks, such as those three to four pounds, are cooked just over an hour.

Duck is not usually served stuffed. The classic preparations rely on slightly acidic sauces and accompaniments to the finished duck, but stuffing is rare because the short amount of time duck needs in the oven doesn't allow stuffing to be properly cooked.

Duck is jointed and carved like chicken. The legs are removed and jointed. The breast is longer, so when carving roast duck, cut slices diagonally from the tail, moving toward the front of the breast.

Wing Tips

Skim off and reserve the clear fat from the roasting pan and save it for excellent roast potatoes. See p. 269 for the technique for roasting potatoes in goose fat, but use the duck fat instead.

Roast Duck and More: Recipes

Duck's dark rich meat takes well to acidic flavors such as orange and cranberry, and the recipes below reflect this autumnal flavor. Duck is not heavy in and of itself, but it tends to feature in elegant meals that can be quite filling, such as the Italian-inspired duck with white beans below.

Simple Roast Duck with Variations

Like roast chicken, you can do a lot with a simple roast duck. The classic orange preparation involves little more than the addition of a whole orange to the most basic recipe below, and other fruits can be employed with similar flair. Although it's possible to use various spice rubs and basting liquids with roast duck, in general, duck is eaten rarely enough in American homes that most people prefer to enjoy the pure duck flavor, perhaps accented with a fruit.

Pan juices from duck can make the best sauce of all. Serve duck with potatoes and fresh, simply prepared vegetables such as green peas.

Serves 4

1 4–5-pound duck, with giblets

1 lemon (optional)

Salt and freshly ground black pepper

1 tablespoon all-purpose flour

1. Remove the giblets from the interior. Rinse and pat dry the duck.

2. Place the giblets, except for the liver (save and freeze for use in the pate on p. 139), in a saucepan. Cover with 2–3 cups water and bring to a simmer. Do not boil. Lower heat and simmer gently for about an hour. Strain out the giblets and discard, reserving the stock.

3. Meanwhile, preheat oven to 350°. Prick the skin of the duck all over with a fork or tip of a sharp knife. If using lemon, cut it in half and rub it all over the skin. Rub salt and pepper all over the outside, and place the duck on a roasting rack in a shallow roasting pan.

4. Place in the oven and roast for 1 hour and 15 minutes for a medium-rare breast, and up to 1 hour and 35 minutes for a well-done breast. Remove from the oven. Set the duck aside on a warmed platter.

5. Skim the fat off the pan juices. Pour the pan juices into a small saucepan over medium heat and blend in the flour, whisking to remove all lumps. Slowly pour in 1 1/2–2 cups of the giblet stock. Bring to a gentle boil, stirring till sauce is thick and smooth. Carve the duck and pass the sauce separately.

Variations

Duck a l'Orange

Using a sharp knife or vegetable peeler, peel just the orange part, the zest, off 1 orange, avoiding the bitter white pith beneath. Trim off the pith and discard, and cut the orange's flesh into quarters. Place the orange flesh inside the duck's cavity before roasting.

Finely mince the zest and add it to the skimmed pan juices when making the gravy above. Finish the gravy and stir in 1/4 cup orange juice and 2 tablespoons Grand Marnier (or Cointreau or other orange liqueur), if desired. Carve the duck and serve with the sauce.

Duck with Cranberry

Roast the duck according to the instructions above. Measure 1/4 cup out of 1 (14-ounce) can whole cranberry sauce, and strain the whole cranberries out of the 1/4 cup, reserving this strained sauce to brush over the duck 10 minutes before end of roasting.

When making the gravy, add the remaining whole cranberry sauce to the skimmed pan juices along with 1/4 cup red wine. Reduce the stock in the gravy to 1 cup. Carve duck and serve with the sauce.

Wing Tips

Cook your duck giblets in chicken stock for an even richer gravy.

Autumn Duck with White Beans

This Italian-inspired dish pays homage to the natives of Tuscany, who are known in Italy as "bean-eaters." Jointed duck is pan-fried till crispy, then cooked with creamy white cannellini (white kidney) beans, accented with the pungent flavors of rosemary and sage. The finished dish is rich, fragrant, warming, and deeply satisfying. Serve with crusty white bread, a garlicky green salad, and a bottle of Chianti.

Serves 4–6

1 pound uncooked white beans, such as cannellini or navy beans

1 large onion, chopped

2 cloves garlic, minced

1 4–5-pound duck, jointed

Salt and freshly ground black pepper

2 tablespoons olive oil

1 cup canned whole tomatoes, with juice

1 cup dry white wine

1 teaspoon dried rosemary

1 teaspoon dried sage

1. Soak the beans in cold water overnight. Rinse and cover with cold water in a large saucepan. Add onion and garlic and cook for 1 1/2 hours, adding more water if necessary, until tender but not mushy. Drain the beans, reserving 2 cups of the cooking liquid. Return the beans to their cooking pot.

2. Wash and pat dry the duck pieces and sprinkle with salt and pepper. Heat a large heavy skillet, preferably cast-iron, over medium-high heat. Add olive oil to the hot skillet. Place the duck pieces in the hot oil and cook until well-browned, about 10–12 minutes, turning occasionally so the pieces brown evenly.

3. Add the duck to the beans in the large saucepan. Stir in the tomatoes, wine, rosemary, and sage along with the 2 cups of reserved cooking liquid from the beans. Bring to a boil and reduce heat. Cover loosely and simmer over a low heat about an hour, till duck is tender and sauce has reduced. Serve hot.

Duck Salmi

Salmi is essentially an elegant French way to deal with leftovers. It's a rich ragout, or stew, of roasted game cooked with red wine or port. The word comes from the French "salmigondis," meaning medley or mixture.

If you made a stock with the duck giblets, use that instead of chicken stock. Serve the salmi with mashed potatoes.

Serves 6

2 tablespoons butter

1 small onion, minced

2 cloves garlic, minced

1/2 pound button mushrooms, sliced

2 tablespoons tomato paste

2 tablespoons all-purpose flour

3 cups chicken stock

1 cup port or strong red wine

2–3 cups cooked duck meat, sliced

1/2 cup black olives, pitted and sliced

1/2 teaspoon freshly ground black pepper

Salt

Chopped fresh parsley for garnish

1. Melt the butter in a large saucepan over medium heat. Saute the onion till very lightly browned, then add the garlic and mushrooms and cook till softened.
2. Stir in the tomato paste and sprinkle the flour over all. Cook 2 minutes, then slowly blend in the chicken stock, stirring to prevent lumps from forming.
3. Add the wine and bring to a boil. Reduce heat and simmer 5–10 minutes, till sauce is slightly reduced and thickened. Add the duck, black olives, and pepper. Taste and add salt if necessary. Garnish with chopped parsley and serve hot.

Don't Fowl Up

If you only have canned olives, leave them out of the salmi. The texture of canned olives is too mushy in this dish.

The Least You Need to Know

➤ Duck is all dark meat, with a thick layer of fat directly beneath the skin.

➤ Duck's richness of flavor takes well to acidic, fruit-based sauces.

➤ To let the fat drain out and allow the skin to become crisp, it's necessary to pierce the duck's skin all over with the tip of a sharp knife before roasting. If you neglect this step, the duck will be greasy.

➤ Unlike chicken (and almost all other poultry), duck can be served a bit rare, with the breast meat having a slightly rosy hue.

Chapter 33

Duck, Duck . . . Goose!

In This Chapter

➤ The noble fowl

➤ Loose as a goose: Tips for better cooking

➤ Great goose recipes

Goose is the ultimate in poultry, rich, fat, and gamy—and it's one of the few foods in the world where the fat is prized equally with the flesh.

The Noble Fowl

The British chef Keith Floyd refers to goose as the queen of poultry. Certainly there's something particularly elegant about the bird that gives us foie gras, one of the world's most sought-after luxury foods. The fattening of goose livers by force-feeding the geese dates back to the ancient Egyptians.

The flesh of goose is very dark, but cooked, it's quite lean. The goose is padded with fat between its skin and meat, however, so it must be carefully cooked to drain out as much of the fat as possible. The fat should be saved after roasting the goose. It's prized by cooks for its flavor, most especially for roasting potatoes and, in France, for its use in dishes such as cassoulet, the rich bean and meat stew from the south of France.

Anything you can do to a duck, you can do to a goose, with few exceptions. Goose must be pricked all over like duck to let the fat escape, but goose is also often blanched in boiling water to tighten the skin and force out the fat. A 10-pound goose can release up to five cups of fat, so no matter how big it looks in the package, expect it to shrink considerably by the time it reaches the table. Plan on about one pound of goose per person, although, like duck, goose has far less meat on its bones per pound when compared to chicken.

Goose is usually roasted stuffed with a nonabsorbent stuffing, such as a fruit mixture (see below), to keep the stuffing from absorbing the fat dripping out of the goose.

Geese for roasting range from eight to fifteen pounds. The ones force-fed to fatten their livers can be nearly thirty pounds but these usually do not come to market for roasting. Their tougher flesh is used for making pates and confit, which is a method of preserving and tenderizing poultry with fat.

Geese can usually be found frozen in supermarkets during the year, and around Christmas time, geese are available fresh from gourmet markets and butchers. Indeed, upmarket butcher shops in New York City offer free-range geese for upwards of $20 a pound during the Christmas season. But there are far more affordable geese to be had if you're looking, especially if you buy a frozen bird, and because of its high fat content, goose freezes very well.

If you're fortunate enough to find a fresh goose at a price that won't keep your kids from going to college, make sure you buy one with evenly dark pink flesh and the plumpest breast. If the feet are still on it, as you might see in an Asian market, try to find feet that aren't dark red and hairy, which means it's an older bird. Younger birds are more tender.

Loose as a Goose: Tips for Better Cooking

Wash the goose thoroughly inside and out before cooking, removing giblets. Prick the skin all over with a fork or the tip of a sharp knife to help the fat escape. Pull off the loose fat visible around the cavity, cut it into small pieces, and put it in the bottom of the roasting pan. Roasting will render it into valuable cooking fat, as discussed below.

Always put some water in the bottom of the roasting pan before starting to roast, about one cup, most especially when you've put fat in the bottom. This is to prevent the first juices that will drip out of the bird from burning when they hit the bottom of the hot dry roasting pan. The water will keep the fat from spitting and burning, and also help prevent the meat juices draining from the goose from burning black on the bottom of the pan.

Some cooks believe that you can help crisp the skin and eliminate more fat if you dip the goose into boiling water for about a minute, then let it dry thoroughly overnight, uncovered on a rack in the refrigerator, before roasting. It's probably more helpful to baste the bird occasionally with a ladle of boiling water while it's in the oven. The heat of the water helps loosen the fat from the skin and encourages it to drain out through the holes you pricked.

While it's true that you don't have to baste duck, it's important to remember that goose has a lot more fat than duck under the skin. Your job when cooking it is to get all that fat out of there, or as much as possible. If you don't, the skin will be soggy, greasy, and chewy instead of tender-crisp and delectable.

Don't overcook goose. The oven should be no lower than 300°, no higher than 350°, except for a few minutes when starting cooking, and closer to 325°. A too-low oven won't melt the fat and let it drain well, and a very hot oven would cause all the fat draining out to smoke and spit. Cooking at 375° for ten to fifteen minutes when starting to roast will get the fat flowing, but don't forget to turn the oven down. If the fat is spitting even at a lower temperature, add an extra 1/2 cup of just-boiled water to the roasting pan.

Unlike duck, you don't want to have the breast of goose rare, but just cooked. Overcooked, it can be dry and tough. Plan on about fifteen minutes per pound for a stuffed goose, give or take a little. Use a digital instant-read thermometer to find when the thigh has reached 175° to 180°.

Goose is carved like chicken, although the breast is much longer. Make angled cuts on each side of the breast, starting near the legs, and work your way to the front.

The sheer quantity of fat draining into the roasting pan will astonish you, but in the case of goose, it's like liquid gold. After you've roasted the goose, skim the fat off the top of the roasting juices, strain it through a paper-towel lined strainer, and put it in a clean container in the refrigerator to solidify. The solids in the bottom of the pan are called cracklings. These browned fat particles are delicious mixed right into the gravy. Some cooks reserve them to sprinkle over salads or to flavor vegetables while cooking.

In this form, the fat will stay good for several weeks. If you want to purify this fat to preserve it for longer storage, up to many months, scoop all the solid white fat out of the container into a clean roasting pan, discarding any impurities in the bottom of the container. Put it in a 350° oven for one hour, until it's completely clear. The fat may spit a little to start. (You're trying to cook out all the water and impurities.) Strain out any solids in the roasting pan and discard. Let the fat cool and then put the clear liquid fat into a clean glass

Wing Tips

The main thing you want goose fat for is roasted potatoes. Parboil halved potatoes for fifteen minutes, leaving them quite firm, and heat the clear fat in a separate casserole in a 350° oven. Put the partially cooked potatoes in the hot fat, toss gently to coat, and roast for forty-five to sixty minutes until they're crispy and golden on the outside, tender and creamy inside.

Wing Tips

Use the goose fat for frying meat for stews, to add flavor and richness to gravies in place of butter, in small quantities to season vegetables and beans while cooking, in pates, and most particularly for roasting potatoes. Goose fat is a highly prized commodity in France, extremely expensive to buy, but you can render your own for the price of your goose. Even if you only use it for roast potatoes a couple times a year, you'll be very glad you did.

or plastic container. When it's completely cool, seal the container tightly and store the fat in the refrigerator. You'll probably have a little less than a quart, and it will stay fresh for many months. (Alternately, freeze the less-pure fat and keep it for up to six months.)

Don't Fowl Up

You can use a bulb baster or a spoon to skim off the fat, but the best way to separate fat from pan juices with any roast poultry is with a fat separator. These very inexpensive plastic devices are pitchers with the spout starting at the bottom instead of at the lip of the pitcher. When you pour in all the pan juices and fat, the fat quickly rises to the top, and then the pan juices for gravy can be poured off the bottom. As soon as the fat reaches the spout entrance at the bottom of the separator, you're done.

Great Goose Recipes

Roasting goose is the time-honored way to render the fat and make the skin crisp. It's not hard, but you have to pay attention. Braising, however, leaves the meat much more tender and flavorful, and renders out even more fat. You'll be giving up the crisp skin, but you'll have extra fat for a whole winter's worth of roasted potatoes.

Roast Goose with Sausage Stuffing

Sausage may seem like a heavy stuffing for such a fatty bird, but sausage's spiciness, lightened with bread and celery, is a perfect match for the richly flavored meat. Further, a thick and moist stuffing is less likely to soak up too much goose fat while cooking. Use a mild Italian sausage, lightly sweet, but with a good taste of fennel seeds. You can use packaged bread crumbs, but for the best flavor, trim the crusts off sourdough bread and pulse the bread in your food processor or blender to make fresh crumbs. Make sure you reserve the goose's liver to chop up in the stuffing. It adds a great deal of depth and suaveness of flavor.

The standard accompaniment for roast goose is applesauce, the fruit's acid cutting the rich flavor of the meat. Goose is also delicious with a fruit stuffing. If the sausage stuffing isn't to your taste, try either of the variations below.

Serves 6–8

1 12–14-pound goose

Salt and freshly ground black pepper

For stuffing:

2 tablespoons butter

1 large onion, chopped

2 stalks celery, thinly sliced

1/2 pound sweet Italian sausage or any mild breakfast sausage

2 cups fresh white breadcrumbs

The liver from the goose, finely chopped

1/2 cup walnuts, chopped

1/2 teaspoon dried sage

1/2 teaspoon dried thyme

1/4 teaspoon nutmeg

1/2 cup chicken stock

For gravy:

2 tablespoons butter

1/4 cup red wine or port

1. Wash and pat dry the goose. Prick the skin all over with a fork or the tip of a sharp knife. Rub with salt and pepper. Set on a roasting rack in a shallow pan. Preheat the oven to 375°.

2. To make the stuffing, melt the butter in a large skillet over medium heat. Add the onion and celery and saute until translucent. Pour into a bowl and add the remaining stuffing ingredients. Mix well, using your hands if necessary to work the sausage throughout (if the sausage is in skins and not loose, squeeze it out of the skins into the bowl and discard the skin).

3. Stuff the mixture into the cavity of the goose. Lay it breast-side down on the roasting pan. Add 1 cup of water to the bottom of the pan and put into the oven. Roast at 375° for 15 minutes, then reduce the heat to 325°.

continues

continued

4. Roast for 2 hours, basting every 15 minutes with either the pan juices or a ladleful of boiling water if desired.

5. Then turn the goose breast-side up and drain off the fat and pan juices that have collected in the pan. (If you want roast potatoes, you can use this fat in a separate pan to start cooking them now. Reserve the pan juices for gravy, if desired.)

6. Roast another hour, until the legs move slightly and the juices are mostly clear but slightly yellow.

7. Remove from oven and allow to sit about 15 minutes before carving. Blend the pan juices in a small saucepan over medium heat with butter and red wine or port and heat through. Carve the bird and serve gravy separately.

Don't Fowl Up

Unlike chicken, the legs of a goose will never move easily in their sockets when the bird is done. Base your judgment on temperature of the meat (finished at 180°) and length of time in the oven and whether the juices are mostly clear and slightly yellow.

Stuffing Variations

Any of these stuffing recipes can be used with chicken or any other fowl, and any other stuffing recipe in this book or elsewhere can be used with a goose. The recipes in this chapter are tailored to the rich flavor of a goose, but mixing and matching flavors can be good when it comes to roasting poultry.

Prune and Cognac Stuffing

This unusual stuffing is superb in goose and should be saved for a special occasion or holiday. Prunes are not usually America's ideal of high elegance, but the French know well that their concentrated sweetness makes a moist delicious stuffing. Soaked overnight in cognac, the prunes have a warm fruity richness that complements the dark goose meat perfectly.

1 cup prunes, pitted and chopped

1/2 cup cognac

2 tablespoons butter

1 large onion, minced

1 goose liver, chopped

2 cups fresh white breadcrumbs

1/2 teaspoon dried sage

1/4 teaspoon nutmeg

1. Put the prunes in a small glass bowl, cover with cognac, and stir. Soak overnight, covered, on the countertop.

2. Melt the butter in a skillet over medium heat and saute the onions until softened but not browned. Transfer the cooked onions to a large bowl and mix in the prunes with their liquid and the remaining stuffing ingredients.

3. Combine well and stuff the goose loosely in the body cavity just before it goes in the oven. Roast according to instructions above.

Apple and Chestnut Stuffing

A festive and Christmas-y stuffing, this one draws on the sweetness and acidity of the apples which blend perfectly with the slightly smoky flavor and toothsome texture of the chestnuts.

1 pound fresh chestnuts

3 tablespoons butter

1 large onion, chopped

2 medium tart apples (such as Granny Smith), peeled, cored and chopped

2 cups fresh white breadcrumbs

1 teaspoon salt

1 tablespoon fresh parsley

1/2 teaspoon dried marjoram

1/2 teaspoon dried thyme

1/4 teaspoon freshly ground black pepper

1. Cut an X in the bottom of each chestnut with a sharp knife to let the steam escape when roasting. Heat a cast-iron skillet over medium-high heat and put the chestnuts into the dry pan. Heat the chestnuts in the pan for 3–4 minutes, shaking regularly, then remove and let cool.

2. When the chestnuts are cool enough to handle, peel off the shells and place the nuts in a saucepan. Cover with 2 cups of water. Bring to a boil and simmer for about 20 minutes. Drain the chestnuts, cool them, and then chop coarsely.

3. Melt the butter in skillet over medium heat. Add the onions and saute until translucent. Stir in the apples and chestnuts and saute another 2–3 minutes. Place in a large bowl and mix in remaining ingredients.

4. Stuff the goose loosely in the body cavity just before it goes in the oven and roast according to instructions above.

Don't Fowl Up

Never stuff a goose or any other fowl until just before it goes in the oven. Letting a bird sit around stuffed, even in the refrigerator, can allow harmful bacteria to grow.

The Least You Need to Know

➤ Goose is a highly fatty bird, and it's important during cooking to let as much fat as possible drain out.

➤ A 10-pound goose may yield as much as five cups of fat.

➤ Save the highly flavorful fat, though, for cooking or roasting potatoes.

➤ The richness of goose makes it a special-occasion bird, calling for a special stuffing. Goose goes well with fruity stuffings such as one made with prunes soaked in cognac.

Chapter 34

Call of the Wild: Other Game Birds

In This Chapter

➤ What are game birds?

➤ Rules of the game: Tips for better cooking

➤ Playing the game: Recipes for game birds

The flesh of "wild" birds, even when raised domestically, tends to be lean, sometimes so lean that you have to add extra fat between the skin and flesh.

What Are Game Birds?

The game birds most commonly available in the US are squab, guinea fowl, pheasant, partridge, and quail.

Any of these birds that you find in the supermarket have been raised on a farm, although they're still considered game birds. The ancient Egyptians raised quail for food, the ancient Greeks domesticated the squab, and both partridge and guinea fowl have been bred for eating for centuries. These birds remain a breed and type that is found in the wild, however (unlike, say, the domestic chicken), so they are still considered to be game.

Pheasant is a slightly more recent upstart in North America, although they have been both hunted and bred in Europe for thousands of years, dating back to the ancient Romans. Pheasant were found unable to survive in the wild in North America in the late 1700s, and only as late as 1881 were they being successfully bred in captivity here.

The problem with game birds is not that they're farmed, but that mass breeding has often led to a similarity in flavor from species to species. One small, dark-meated bird tastes much like the other, and though there's some charm in their petite sizes, the meat is often lacking distinguishing characteristics.

The best way around this if you're in the market for game birds is to try to find a local purveyor. If you're fortunate enough to live in an area where there's a greenmarket or farmer's market, you may be able to find small farmers offering hand-raised fowl, most often free-range, that they've bred and raised from egg to table. These birds, who have had access to sky and water and assorted grain, not to mention the occasional insect, will have the best flavor available. Another alternative is to have friends who hunt and who will occasionally hand on a brace of pheasant or other birds.

Lastly, you can buy the frozen birds at the store and prepare them with care and attention to detail, surrounded by the best ingredients, that may allow you to salvage the flavor and even produce a downright delicious dish. So don't despair if all you can find is the frozen version.

Roost Rap

A "brace" of any type of bird is two birds.

Feathered Facts

Guinea fowl were quite popular in Colonial America and often raised at home. Guinea fowls, with their piercingly loud cries, used to serve as watch birds on farms. Their popularity waned in the latter part of the last century, but they were once a common sight on farms in America.

Squab

Squab are baby pigeons, eaten before they're 6 weeks old, while they're too young to fly. The flesh is dark, tender, and delicate. They're usually no bigger than one pound, and they can contain a good amount of meat for their size. The breasts are quite plump. Squab are good roasted whole, or split and grilled over a charcoal fire, or split and quickly broiled.

Guinea Fowl

Guinea fowl are very lean-fleshed birds with a slightly musky flavor. Originally from Africa, the Portuguese brought them to Europe in the 1500s. The breasts have light, mild-flavored meat, and the legs are dark with a stronger flavor. Larger guinea fowl, some weighing up to three pounds, are good braised, which ensures that the lean meat stays moist and tender. Smaller guinea fowl, usually under a pound, are often marinated to tenderize them and broiled or grilled.

Pheasant

Pheasant is one of the most widely available game birds, with beautiful brown and dark green plumage. The flesh has a mild, vaguely sweet flavor. Actual wild pheasant, rarely found in the US, tastes much stronger than the domestic type and the flesh is chewier. Commercially available pheasant is so mild and tender that the bird takes well to practically any recipe, particularly anything that requires chicken. Certain methods can help bring out the gamy taste, such as cooking the pheasant with juniper berries and wine.

Partridge

Partridge is the name that encompasses a wide variety of game birds. Grouse are partridges, though not all partridges are grouse. Grouse is rarely commercially available in the US, though in the British Isles it is considered one of the finest game birds. In the US, the most common type is the chukar partridge, with meaty legs and dark, lean flesh.

Quail

Quail are the tiniest of commercially available game birds in the US, usually less than half a pound in size. They look like tiny toy chickens, and they make a particularly charming presentation, especially in the classical French style on large croutons that have been spread with a paste of the quail's liver. The meat is delicate and flavorful, and the skin is very thin and tender and can be cooked to a crisp finish. The flesh is quite pale but with a distinctive flavor. Because they're so tiny, quail can be deep-fried whole or split and rapidly broiled or grilled. Quail are very lean, and thus often served with the breasts quite rare, to keep them from drying out.

Feathered Facts

In the old days, the gamy flavor of wild birds was traditionally accentuated by "hanging," leaving the whole bird, with feathers and innards intact, in a cool place such as a pantry from a couple of days and up to two weeks. Pheasant was hung until it actually began to decompose. In this condition, the pheasant was considered "high" and the flesh was thought to be far more flavorful. It was said that the pheasant was ready when the feathers started to fall out. For health reasons, however, most states have laws against hanging before selling commercially.

Wing Tips

If you have a particularly gamy bird and you wish to decrease the wild flavor and odor, marinate for at least six hours, turning occasionally, in two quarts of water mixed with 1/2 cup cider vinegar and three tablespoons salt. If the bird has had a heavy diet of fish and this is discernible in the smell of the flesh (as it is in some wild ducks), soak the bird at least six hours in two quarts of buttermilk, turning occasionally.

Wing Tips

If you want to increase the wild game taste of your game birds without hanging them (which accentuates the game taste through decomposition), you can marinate the bird in two cups of red wine, 1/4 cup whole juniper berries, three cloves garlic, crushed, and one teaspoon dried rosemary. This is similar to the traditional marinade for game such as wild boar. The juniper flavor brings out the sweet, gamey taste of the meat.

Roost Rap

Barding is draping bacon or salt pork over lean fowl or pushing it under the skin. For really lean cuts of meat that might be very dry when cooked, there's larding, where fat such as bacon is cut into strips called lardoons and threaded directly through the meat with a larding needle. This is an extremely compli-cated procedure that is never called for with today's domesticated breeds.

Rules of the Game: Tips for Better Cooking

The big secret to keeping game birds moist is barding. To bard a bird, strips of fat such as bacon or salt pork are cut into squares and either draped over the bird or inserted between the skin and the meat. The fat drips down over the fowl during cooking and prevents it from drying out.

When you bard on the surface of the skin, however, you keep the bird from browning, so you may want to remove the barding strips about ten minutes before the end of cooking time so that the breast can brown properly.

Playing the Game: Recipes for Game Birds

Below are some classic game recipes, such as the roasted quail on croutons, as well as some more unusual dishes, like guinea fowl with a sauce of blackberries and vinegar. You can use any of these preparations for the other game birds.

As with chicken, trussing game birds is essentially an aesthetic exercise, with no effect on the flavor and cooking time of the bird. If you wish to truss your game bird for the sake of an especially elegant presentation, however, you can simply tie the drumsticks firmly together with a length of clean kitchen string or linen trussing twine. Remember to cut off the trussing string before carving and serving.

Grilled Squab with Honey-Ginger Sauce

Squab are butterflied and quickly grilled to keep their dark, tender meat juicy. Brushed with honey and soy sauce and spiked with fresh ginger just before leaving the grill, they're served with grilled scallions to offset the sweetness of the sauce. If you don't want to grill, cook the squab under the broiler.

Serves 4

4 squab

Salt and freshly ground black pepper

Olive oil

2 tablespoons honey

2 tablespoons soy sauce

1 tablespoon grated fresh ginger

4 whole scallions, washed and roots trimmed off

1. Butterfly the squab by using poultry shears or a sharp knife to split them right up the back. Open the squab out and press down on the breast to flatten. Rinse and pat dry. Brush lightly with olive oil and season on each side with salt and pepper.

2. Mix the honey, soy, and ginger in a small bowl and set aside. Brush the scallions lightly with olive oil.

3. Prepare a medium-hot fire in an outdoor grill. Place the squab on the grill breast-side down, and grill 6–7 minutes, till the breast is crispy and brown. Lay the scallions to cook on the edges of the grill, turning several times till softened and lightly browned.

4. Turn the squab and brush the upper side with the honey glaze, and grill another 6–7 minutes. Remove from grill and serve immediately with grilled scallions.

Guinea Fowl with Blackberries

The bird is quickly roasted breast-side down in a hot oven before being jointed and served with a tart sauce with fresh berries and a splash of vinegar, lightly thickened with butter. Serve with mild-flavored vegetables on the side, such as new peas and mashed potatoes, to let the flavor of the bird and berries shine through. If fresh berries are not available, you can use frozen, thawed and partially drained, but your sauce won't have the same vibrancy. If the sauce is too tart for your taste, add a teaspoon of brown sugar.

Serves 4

2 2-pound guinea fowls

Salt and freshly ground black pepper

Juice of 1 lemon

1 cup fresh blackberries (or raspberries)

1/2 cup chicken broth

1 tablespoon red wine vinegar

4 tablespoons (1/2 stick) butter

1. Preheat the oven to 400°. Rinse and pat dry the guinea fowl and season them inside and out with salt and pepper. Squeeze the lemon juice over each.

2. Place the guinea fowl breast-side down in a shallow roasting pan and roast for 30 minutes.

3. While the guinea fowl are roasting, put the berries in a non-aluminum saucepan. Stir in the chicken stock and bring to a boil. Reduce heat and simmer gently for 2–3 minutes, till berries are softened. Stir in the vinegar, then blend in the butter and stir till melted. Remove from heat and keep covered so it stays warm till guinea fowl are done.

4. Carve the guinea fowl onto warmed serving plates, top with the sauce, and serve immediately.

Pheasant Normande

This is a classic preparation of pheasant with apples, cream, and Calvados, the French apple brandy made of distilled fermented apple juice. Apple jack is a good American approximation. If you absolutely can't find Calvados or apple jack, you can substitute brandy. You want a sweet eating apple for this dish, such as Golden Delicious, Rome, or Fuji.

Classic Normandy preparation requires you to set the Calvados aflame after adding it to the pan, but in this recipe, the sauce is simply boiled for a few moments to evaporate the alcohol. It's a very rich dish, so serve it with a tartly dressed salad to cut the creamy flavor.

Serves 4–6

2 medium pheasants (about 3 1/2 pounds each)

3 tablespoons butter

1 small onion, diced

1 clove garlic, minced

1/2 cup Calvados or apple jack

2 sweet apples, peeled, cored, and thinly sliced

3/4 cup Elaborate Chicken Stock (p. 51)

1 cup heavy cream

1 teaspoon salt

Freshly ground black pepper

1. Rinse and pat dry the pheasants. Melt the butter in a large skillet over medium-high heat. As soon as the foam subsides, add the pheasants and saute, turning to brown on all sides.

2. Add the onion and garlic and cook till softened and lightly browned.

3. Pour in the Calvados or apple jack. Bring to a boil and cook several minutes till some of the liquid has evaporated. Add the sliced apples and stock, and simmer gently for 5 minutes, till apples start to soften.

4. Pour in the cream and add salt and pepper. Bring to a boil, reduce heat, cover loosely and simmer very gently for 45 minutes, till pheasant is tender.

5. Remove the pheasants from the pan and carve onto a serving dish. If the sauce is very thin, boil it for a few moments to reduce and thicken. Pour the sauce over the carved pheasants and serve immediately.

Provençial Partridge with Red Wine and Black Olives

Partridges are quickly roasted in a hot oven before being served with a mostly acidic sauce of tomato and olives, underpinned with bacon and butter, that complements the dark meat. Use the best black olives you can find, not canned olives. Tiny flavorful French Niçioise olives would be ideal, though they're too little to pit conveniently. If you leave the pits in, remember to warn your dinner guests to fend for their own teeth. Serve with scalloped or roasted potatoes.

Serves 4

4 medium (1 pound) or 2 large (1 1/2-2 pound) partridges

4 tablespoons (1/2 stick) butter, softened

Salt and freshly ground black pepper

4 slices of bacon

1 small onion, diced

1 tablespoon flour

1 tablespoon tomato paste

1/2 teaspoon thyme

1 cup dry red wine

1 cup chicken stock

1/2 cup small black olives

1. Preheat the oven to 375°. Butterfly each of the four small partridges by splitting up the back and removing the backbone. (If using two larger partridges, split each in half completely and cut off the backbone.) Rinse and pat dry the partridges, and press down on the breastbone to open each out and flatten.

2. Using 2 tablespoons of the butter, rub each bird under the skin with butter. Season with salt and pepper. Place a slice of bacon across each butterflied partridge (or on each half) and place the birds in a shallow roasting pan.

3. Roast for 20 minutes for four smaller birds, 25 minutes for two larger birds.

4. While the birds roast, melt the remaining 2 tablespoons of butter in a skillet over medium heat. Add the onion and saute till softened and lightly browned.

5. Stir in the flour, tomato paste, and thyme, then slowly blend in the red wine, stirring till no lumps remain. Bring to a boil and let wine reduce for several minutes, then stir in the chicken stock and bring to a boil. Add the olives, reduce heat, and let sauce bubble till it's thick and smooth, 6–8 minutes.

6. When the pheasants are ready, place on warmed serving plate and spoon the sauce over. Serve immediately.

Roast Quail on Croutons

This is a classic quail preparation, with the tiny hearts and livers chopped, mixed with cognac and anchovies, and spread on little toasts, also called croutons. These are broiled and then topped with the roasted quail and served immediately, with the pan juices dripping down to soak the bread.

It's a lovely and elegant main course, and it's definitely a finger food. Quail are almost always meant to be eaten with the fingers, so provide bowls of warm water and little towels for diners to wipe their fingers.

Serves 4

4 large slices sourdough bread (or 8 small slices)

8 quail

2 heads garlic

8 sprigs fresh rosemary

Salt and freshly ground black pepper

8 slices bacon

8 anchovy fillets

1/4 cup cognac

1. Make the croutons by trimming the crusts off the bread (and halving each slice if using large slices such as from a large round loaf). Toast each till very crisp. Set aside.

2. Preheat your oven to 400°. Remove the giblets from each bird and set aside. Wash and pat dry the quail before putting a sprig of rosemary and 2–3 cloves of garlic in the cavity of each. Season the outside of each quail with salt and pepper and drape a slice of bacon across the breast of each.

3. Arrange the quail on a flat rack in a shallow roasting pan. Roast for 25 minutes.

4. While the quail are roasting, finely chop up the hearts, livers, and anchovies and blend with the cognac. Spread this mixture on each slice of toasted bread and lay them on a baking sheet.

5. As soon as you remove the quail from the oven, switch on the broiler. Pop the baking sheet under the broiler and cook 2–3 minutes, till the liver and hearts are cooked. Remove, lay two toasts on each plate, and top each toast with a roasted quail. Drizzle the pan juices over all and serve immediately.

The Least You Need to Know

➤ The game birds most commonly available in the US are squab, guinea fowl, pheasant, partridge, and quail.

➤ Most game birds are so lean that you need to add extra fat to keep them from drying out when cooked. This can be accomplished by draping slices of bacon over the bird's breast and the technique is called barding.

➤ Game birds should be roasted quickly to keep the meat moist.

➤ Game birds such as squab can be butterflied for fast, even cooking on the grill.

Glossary

Adjust To taste a dish and add more salt, pepper, flavorings, etc. It's much easier to add more than to take away excess, so use a light hand when salting at the start of cooking.

Al dente An Italian term meaning, literally, "to the tooth," pasta in this manner is cooked through but still slightly firm, not overly soft.

Bacteria Bacteria can be found naturally in many foods, and not all bacteria are harmful. However, chicken in particular can harbor certain bacteria (*see Salmonella, Campylobacter*) that can be dangerous to human health if not destroyed by proper cooking.

Baking sheet A flat metal pan with a rim along one side, used for baking foods that will not drip or run.

Barding To drape bacon or salt pork over lean fowl or to push it under the skin so that there will be extra fat on the meat while cooking, to keep it from drying out.

Baste To spoon pan juices, fats, or a marinade or sauce over a food as it roasts, broils, or grills, in order to stop the food from drying out in the cooking heat.

Beat To mix rapidly in order to break up lumps and incorporate air.

Black peppercorn The whole spice which is ground for black pepper; the tiny, dried black berry can be simmered whole in stocks and sauces.

Blanch To plunge a food into boiling water for a moment or two to set color or, when making stock, remove impurities from the surface of the chicken bones.

Blend To stir one ingredient into another so that no lumps remain.

Boil To heat a liquid until bubbles rise continuously and break on the surface.

Bone To remove bones from meat.

Braise To brown a food in a small amount of fat and then cook slowly for a long time in a small amount of liquid in a covered pan.

Brine To soak poultry (or another food) in salted water to plump and season.

Broil To cook a food under direct heat (usually a coil found in the top of an electric oven), allowing quick cooking with a minimum of fat.

Broiler-fryer The standard chicken, usually under 3 months old, and generally ranging from two to four pounds. Used for nearly all cooking methods except long, slow stewing.

Butterfly To slice a chicken (or other piece of meat or seafood) open all the way up the back, opening out and pressing down so that the whole piece of meat lies flat.

Campylobacter A bacteria increasingly present in commercially produced chicken that is considered the leading cause of diarrhea in adults. To be certain of destroying campylobacter in chicken, cook until the internal temperature reaches 180°.

Capon A castrated male chicken raised on a fatty diet till it reaches six to ten pounds. The meat is very tender and marbled with fat.

Chipotle A smoked jalapeno pepper, usually found canned in a red adobo sauce. The flavor is deep and smoky and decidedly different from plain jalapenos.

Coarsely chopped To cut an ingredient in large pieces without regard for evenness of size.

Cover To place a lid on a pan of cooking food so that the steam cannot escape, thereby increasing the heat and cooking the food more quickly. To cover loosely is to set the lid askew so that steam is able to escape.

Cubed To cut an ingredient into even-sized, square pieces; cubed food is usually slightly bigger than diced food.

Dark meat The meat of the thighs and drumsticks on chicken, which is darker due to being a different muscle type than that of the breast and wings; the meat is moister with a slightly higher fat content than white meat.

Deglaze To incorporate into a sauce the browned bits left from frying a food by swirling a liquid such as wine, water, or stock in the bottom of the pan.

Diced Food cut into small, even-sized cubes.

Dredge To coat a food with a dry ingredient such as flour or breadcrumbs before frying, usually by dragging the food through the dry ingredient on a plate or by shaking it in a bag with the dry ingredient.

Drumstick The lower part of the leg of the chicken.

Duck A domestically raised game bird with all dark meat.

Food Safety and Inspection Service (FSIS) A branch of the US Department of Agriculture (USDA) that ensures accuracy of labeling in meat and poultry, and insures that a chicken labeled, say, "natural" contains no artificial ingredients, added colorings, and has been minimally processed.

Free range A chicken that has had occasional access to the outdoors while being raised, as opposed to mass-produced battery chickens, which are confined in a limited space. Real free-range chickens have more flavorful meat.

Fresh Poultry can be labeled fresh if its internal temperature has never been below 26°, even though it may feel rock hard in your hands.

Frozen A bird that has been stored at lower than 26° may be labeled "hard chilled," but for all intents and purposes, it's frozen.

Game hen *See Rock Cornish game hen.*

Giblets The chicken's internal organs, usually found wrapped in plastic or paper in the inside cavity of whole chickens. The giblets consist of the heart, liver, gizzard, and neck of the bird, and all are edible.

Gizzard An internal organ that is part of the bird's digestive tract, gizzards are tasty and chewy, especially when floured and fried.

Guinea fowl Very lean-fleshed birds with a slightly musky flavor and light, mild-flavored breast meat.

Habanero A brightly colored, very hot South American chili. Small and shaped rather like a lantern, habaneros range from red to green to fiery yellow and orange. They add a citrus flavor along with their heat.

Heart The cleaned heart of the chicken, found among the giblets. Can be eaten floured and fried, or stewed with the other giblets for a stock to use in giblet gravy.

Jalapeno A dark green chili about two inches long that can be quite hot. To make the heat milder, remove the seeds and inner membranes when chopping.

Jelly Fruit juice and sugar stewed with pectin; jelly is clear and does not have any pieces of whole fruit in it, unlike jam or preserves, which contains pieces of the fruit.

Jelly roll pan A metal baking sheet with a rim around all four sides.

Joint To cut a chicken into pieces along its natural divisions (i.e., wings, drumsticks, thighs).

Keep warm *See Warm.*

Leg The whole thigh and drumstick, which can be cooked still connected and need not be jointed into separate pieces.

Liver An internal organ of the bird high in minerals and folic acid; more than one liver may come in a package of giblets. Flour and fry to eat, or save them up to make pate. It's best to leave liver out of stocks.

Low oven An oven set at its lowest temperature, usually about 180°, to keep food warm while other parts of a meal are being cooked. Some oven dials have a setting for this purpose marked simply "warm."

Marsala A red wine to which other alcohol has been added for a strong flavor. Used in sauces of many Italian foods.

Medium fire A charcoal fire on the grill that has been let burn down till coals are still red but have some white ash at the edges.

Neck The neck is not technically an internal organ, but it is almost always packaged as part of the giblets. It has strips of dark meat on it that add flavor when the neck is simmered for stock.

Organic A chicken that has been raised without any chemical additives (such as antibiotics) in its feed. Federal law currently does not allow chickens to be labeled as "organic."

Paillard The French term for a chicken breast piece beaten into an even thickness, for aesthetic appeal and ease in cooking.

Peppercorns *See Black peppercorns.*

Pheasant One of the most widely available game birds, with beautiful brown and dark green plumage. The flesh has a mild, vaguely sweet flavor.

Preserves Whole or chopped fruit cooked with sugar to make a spread for bread, also can be used in sauces and gravies.

Quail The tiniest of commercially available game birds in the US, usually less than half a pound in size, they look like tiny toy chickens, with tender, delicate meat.

Ragu The Italian word for a highly seasoned, long cooked, thick stew of meat or poultry.

Reduce To cook until the water in a sauce or liquid has started to evaporate and the sauce is thickened.

Roast To cook in a dry heat, usually in the oven, allowing the outside of a food to brown while the inside becomes tender and moist.

Roasting pan An open pan for browning a food in the oven over dry heat. The best roasting pans have low sides to allow the heat to better reach the food and brown evenly.

Roasting rack A flat or V-shaped metal rack to hold a food up off the bottom of the roasting pan. This allows fat to drain off and keeps the food from essentially boiling in its own liquid.

Rock Cornish game hen A hybrid between strains of the meaty American White Rock chicken and the flavorful English Cornish hen, game hens should be bought as small as possible, closer to one pound than the too-large 2-pound birds sometimes seen.

Salmonella A harmful bacteria that can be present in both chickens and raw eggs and that can cause gastrointestinal disorders in humans. To destroy salmonella, the USDA recommends cooking the meat to an internal temperature of 180°.

Schmaltz Rendered chicken fat, used for cooking.

Season To add salt and pepper, or a herb, spice, or flavoring.

Self-basted The label on poultry that has been injected with a mixture of oil, seasoning, and stock or water to keep it moist while cooking.

Simmer To raise a liquid to just below a boil, with only the occasional bubble rising and breaking on the surface.

Skim To remove fat or scum from the top layer of a liquid, such as spooning the fat from the top of chicken stock.

Sprinkle To lightly scatter an ingredient, such as salt or Parmesan cheese, over the surface of a food.

Squab Baby pigeons, eaten before they're 6 weeks old, at less than a pound each. The flesh is dark, tender, and delicate.

Stewing hen A bird raised to produce eggs and not brought to market till much older and heavier than the average broiler-fryer. A stewing hen can weigh from five to seven pounds, and must be cooked long and slow to keep the meat from being tough or stringy.

Strain To pour a liquid through a sieve, strainer, or colander to remove solids, as when straining finished chicken stock to remove the pieces of bone and vegetable.

Sweat To soften chopped vegetables by sauteing very lightly in butter, then covering and leaving to steam; the result is vegetables that are softened and translucent but not browned.

Thigh The upper part of a chicken leg; boned, it can serve as a dark meat alternative to the breast meat in any recipe.

US Department of Agriculture (USDA) A department of the federal government that monitors the production and distribution of all livestock and produce in the US. USDA officials monitor the processing of all commercially produced chicken in the US.

Warm, keep warm To stop a food from growing cold while preparing other ingredients or dishes. The food to be kept warm can be set on an ovenproof dish or platter and simply covered in aluminum foil or with a lid, if it doesn't have to sit for more than five to ten minutes, but if you're holding a platter of, say, fried chicken while you finish cooking the potatoes, you may want to put the platter in a low oven, set at 180°. Don't cover crisp foods in a warm oven, as steam under the cover may soften them.

Water bath To hold a pool of water around a pan in the oven to keep the ingredients from scorching. Pate is cooked in a loaf pan which is set into another, larger pan and water is poured into the larger pan till it goes halfway up the side of the loaf pan, to keep the pate from getting drying out in too much direct heat.

Whisk To rapidly stir an ingredient into another ingredient, using a fork or a metal or wooden whisk, to incorporate air and/or to prevent lumps from forming.

White meat The breast and wing meat of the chicken.

White pepper A ground spice made from the core of the black peppercorn after the black surface has been removed. White pepper puts more heat into a sauce than black, but black pepper may be substituted for it at any time.

Wing tip The pointed end of the wing piece, which is almost always removed when jointing a chicken or trimming wings for Buffalo Wings or other spiced wings. Save wing tips in a bag in the freezer until you have enough to make stock (two cups of wing tips will make about one quart of stock). When roasting the chicken whole, the wing tip stays on.

Sources

Poultry and Game

D'Artagnan
399-419 St. Paul Avenue
Jersey City, NJ 07306
800-327-8246
Ducks, geese, other wild game and fowl.

Wild Game
2315 West Huron Street
Chicago, IL 60612
312-278-1661
Poultry and game birds.

Foggy Ridge Gamebird Farm
P.O. Box 88
Thomastown, ME 94861
207-273-2357
*Game birds, including pheasant,
partridge, quail.*

Prime Cut
1300 Boston Post Road
Guilford, CT 06437
203-453-9986
Duck, goose, pheasant, turkey.

**For herbs, spices, and flavorings,
including Asian and Mexican supplies:**

Balducci's Mail Order
42-26 12th Street
Long Island City, NY 10012
800-BALDUCCIS

Dean & DeLuca
560 Broadway
New York, NY 10012
800-221-7714

Penzey's Spice House
P.O. Box 1633
Milwaukee, WI 53201
800-574-0277

Williams-Sonoma
P.O. Box 7456
San Francisco, CA 94120
800-541-2233

Zabar's Mail Order
2245 Broadway
New York, NY 10024
800-221-3347

Index

C

X-Z